Professional Crystal Reports for Visual Studio .NET

David McAmis

Wrox Press Ltd. ®

Professional Crystal Reports for Visual Studio .NET

Reprinted November 2002

Published by Wrox Press Ltd,
Arden House, 1102 Warwick Road, Acocks Green,
Birmingham, B27 6BH, UK
Printed in the USA
ISBN 1-86100-774-4

Trademark Acknowledgments

Wrox has endeavored to adhere to trademark conventions for all companies and products mentioned in this book, such as the appropriate use of capitalization. Wrox cannot however guarantee the accuracy of this information.

Credits

Author
David McAmis

Additional Material
Helen Callaghan
Mike Foster
William Sempf

Technical Reviewers
Carl Burnham
Cristof Falk
Martin Halford
Mark Horner
Michael Oyach
Phil Powers De George
David Schultz
William Sempf

Commisioning Editor
Paul Jeffcoat

Managing Editor
Laurent Lafon

Technical Editors
Catherine Alexander
Helen Callaghan
Mike Foster
Jon Hill

Project Manager
Nicola Phillips

Production Coordinator
Neil Lote

Proof Reader
Chris Smith

Cover
Natalie O'Donnell

Index
Martin Brooks

About the Author

David McAmis is a Crystal Certified Consultant and Trainer, living and working in Sydney, Australia as a partner in Avantis Information Systems. As a consultant for Avantis, and on behalf of Crystal Decisions, David creates Windows, web, and mobile applications incorporating Crystal technology across a wide number of platforms, databases and ERP systems to deliver innovate solutions for common business problems.

In his varied career, he has held the roles of consultant, technical trainer, university lecturer, and consulting services manager, and has served as vice-president of a software and services company in the US. David holds a B.S. degree in Management Information Systems and is a Microsoft Certified Professional, as well as a certified trainer and consultant for numerous software products.

David has been working with Crystal Reports since version 4.5 and is an active member of the beta and user group community and a self-confessed "Raving Fan". In his career as a Crystal developer and trainer, he has travelled the world and taught over 800 students. You can reach him at dmcamis@hotmail.com.

There is an incredible team of people that make Wrox books happen and this one was no exception – none of this would have been possible without the professional talents (and patience) of Paul, Nikki, Catherine, Mike, Helen, and the rest of the Wrox editorial team, including countless reviewers whose comments helped shape the book's content. I would like to give special thanks to Bill Sempf for his work, both as a reviewer and contributor.

Behind the scenes, there are many people I work with on a day-to-day basis, especially Colin, Pearl, Alice, and Lisa, who have been a sounding board and have had to hear about this project for the past four months. As always, a big thank you needs to go out to the Crystal Decisions Asia Pacific team for their support and assistance, and to Chris and Craig in particular for their faith and confidence in me, and for continually keeping me challenged.

And on a personal note, there is a worldwide network of friends and family who offer their support and encouragement on a daily basis, which I couldn't do without. Thanks to Mark and E'mer for the late night advice and to my family for their love and support. Nunc scio quit sit amor.

Professional *Crystal Reports*
for *Visual Studio .NET*

Table of Contents

Table of Contents

Table of Contents

Table of Contents

Professional *Crystal Reports*
for *Visual Studio .NET*

Introduction

Welcome to *Professional Crystal Reports for Visual Studio .NET*. Crystal Reports is one of the world's leading software packages for creating interactive reports. The reports let users view data and the trends therein, and they can be published on the Web or integrated within applications. With more than four million licenses shipped, Crystal Reports is the leader among Windows report writers. Crystal Reports has been in the Visual Studio box since 1993, but the latest version, Crystal Reports .NET, is now integrated more closely than ever before with Visual Studio .NET. This book will detail the functionality provided with Crystal Reports for Visual Studio .NET, and how, when, and where you should integrate reports into your .NET applications.

Why incorporate reports into applications? Virtually all applications need to present data to users, but any work beyond basic formatting – charts or conditional formatting, for example – can be very complex to program manually. In this book, we will provide you with the practical, high value, real-world information that you need to understand the array of tools that Crystal Reports for Visual Studio .NET provides for developers, so that you can immediately begin creating rich reports that can be integrated into your Windows and web-based applications.

We begin with an overview of Crystal Reports for Visual Studio .NET, introducing the technology and what we can use it for, and the benefits of integrating Crystal Reports with the .NET Framework. We then go on to create some reports, and learn how to integrate them into both Windows and web-based applications. We examine XML Web Services, and how to work with ADO.NET and formulas and logic in our reports, then finish by developing distributed reporting applications, and looking at how to deploy the applications we have created throughout the book.

This book does not attempt to be all-inclusive, and it will not teach basic .NET techniques. To be able to deliver a functional guide to Crystal Reports for Visual Studio .NET, we assume that you have a grasp of essential programming techniques, in this case, a knowledge of programming in Visual Basic .NET, and experience using Visual Studio .NET, and that you can apply these skills to a new technology.

Examples are carefully chosen to demonstrate the capabilities of Crystal Reports for Visual Studio .NET and aid you in understanding the techniques that you can apply when you begin to use this technology in your .NET applications.

Who Is This Book For?

This book is for programmers who want a comprehensive guide to the functionality included with Crystal Reports for Visual Studio .NET. It's assumed that you have some knowledge of .NET and experience with Visual Studio .NET.

This book is mainly aimed at readers who have some experience with Crystal Reports. However, the book will prove valuable for readers who are new to Crystal Reports, and want a guide to this free reporting tool they've discovered within Visual Studio .NET.

What You Need to Use This Book

There are software and knowledge requirements for successful progress through this book.

Software

- ❑ Microsoft Windows 2000 or XP Professional
- ❑ Visual Studio .NET Professional or higher
- ❑ SQL Server 2000 or MSDE

Knowledge

- ❑ Some knowledge of the Visual Studio .NET development environment is assumed
- ❑ Some very basic knowledge of SQL is assumed

What Does This Book Cover?

This book covers the features of Crystal Reports for Visual Studio .NET that you'll find yourself using time and again to build complex reports and integrate them into different .NET applications. We start by explaining how Crystal Reports fits into the .NET platform and how it differs from previous versions of Crystal Reports. Then, we discuss the key techniques we can use:

- ❑ Creating reports using the Expert
- ❑ Integrating reports into Windows and web-based applications

- ❏ Creating XML Report Web Services
- ❏ Working with ADO.NET
- ❏ Using Formulas and Logic in our reports
- ❏ Developing Distributed Reporting Applications
- ❏ Deploying our applications

Chapter 1 – Crystal Reports.NET Overview: In this chapter, we take our first look at Crystal Reports for Visual Studio .NET (Crystal Reports.NET), including how the product is different from other version of Crystal Reports, how to find and run the sample applications that are included, and where to find the tutorials that will get you up to speed with the product. We will also take a look at the new Crystal Reports.NET architecture, and learn how it fits in to the .NET Framework. Whether you are an experienced application developer looking to move to Visual Studio .NET or you are developing your first application and have never heard of Crystal Reports, it all starts here.

Chapter 2 – Getting Started with Crystal Reports.NET: In this chapter, we will be looking at the Crystal Reports Designer within Visual Studio .NET and learn how to create and import reports for use in Windows or web applications. By the end of the chapter, we will have the skills to develop our own basic reports and can move on to the actual integration of these reports into our application. If you have used Crystal Reports before, some of the material in this chapter will be familiar.

Chapter 3 – Report Integration for Windows-based Applications: In this chapter, we are going to look at how to integrate and view the reports that we created in the last chapter from Windows applications, and how to customize our reports at run time using the rich object models provided. Throughout the chapter we will be looking at code examples to illustrate the use of various features and by the end of the chapter, we should be familiar with the majority of report integration concepts, and be ready to apply them to our own application development.

Chapter 4 – Report Integration for Web-based Applications: In this chapter, we are going to look at how to integrate and view reports from within web-based applications created with Visual Studio .NET. In addition, we will look at some of the run-time customizations that can be made to our reports, as well as some issues around web-application deployment. As we go through this chapter, we will be building forms for use in web-based reporting applications, which demonstrate many of the features of Crystal Reports.NET that can be used in our own web applications.

Chapter 5 – Creating XML Report Web Services: We have now seen how to integrate reports into Windows and web-based applications, but now we need to learn how to leverage those skills and work with XML Report Web Services. This chapter will teach us to identify what an XML Report Web Service is and understand how it can be used in our application. We will also create a Report Service from an existing Crystal Report and utilize the service with the Crystal Windows or Web Viewer.

Chapter 6 – Working with .NET Data: In this chapter we take a step back to look at what lies underneath the reports we have created – the data our report is based on and how Crystal Reports.NET uses this data. We will look at the way Crystal Reports works with different data sources and how it interacts with ADO.NET. At the end of this chapter, we will have an understanding of how Crystal Reports.NET interacts with different data sources, the options for working with these data sources, and how to use ADO.NET as a data source for our report development.

Chapter 7 – Formulas and Logic: This chapter will narrow our focus to look at where the majority of Crystal Reports development time is spent: writing formulas and logic. We will discover the best way to add calculations and logic to our reports, and learn enough syntax and code to handle most situations. We will also see how to differentiate between the two different 'flavors' of the Crystal Formula Language, and how to write our own record selection and conditional formatting formulas.

Chapter 8 – Working with the Crystal Reports Engine: In this chapter, we will be looking at the Crystal Reports Engine, the functionality it provides and some of the advanced integration techniques that we can use in our own application. We learn to identify when to use the Crystal Reports Engine namespace, how to integrate it into our application, and how to use the features contained within the properties, methods and events associated with the engine.

Chapter 9 – Distributing Your Application: Finally, with our development and testing finished, we will, in this chapter, look at one of the last steps in the software development life cycle – the actual deployment of our application to the end users. We will examine the tools Visual Studio .NET provides to help distribute applications, and how these tools can be used to distribute applications that integrate Crystal Reports. This chapter has been designed so that if you are only interested in deploying Windows applications, you can turn immediately to that section and get started. Likewise, if you are developing web applications, there is a separate section for web deployment. By the end of this chapter, we will be able to identify the set-up and distribution tools within Visual Studio .NET, and understand how they can be used to package and distribute our application. We will also be able to create a set-up package from an application that integrates Crystal Reports and successfully install it on a target machine.

Style Conventions

We have used a number of different styles of text and layout in this book to help differentiate between the different kinds of information. Here are examples of the styles we used and an explanation of what they mean.

Code has several font styles. If it is a word that we are talking about in the text – for example, when discussing a `For...Next` loop – it is in `this font`. If it is a block of code that can be typed as a program and run, then it is in a gray box:

```
Private Sub Button1_Click(ByVal sender As System.Object, _
    ByVal e As System.EventArgs) Handles Button1.Click
End Sub
```

Sometimes, you will see code in a mixture of styles, like this:

```
Private Sub Button1_Click(ByVal sender As System.Object, _
    ByVal e As System.EventArgs) Handles Button1.Click

    MsgBox(TextBox1.Text)

End Sub
```

In cases like this, the code with a white background is code that we are already familiar with. The line highlighted in gray is a new addition to the code since we last looked at it. Code with a white background is also used for chunks of code that demonstrate a principle, but which cannot be typed in and run on their own.

Advice, hints, and background information comes in this type of font.

Important pieces of information come in boxes like this.

Important Words are in a bold type font.

Words that appear on the screen, or in menus like File or Window, are in a similar font to the one you would see on a Windows desktop.

Keys that you press on the keyboard like *Ctrl* and *Enter* are in italics.

Commands that you need to type in on the command line are shown with a > for the prompt, and the input in **bold**, like this:

```
>something to type on the command line
```

Customer Support

We always value hearing from our readers, and we want to know what you think about this book: what you liked, what you didn't like, and what you think we can do better next time. You can send us your comments, either by returning the reply card in the back of the book, or by e-mail to feedback@wrox.com. Please be sure to mention the book's ISBN and title in your message.

Sample Code and Updates

As you work through the examples in this book, you may decide that you prefer to type in all the code by hand. Many readers prefer this because it is a good way to get familiar with the coding techniques that are being used. However, whether you want to type the code in or not, we have made all the source code for this book available at the Wrox.com web site.

When you log on to the Wrox.com site at http://www.wrox.com/, simply locate the title through our Search facility or by using one of the title lists. Now click on the Download Code link on the book's detail page and you can obtain all the source code.

The files that are available for download from our site have been archived using WinZip. When you have saved the attachments to a folder on your hard drive, you need to extract the files using a de-compression program such as WinZip or PKUnzip. When you extract the files, the code is usually extracted into chapter folders. When you start the extraction process, ensure your software (WinZip, PKUnzip, and so on) has Use folder names under Extract to: (or the equivalent) checked. The book assumes all of the code is located on your C:\ drive, so the path of the examples described in the book will begin C:\CrystalReports\ChapterXX\, where XX is the chapter number. If you extract the code to somewhere other than the C:\ drive, please keep this in mind when you are working with the examples.

Even if you like to type in the code, you can use our source files to check the results you should be getting – they should be your first stop if you think you might have typed in an error. If you don't like typing, then downloading the source code from our web site is a must! Either way, it will help you with updates and debugging.

Registration for code download is not mandatory for this book, but should you wish to register for your code download, your details will not be passed to any third party. For more details you may view our terms and conditions, which are linked from the download page.

Errata

We've made every effort to make sure that there are no errors in the text or in the code. However, no one is perfect and mistakes do occur. If you find an error in this book, like a spelling mistake or a faulty piece of code, we would be very grateful for feedback. By sending in errata, you may save another reader hours of frustration, and of course, you will be helping us provide even higher quality information. Simply e-mail the information to support@wrox.com; your information will be checked and if correct, posted to the errata page for that title, or used in subsequent editions of the book.

To find errata on the web site, log on to http://www.wrox.com/, and simply locate the title through our Search facility or title list. Then, on the book details page, click on the Book Errata link. On this page you will be able to view any errata that have been submitted and checked through by editorial.

Technical Support

If you wish to directly query a problem in the book with an expert who knows the book in detail then e-mail support@wrox.com. A typical e-mail should include the following things:

❑   The **book name**, **last four digits of the ISBN** (7744 for this book), and **page number** of the problem in the Subject field.

❑   Your **name**, **contact information**, and the **problem** in the body of the message.

We *won't* send you junk mail. We need the details to save your time and ours. When you send an e-mail message, it will go through the following chain of support:

1.   **Customer Support** – Your message is delivered to one of our customer support staff, who are the first people to read it. They have files on most frequently asked questions and will answer anything general about the book or the web site immediately.

2.   **Editorial** – Deeper queries are forwarded to the technical editor responsible for that book. They have experience with the programming language or particular product, and are able to answer detailed technical questions on the subject. Once an issue has been resolved, the editor can post the errata to the web site.

3.   **The Authors** – Finally, in the unlikely event that the editor cannot answer your problem, they will forward the request to the author. We do try to protect the author from any distractions to their writing, however, we are quite happy to forward specific requests to them. All Wrox authors help with the support on their books. They will mail the customer and the editor with their response, and again all readers should benefit.

> Note that the Wrox support process can only offer support to issues that are directly pertinent to the content of our published title. Support for questions that fall outside the scope of normal book support is provided via the community lists of our http://p2p.wrox.com/ forum.

p2p.wrox.com

For author and peer discussion, join the **P2P mailing lists**. Our unique system provides **programmer to programmer™** contact on mailing lists, forums, and newsgroups, all *in addition* to our one-to-one e-mail support system. Be confident that your query is being examined by the many Wrox authors, and other industry experts, who are present on our mailing lists. At p2p.wrox.com you will find a number of different lists that will help you, not only while you read this book, but also as you develop your own applications.

To subscribe to a mailing list just follow this these steps:

1. Go to http://p2p.wrox.com/ and choose the appropriate category from the left menu bar.

2. Click on the mailing list you wish to join.

3. Follow the instructions to subscribe and fill in your e-mail address and password.

4. Reply to the confirmation e-mail you receive.

5. Use the subscription manager to join more lists and set your mail preferences.

Professional *Crystal Reports*
for *Visual Studio .NET*

Crystal Reports.NET Overview

Crystal Reports has enjoyed a long association with Microsoft and has shipped with Visual Basic (and subsequently Visual Studio) as the default report writer since 1993. Developers have traditionally had a love-hate relationship with Crystal Reports – they loved the functionality it provided and the free run-time license, but hated having to upgrade to the latest version to get the features they required, and the fact that reports could not be created or modified programmatically, but only through the UI (either the developer UI with Visual Studio or with the consumer UI with the Crystal Reports retail package).

Just as the release of Visual Studio .NET represents a significant leap for the Microsoft development platform, the release of Crystal Reports for Visual Studio .NET is also a milestone for the Crystal Decisions development team. Following the Microsoft .NET strategy, the product has been redeveloped to take advantage of the .NET Framework and is now a fully featured product in it's own right – developers no longer have to wait to upgrade to the latest release to get the features they need.

In this chapter, we are going to take a first look at Crystal Reports for Visual Studio .NET (Crystal Reports.NET), including how the product is different from other versions of Crystal Reports, how to find and run the sample applications that are included, and where to find the tutorials that will get you up to speed with the product. We will also take a look at the new Crystal Reports.NET architecture, and learn how it fits into the .NET Framework.

Whether you are an experienced application developer looking to move to Visual Studio .NET or you are developing your first application and have never heard of Crystal Reports, it all starts here.

What is Crystal Reports?

In simplest terms, Crystal Reports is a report design tool that allows you to create reports that can retrieve and format a result set from a database or other data source. In addition to simply reading data from a data source, Crystal Reports has its own formula language for creating calculations and a number of features that can be used to turn raw data into presentation-quality reports, with graphs, charts, running totals, and so on.

If we were to look at all of the different types of reports that could be created using Crystal Reports, you would find that they are as varied as the developer or end user who created them.

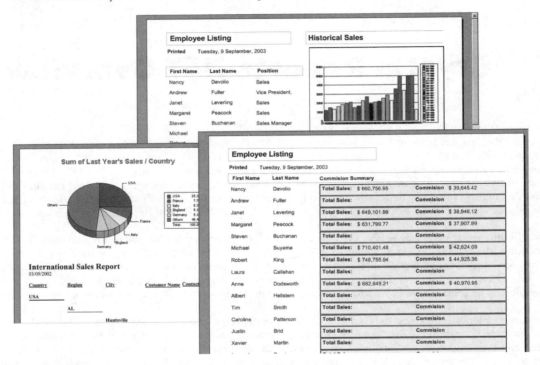

You can create reports that range from a simple list with only a few columns to a complex management report that shows multiple graphs, tables, and Key Performance Indicators (KPIs). The flexibility of the report designer itself means that it can be used for many different types of reports and output, depending on your needs.

In addition to a powerful toolset for actually creating reports, Crystal Reports also features a number of APIs and tools specifically created for developers to allow them to integrate these reports into their own applications. To help understand these features and how they are used, we are going to have a brief look at the history of the products leading up to this release of Crystal Reports.NET

A Brief History

In the beginning, a small company in Vancouver called Crystal Services developed a DOS-based reporting add-on for ACCPAC accounting in 1988. A few years later, in 1992, the company released Crystal Reports, touting it as the "world's first Windows report writer" and it wasn't too long after that Microsoft standardized on Crystal Reports as the reporting engine for Visual Basic and the rest is history.

Within a year of that historic partnership between Crystal Services and Microsoft, over a million licenses of Crystal Reports were shipped, giving it a foothold within the developer community and ensuring long-term success. Since that time, Crystal Reports has evolved alongside the available platforms and development tools, moving from floppy distribution to CDs, from 16 to 32-bit, and from a .DLL print engine to ActiveX control to Automation Engine to .NET Classes.

Over the years, the user interface for creating reports hasn't changed much – the basic features are still the same, even though the look and feel of the icons and menu bars may change depending on the UI design standards of the day. What has really changed over the years and releases of Crystal Reports is the functions and features that have been developed, culminating in a product that can easily hold its own with just about every other report writer on the market. To have a look at some of those features, we are going to delve in to just exactly what you can do with Crystal Reports.NET.

What Can You Do with Crystal Reports.NET?

To start with, Crystal Reports.NET includes an integrated Report Designer available within the Visual Studio IDE that you can use to create report files (.rpt) to integrate with your application.

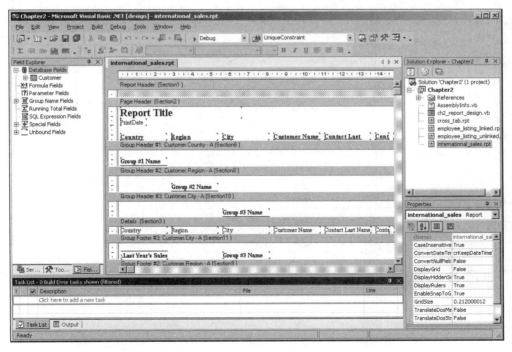

This Report Designer (covered in Chapter 2) features a number of "experts" (or wizards) to help you get started creating a report and will guide you through the report development process, from selecting a data source and the field that will appear on your report, to determining what records should appear.

Once you have a basic report designed, you can then add features like formula fields, running totals, graphs, and so on to make your report design as complex as required. Reports come in all shapes, sizes and forms. You may want to create a report that can be used to print an invoice from your application or you want to compile statistics for a management report or produce an inventory count sheet. You don't even have to constrict yourself to a particular size or shape – reports can be created that print shipping labels or address labels and can include bar codes, pictures, graphics, and so on.

> To get an idea of the types of reports that can be created using Crystal Reports, check out the Sample Reports available from the Crystal Decisions web site at http://community.crystaldecisions.com/fix/samplescr.asp.

After you have created a report, you need some way to display this report from your application, and Crystal Reports.NET has two different viewers to make this happen. The Windows Forms Viewer (which we look at in Chapter 3) can be used with windows applications to preview any reports you have integrated into your application and features a rich object model that allows you to control the appearance of the viewer and some aspects of the report at run time.

Employee Sales Summary

Printed   Tuesday, 9 September, 2003

	Davolio	Dodsworth	King	Leverling	Peacock	Suyama	Total
Active Outdoors Crochet Glove	$22,830	$19,755	$62,647	$12,608	$44,810	$24,335	$186,984
Active Outdoors Lycra Glove	$32,055	$39,532	$44,213	$36,371	$64,153	$27,656	$243,980
Descent	$400,063	$405,792	$422,025	$369,674	$364,773	$329,386	$2,291,713
Endorphin	$81,634	$80,021	$71,698	$55,693	$72,341	$88,863	$450,250
Guardian "U" Lock	$9,131	$2,491	$13,409	$250	$963	$255	$26,500
Guardian ATB Lock	$8,621	$17,703	$638	$3,337	$3,299	$22,124	$55,722
Guardian Chain Lock	$5,129	$7,114	$7,507	$3,116	$1,003	$78	$23,947
Guardian Mini Lock	$4,275	$508	$1,329	$3,807	$5,375	$13,326	$28,620
Guardian XL "U" Lock	$6,726	$2,706	$11,179	$2,159	$9,919	$5,376	$38,064
InFlux Crochet Glove	$7,563	$15,555	$8,159	$11,298	$7,063	$21,405	$71,044
InFlux Lycra Glove	$6,091	$13,983	$17,696	$856	$16,415	$19,496	$74,537
Micro Nicros	$8,962	$9,330	$12,210	$17,360	$6,187	$16,492	$70,541
Mini Nicros	$41,679	$21,923	$16,227	$23,156	$13,682	$13,947	$130,613

Current Page No: 1   Total Page No: 1+   Zoom Factor: 100%

You can add this viewer to any form in your application and either have it as the sole content of the form, or place it alongside other form components. You can control the viewer's appearance, changing toolbars, and other visual aspects, even creating your own icons and buttons to control the viewer and its actions.

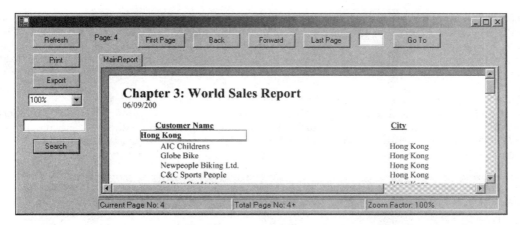

For web-based application, there is also a Web Forms Viewer (Chapter 4) that has similar functionality and allows you to view reports you have integrated into your web applications. You can add this viewer to web pages within your application and show a report either on its own page, or in a frameset, or side by side with other application content – it is up to you.

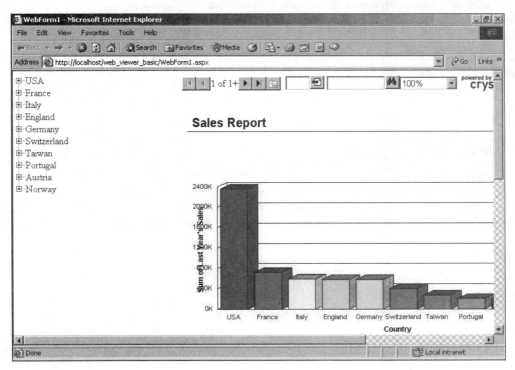

For complete control over your report, regardless of whether your are viewing it through the Windows or Web Forms Viewers, you also have access to the Report Engine (see Chapter 8), which will allow you to control even the most minute aspect of your report before you view it using one of the aforementioned viewers. Using the Report Engine, you can control the report's formatting and features, set database credentials and call direct methods to print, export, and so on.

For creating distributed applications, Crystal Reports.NET has a number of features specifically designed for creating and consuming XML Report Web Services, either through a generic Web Service that ships with Crystal Reports.NET (which allows you to utilize a report without having to publish it as a Web Service) or by creating your own Web Services from report files. (In any case, Chapter 5 will guide you through the process of both creating and consuming XML Report Web Services.)

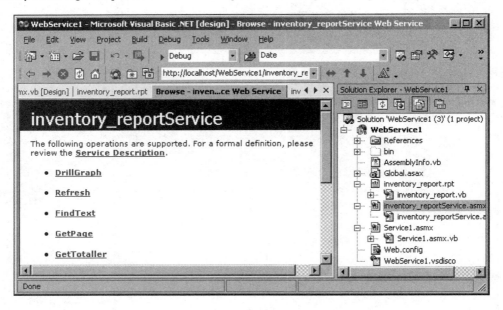

Finally, Crystal Reports.NET is also tightly integrated with Crystal Enterprise, a report scheduling and distribution system that provides a true multi-tier back-end processing platform for reports and allows you to use a scheduling engine and distribution framework to distribute reports to thousands of users.

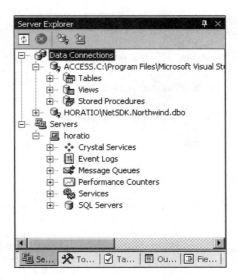

If that wasn't enough functionality jam-packed into this release, there are also a number of tools included for distributing reports with your application that are covered in Chapter 9.

How is Crystal Reports.NET Different from Previous Versions of Crystal Reports?

Crystal Reports.NET is a brand-new product that is only available with the Visual Studio .NET suite. It shares some common features with the retail version of Crystal Reports and was built on the Crystal Reports 8.x technology, but components of Crystal Reports.NET have been re-written using C# and are designed to take full advantage of the .NET Framework.

Integrated Design Environment

Unlike the standalone versions of Crystal Reports, Crystal Reports.NET is part of the Visual Studio .NET Integrated Development Environment (IDE). Using the integrated Report Designer, you can create or modify reports from within the Visual Studio .NET IDE. (If you have used the Report Design Component from previous versions of Crystal Reports, the concept will be familiar.)

Any Language, Any Time

Keen to make amends to developers who have felt slighted in the past, Crystal Reports.NET follows the Visual Studio .NET mantra of "any language, any time" and is not too picky about the language you use to write reporting applications. For all .NET languages the report designer remains the same, and the code used to control viewing reports and report engine calls will only vary slightly between languages, due to different syntax rules and conventions. For example, if you were binding a report to a Web Forms Viewer in VB.NET, the syntax would look something like this:

```
crystalReportViewer1.ReportSource = my_Report1
```

While, the same code can be ported to C#, with only one rather minor syntax change:

```
crystalReportViewer1.ReportSource = my_Report1;
```

Clearly, it is going to be a lot easier to switch between languages when required – this also means that the ease of use that Visual Basic developers enjoyed with previous versions of Crystal Reports can be used across all of the .NET languages.

Integration Methods

Another difference is that the way that we integrate reports into both Windows and web applications has changed. In the past, Crystal Reports developers had a number of different integration methods they could choose from for Windows applications, such as an ActiveX control, Automation Server, or direct calls to the Crystal Reports Print Engine. For web applications, Crystal Reports shipped its own web component server and report viewers, allowing developers to integrate reporting into their applications.

While the report integration solution provided for Windows development seemed to make most developers happy, the web integration provided with Crystal Reports left something to be desired. There were inherent problems with configuration, scalability, and reliability, meaning that the Crystal Reports web development platform could not be used to create scalable enterprise applications.

With the introduction of Visual Studio .NET, is it now possible to bring both Windows and web development into the same framework. The Crystal Report Engine is now a COM+ object wrapped around an updated version of the Crystal Reports Print Engine you may have worked with in the past. The Report Engine can be used to customize features at run time and also takes care of report processing.

When working with Crystal Reports for Visual Studio .NET, you have a choice of either leaving the report on the local machine (and using that machine's resources to process and display the report results using the Windows Forms Viewer), publishing it to a web server (and using the Web Forms viewer) or publishing it as a Report Web Service – which can be consumed and viewed by either the Windows or Web Forms Viewer.

Each of these integration methods will be covered in its own chapter, starting with Chapter 3: Report Integration for Windows-Based Applications.

Ease of Use

Integrating a report into a Windows application is as simple as dragging the Crystal Report Viewer from the toolbar onto a Windows Forms Viewer and binding the viewer to a report file. (You could also create a report using the integrated designer.) The Crystal Report Viewer shown opposite provides a feature-rich client for viewing reports and at design or run time you can customize the appearance and options of the viewer, pass parameters, set properties, and so on.

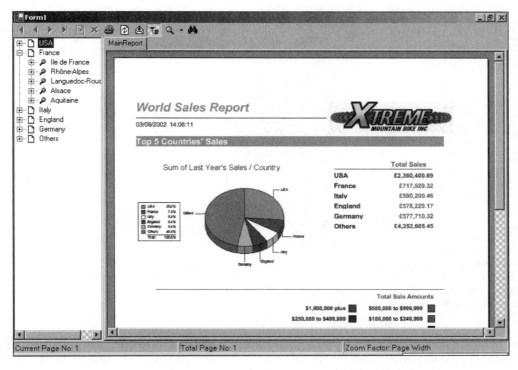

For web development, there is also a Web Forms Viewer that communicates with the Report Engine (either on the local machine or on a remote server) to display a report page in DHTML format. This allows you to quickly integrate reporting into your web applications – there are no runtime files required and the report processing can be performed on the server.

Building Enterprise Applications

In addition to these enhancements, Crystal Decisions has also released Crystal Enterprise – a scalable, platform-independent report distribution, scheduling, and processing engine that can be used in conjunction with Crystal Reports and Crystal Reports.NET to provide the back-end "muscle" to create applications that can support hundreds of users for both real-time and scheduled reports with a clustered, multi-server architecture that can span Windows, Linux, and Unix platforms.

Reports that have been published to the Crystal Enterprise framework can be accessed directly from within Visual Studio .NET, as shown overleaf, and integrated into your application.

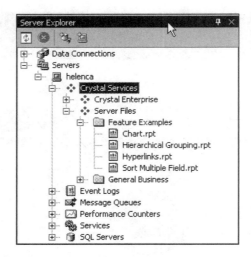

In addition to providing a scalable, multi-tier back end for reporting applications, Crystal Enterprise also has its own security layer (which can use Windows NT authentication, LDAP, etc.), internal structures (folders, objects, rights), and a scheduling engine and distribution capabilities that can be used to build complex reporting applications without have to reinvent a solutions architecture just for reporting.

For example, if you needed to create an application that generates a report every week in PDF format and sends it as an e-mail attachment to 10 different users, you could create that functionality within your own application or you could use the inherent scheduling and distribution capabilities within Crystal Enterprise to make a handful of API calls to do this for you.

Another key area where Crystal Enterprise earns its money is with the clustering technology and multiple-server architecture – imagine in our example from above, there are now 10 reports that go to a hundred different people each day with a copy of the report and a link back to where they can view and search the live report.

The clustering within Crystal Enterprise ensures that these jobs get run regardless of what servers are up or down, and the distributed architecture means that you can add multiple servers to share the processing workload, including servers tasked to specifically run scheduled reports and process on-demand requests.

While the cost of Crystal Enterprise may be off-putting to some developers, its integration with Crystal Reports.NET and distributed architecture (which is beyond the scope of this book) will ensure that you have the scalability you need when your reporting application that serves 10 suddenly needs to serve 10 thousand.

Report Architecture

When we look at Crystal Reports.NET, one of the immediate differences between this version and previous incarnations of the product is the ability to create multi-tier reporting applications. In the past, most Windows applications used a two-tier approach with Crystal Reports, where reports ran on the local machine where the application was installed.

With the introduction of "Crystal Server" for version 4.0 of Crystal Reports, a first attempt was made at developing a client-server version of Crystal Reports; but it wasn't until 1994 when Seagate Software acquired Crystal Reports, and the corporate scheduling product "Ashwin" (which could be used to schedule programs processes, etc.) was introduced that multi-tier report applications became a reality.

The combination of the two products was first introduced in 1995 as "Crystal Info", and later changed name to "Seagate Info". Through the Seagate Info SDK, an additional processing tier was introduced to developers, with a server-based architecture that allowed reports to be run on a separate server and returned to the client.

While the Seagate Info SDK seemed like a good idea, developers were slow to adopt the technology and looked for other ways to create multi-tiered applications. With the introduction of Crystal Reports.NET, developers have found the wealth of tools the product provides, including Web Services, Enterprise integration, and so on, and are now adopting it. Reporting applications using Crystal Reports.NET will generally fall into one of the following categories:

Single-Tier

Crystal Reports integrated with applications created in previous versions of Visual Basic were usually deployed as single-tier applications. In a single-tier application, a developer would use one of the various integration methods to integrate Crystal Reports within their application and would then distribute the report file and all of the Crystal Reports .dll and runtime files required to make the application work. When a report was run, it ran locally as a thick-client application, using the resources of the machine where the application was installed.

With Crystal Reports.NET, you can still create single-tier applications and distribute the runtime files required to run and view a report. Some of the limitations found in applications created with previous versions of Visual Studio tools will still apply, including the need to re-distribute the report file if any changes are required. A much better solution is to consider applications with two or more tiers.

Two-Tier

Most web-applications created with Crystal Reports.NET are considered two-tier applications. In the first tier, shown overleaf, a web application makes a request for a report and the report is processed on the web server that hosts the application.

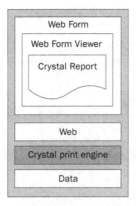

This architecture provides definite advantages over a single-tier app, including off-loading of the report processing and viewing to a server, and a "publish once" mentality for publishing a single copy of a report to a web server that can be accessed by multiple users. However, with this type of two-tier architecture, your application will be limited by the number of users that can physically connect to a single web server, and report processing will add a definite increase to this server's work load if used heavily for viewing reports.

Moving to an even better solution with an even thinner client...

Three-Tier

A true three-tier reporting application, like the one shown below, can be (but doesn't have to be) created using XML Report Web Services (covered in Chapter 5), which are new for Visual Studio .NET. A Report Web Service is a Crystal Report that has been exposed as a Web Service to be used (or consumed) by an application. Applications can connect to a Report Web Service and the underlying report can be viewed either using the Web or Windows Report Viewer, providing all of the functionality (view, drill-down, export) found when integrating reports into a single or two-tier application, but with the report running on a server behind the scenes, resulting in the lightest client resources required for actually viewing a report.

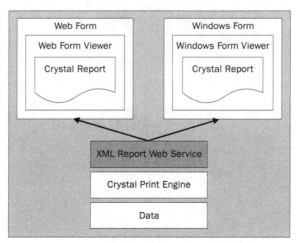

In addition to being able to expose reports as Web Services for internal users, you can also publish Report Web Services to users external to your organization, providing a method for external users to access data held within your own data sources.

Multi-Tier Applications

When working with applications that are to be deployed to large numbers of users, you will probably want to consider moving to a multi-tier architecture (which is just a generalization of the 3-tier concept), where components can be added as the application user base grows.

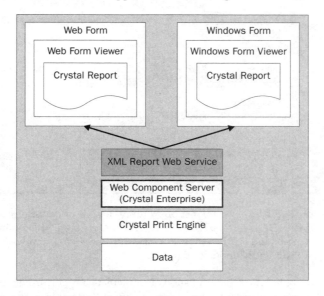

Crystal Enterprise is a web-based, stand-alone solution for secure report delivery and distribution that can be integrated with Crystal Reports.NET. From within the Visual Studio .NET environment, you have access to the reports stored in the Crystal Enterprise framework and a rich object model that exposes all of the Crystal Enterprise features and functionality (scheduling, security, e-mail distribution) for use in your own application.

> **For more information on Crystal Enterprise, check out**
> **http://www.crystaldecisions.com/products/crystalenterprise**

Report Designer

The Crystal Reports Designer, shown overleaf, can be used to create a report from scratch or you can use a number of experts (similar to wizards) to help you get started. The interface is similar to the retail versions of Crystal Reports, and shares enough similarity that existing report developers should have no problems making the transition to the .NET version. With that said, there are some specific options and features that are unique to this version.

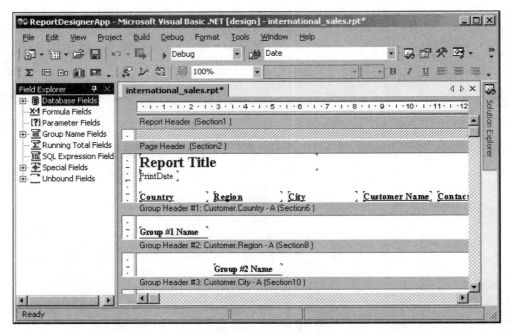

To start, Crystal Reports.NET has extended support for a number of data sources, including ADO.NET, OLE DB (ADO), ODBC (RDO), Access/Excel files (DAO), Crystal Field Definition Files (from previous versions of Crystal Reports), and XML. When working with these data sources, Crystal Reports.NET can utilize either a "Pull" or "Push" mode of data retrieval.

To create a report that "pulls" the required data, you can create a report from a data source just as you normally would and let Crystal Reports handle writing the SQL statement, submitting the statement to the database, retrieving the records, formatting and displaying the records, and so on. This is the most common mode of integrating reports into applications and does not require any additional coding.

In "push" mode, a report can be created from a data source and used within your application, but it is the application itself that is handling the hard work of connecting to the database, populating an ADO.NET (or other) recordset and then "pushing" that recordset to the report. From that point, Crystal Reports will format and display the records it has received.

This method of integration requires more manual coding, but provides more control over the DataSet and report processing. Using the "push" mode to retrieve the data for your report means that you can use optimized SQL and stored procedures via ADO.NET to share database connections with other transactions that occur within your application, and so on.

Incompatibilities

When using the Crystal Reports.NET Designer, you'll notice that there are a number of features that are available in the retail versions of Crystal Reports, which are not supported here. A list of these features has been included below for your reference:

❑ Geographic mapping is not supported in Crystal Reports for Visual Studio .NET. Map objects in Crystal Reports are provided through third-party technology provided by MapInfo and this has not yet been ported over to the .NET Report Designer. If you want to use existing reports that have maps with Crystal Reports for Visual Studio .NET, you can still do so – the map objects themselves will appear blank.

❑ OLAP data sources and the grids that display OLAP information within a report are also not supported. If you are using an existing report that displays an OLAP grid, this area will be shown as a blank.

❑ Crystal Dictionaries, Crystal Queries and Seagate Info Views are not supported. If you need to use an existing report that is based on any of these file formats, you would need to re-create the report directly from the database or data source itself.

> **Note: Up until now we have only looked at previous versions of Crystal Reports. In August 2002, Crystal Decisions released Crystal Reports 9.0, which shares the same file format as Crystal Reports in .NET. It includes a stand-alone report designer (which does not require Visual Studio), as well as an updated report designer for use within the Visual Studio .NET environment, so you could have someone else create reports for your application without having to train them on how to use Visual Studio .NET.**
>
> **Also included are new components for use with .NET – including increased data access, productivity features, and a mobile viewer with associated tools that works with the .NET Mobile Internet Toolkit. For more information on Crystal Reports 9, visit http://www.crystaldecisions.com/products/crystalreports/.**

Crystal Reports.NET Benefits

Now that we have looked at some of the differences between versions of Crystal Reports, and some of the uses (and limitations), we need to have a look at some of the reasons you should be excited about this version and how your applications can benefit from the features we talked about earlier.

Leverage Existing Development and Skills

Crystal Reports can leverage the existing reports you have created, regardless of version. If you already have a suite of reports created in version 7.0, for example, you can quickly import them into Crystal Reports.NET and they are ready to be integrated in your application. But not the other way around – once you have opened or edited a report in Crystal Reports.NET, it uses a Unicode file format that is incompatible with previous versions. In addition, the report design process remains the same, with a number of Experts to guide you through report design, and the same familiar design concepts, formula languages, and features you have used in previous versions.

Tight Visual Studio .NET Integration

From within Visual Studio, accessing a new report is as easy as selecting Project | Add New Item and selecting Crystal Report. There is no need to open a separate application to design reports and all of the reporting features of functionality are available to you, allowing you to programmatically control the look and feel of a report, how it is processed and viewed, and so on.

Windows and Web Report Viewers

For a feature-rich report viewing experience, Crystal Reports.NET includes a report viewer for Windows Forms that has been built using the Windows Forms Classes and provides all of the functionality users have come to expect from Crystal Reports, including drill-down, search, exporting, and so on. In addition to a robust report viewer for Windows Forms, Crystal Reports.NET also includes a thin-client report viewing control for ASP.NET, providing most of the functionality found in the Windows viewer in a "zero-client" (meaning no client is downloaded or installed) DHTML environment, with no additional plug-in or viewer to download.

Easy Deployment

Crystal Reports.NET includes a number of merge modules to make creating setup projects easier. Instead of manually determining the required DLLs and other Crystal-related components, you can simply add one of the merge modules listed below to a setup project:

- ❑ Managed.MSM
  For installing the Crystal Reports.NET managed components, including:

  - ❑ CrystalDecisions.CrystalReports.Engine.DLL
  - ❑ CrystalDecisions.CrystalReports.Web.DLL
  - ❑ CrystalDecisions.Windows.Forms.DLL

- ❑ Database_Access.MSM
  For installing all of the database drivers and all non-managed components (Charting, Export Formats)

- ❑ Database_Access_enu.MSM
  For installing select language-specific components

- ❑ REGWIZ.MSM
  For tracking registration details and license keys

> **One of the most common errors when deploying a Crystal Reports.NET application is forgetting to change the LicenseKey property in your setup project. This must be set or an error involving keycodev2.dll may occur.**

In addition to the merge modules listed above, you may need to include the VC_CRT and VC_STL modules if you are reporting from ADO recordsets, as the Crystal Reports database driver crdb_adoplus.dll relies on the files within these modules.

For more information on deploying your Crystal Reports.NET application, go to Chapter 9.

ADO.NET

With the introduction of ADO.NET, data access has become much easier; and Crystal Reports.NET can take advantage of ADO and the ADO.NET `DataSet`. Instead of having to work out how to access various data sources, Crystal Reports.NET can simply access the ADO.NET `DataSet` as the source for any report you may create.

XML Report Web Services

For sharing reports and creating tiered applications, XML Report Web Services are invaluable. Within the Visual Studio IDE, you can create a Web Service from a report file with two clicks – from that point, Report Web Services can be exposed to users in and outside of your organization and consumed using one of the new viewers included with the product. To optimize the report pages coming over the wire, XML is used to send the report a page at a time to either the Windows or Web Report Viewer, which makes reports viewed from Web Services quick and responsive.

XML Report Web Services are covered in depth in Chapter 5.

Installing Crystal Reports.NET

Crystal Reports.NET ships as a component of Visual Studio .NET and can be installed from the common Visual Studio .NET setup utility. If you are installing Visual Studio .NET for the first time, you may need to complete the Windows Component Update before you can begin – the setup utility will look at your current configuration and determine whether or not you need the updated files and applications. If required, setup will guide you through the update process.

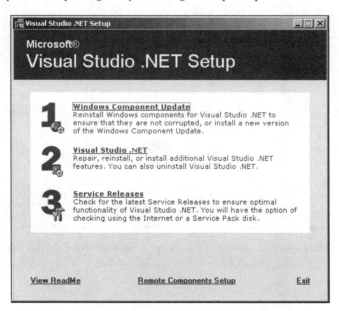

The Component Update installs the following updates to Windows 2000:

- ❑ Microsoft 2000 Service Pack 2 (if you are using Windows 2000)
- ❑ Microsoft Windows Installer 2.0
- ❑ Microsoft Front Page Web Extensions Client
- ❑ Setup Runtime Files
- ❑ Microsoft Internet Explorer 6.0 and Internet Tools
- ❑ Microsoft Data Access Components 2.7
- ❑ Microsoft .NET Framework

After you have completed the component update, you can install Visual Studio .NET. The option to install Crystal Reports for Visual Studio .NET can be found under the Enterprise Development Tools. By default, when you select the Crystal Reports option, all of the related components will be installed as well.

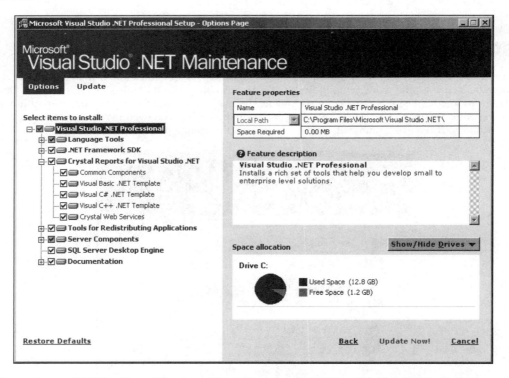

Once it is installed, the Crystal Reports icon will appear on the Visual Studio .NET splash screen and from the Add New Item menu, you should see the option to add a new Crystal Report, as shown opposite.

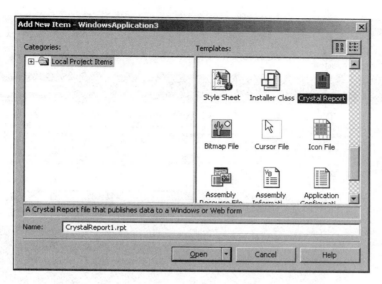

With the installation complete, we can jump right into looking at the samples that are installed with the product and learning about Crystal Reports.NET.

Learning from Sample Applications

Crystal Reports for Visual Studio .NET ships with a number of sample applications to help you get started – the majority of sample applications are simple, but demonstrate some aspect of report integration, feature, or functionality and provide a good learning resource if you are just starting out with Crystal Reports.NET or you are new to this version.

Installing Sample Applications

The Crystal Reports.NET sample applications are installed by default and can be found in the Crystal Reports directory where you have installed Visual Studio .NET. These samples are in self-extracting files that you will need to run before you can open the samples within Visual Studio .NET. These samples are located at X:\Program Files\Microsoft Visual Studio.NET\Crystal Reports\Samples\Code (where X: is the drive where you have installed Visual Studio .NET).

There are two sets of sample applications available, both of which are bundled in self-extracting files – WebForms.exe and Winforms.exe. The first, which will extract to a folder marked WebForms, are written using ASP.NET and demonstrate the use of the Crystal Reports Web Forms Viewer. To view these samples, you will need to use IIS Internet Services Manager to create a virtual directory called "CRSamples" that points to the directory where you extracted the sample files. From that point, you should be able to access these samples from http://localhost/CRSamples.

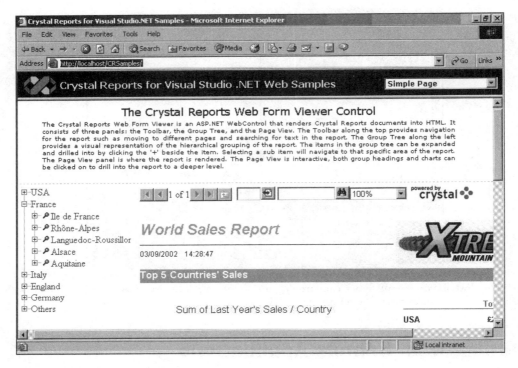

The following samples are included in this set:

Sample	Description
Simple Page	The "Simple Page" sample application demonstrates using the Web Forms Viewer with one of the sample reports (World Sales). The sample demonstrates some of the features of the report viewer, including drilling down into the details of the report, the report group tree, the viewer toolbar and page control options.
Custom Navigation	Demonstrates the amount of customization that can occur within the Web Forms Viewer. By default, the viewer has a set toolbar that appears, but developers who wish to control the look and feel of the entire page can control the toolbar, or even create their own with minimal coding.
Interactivity	Shows how events can be fired when different areas of a report are clicked, which will change the text of the textbox in the upper right-hand corner. It also gives some insight into the events supported by the Web Forms Viewer.

> **Note: There is also the option for "More Samples" that will take you back to the Crystal Decisions web site.**

The second set of sample applications are for Windows Forms, which are extracted from a self-extracting file and found in the **WinForms** folder, and which demonstrate the use of Crystal Reports.NET with Windows applications. There are separate projects for Visual Basic and Visual C# that can be opened and run. Both of these projects demonstrate a simple "Preview" implementation of the Windows Forms Viewer and allow you to select a report to view. Once you have selected a report file (there are a couple located in the **Reports** directory of the **Samples** folder), the report is bound to the viewer; the Print Engine runs the report and uses the viewer to display the results.

Sample Reports

In addition to sample applications, there are also sample report files available for you to use in your testing and development. There are two different sets of reports available in the **Reports** directory of the **Samples** folder – **Feature Examples** demonstrate different features and functionality within Crystal Reports.NET (Charting, Embedded Hyperlinks, Sorting, etc.), and **General Business** reports are typical of reports that may be created and used in business (**Income Statement, World Sales Report**).

All of these reports have been created using the sample Access database that ships with Crystal Reports.NET and are indispensable to use when debugging. If you are having difficulty integrating your report and can't determine whether it is your code, the viewer, or the report designer itself that is not working, you can substitute your report with one of the sample reports and at least eliminate one option!

Sample Data

A sample database has been included with Crystal Reports.NET and the sample reports listed above are based on this database. The "Xtreme Mountain Bike Company" database (`xtreme.mdb`) is an Access database that contains tables for Customers, Orders, Products, Suppliers, and Employees, and does not require a copy of Access to be installed or loaded on to your machine to be used.

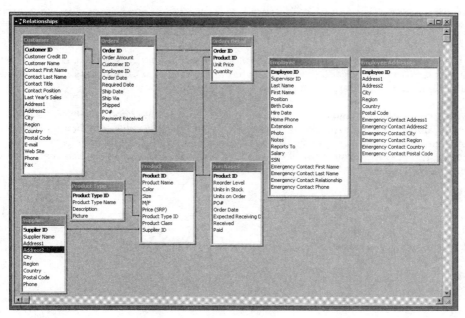

Tutorials

Crystal Decisions has it's own web site dedicated to Crystal Reports.NET and it includes a number of tutorials or walk-throughs that can be used to get up to speed quickly with the product. The web site is located at http://www.crystaldecisions.com/ms/crnet and you will need to register before you can download the tutorials or other materials.

There are a number of tutorials available:

- ❏ Reporting off ADO.NET Datasets
- ❏ Viewing a Report in a Web Application
- ❏ Designing and Viewing a Report in a Windows Application
- ❏ Exposing Reports as Web Services
- ❏ Interactivity and Reports in Web Applications

Most of these tutorials can be completed using the sample database and reports that ship with the product, or you can go through the tutorial using your own reports and data source.

Another key resource for Crystal Reports developers is (www.crystaluser.com), which features a number of Crystal Reports forums, or Crystal Decision's own web site and forums at (www.crystaldecisions.com).

You can also find more information (and post a question if need be) on Microsoft's public newsgroups. The majority of Crystal-related questions, regardless of version or language, get posted to (microsoft.public.vb.crystal), but there are always a few questions posted in the general dotnet newsgroup (microsoft.public.dotnet.general).

> **Note: You will need a newsgroup reader (like Outlook Express) to access these newsgroups.**

There are also a number of good articles at www.dotnet247.com for ASP.NET and other developers, with more than a few articles and questions concerning Crystal Reports integration. You can also find general programming and framework questions there as well.

Finally, Crystal Decisions maintains its own web-based forums at (http://community.crystaldecisions.com) where you can post questions and get some answers. Crystal Decisions does not monitor these forums, but generally the advice is good and you can always find someone who is willing to help. While you are on the site, make sure you register your copy of Crystal Reports.NET for free access to technical support and updates (and the requisite marketing e-mail or two).

Summary

Crystal Reports for Visual Studio .NET is a powerful addition to the Visual Studio .NET toolset and has been developed to take advantage of the new .NET development framework. Using the Crystal Reports Designer, you can quickly create or modify reports without having to leave the Visual Studio IDE. When it is time to integrate your report into either a Windows or web application, Crystal Reports includes a number of viewers that quickly integrate into your application. With a scalable back-end processing architecture, Crystal Reports for Visual Studio .NET should be the only tool you need to integrate reporting into your enterprise applications.

In the next chapter, we'll move beyond the product overview to actually start creating reports and integrating them into our own development.

Professional **Crystal Reports**
for **Visual Studio .NET**

2

Getting Started with Crystal Reports.NET

In the first chapter, we had a look at Crystal Reports.NET, and had a brief overview of some of its features and benefits. With that out of the way, it is time to actually get started using the tool.

In this chapter, we will be looking at the Crystal Reports Designer within Visual Studio .NET and learn how to create and import reports for use in Windows or Web applications. This will include:

❑   Planning Your Report Design

❑   Creating a Report Using an Expert

❑   Working with the Report Design Environment

❑   Report Design Basics

❑   Advanced Report Design Techniques

❑   Optimizing Report Performance

By the end of the chapter, you will have the skills to develop your own basic reports and can move on to the actual integration of these reports into your application. If you have used Crystal Reports before, some of the material in this chapter will be familiar. Crystal Reports.NET builds on the features and concepts found in previous versions of Crystal Reports, but there are some things that are unique to this version, which will be identified throughout this book.

Keep in mind that this book is not designed to be the exhaustive reference on report design – that could take an entire book by itself (and there are a few out there). We have deliberately focused on the integration side, on how to use Crystal Reports with your application. As the title says, this chapter provides just enough information to get you started with Crystal Reports.NET.

The Sample Files

In the C:\CrystalReports\Chapter02\ folder you will find all of the sample reports we build in this chapter:

❑   SalesReport_Basic – a sales report that we will create with the Report Expert

❑   SalesReport_Chart – the same report with a chart that we will add later in the chapter

❑   SalesReport_CrossTab – the same sales report, with a table that we will add later

❑   Demo – a small application that you can use to preview some more advanced sample reports

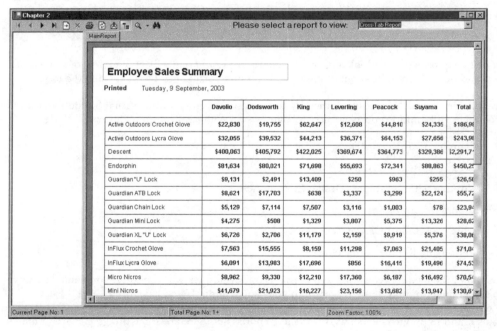

The sample reports utilize the Xtreme sample database that ships with Crystal Reports.NET. By default, this is located in at C:\Program Files\Microsoft Visual Studio .NET\Crystal Reports\Samples\Database\Xtreme.mdb and will have an ODBC DSN that points to this location so Crystal Reports .NET can *see* the database. If for some reason, you don't have this DSN, you will need to create one using the **ODBC Data Source Administrator** found in **Control Panel** under **Administrative Tools**.

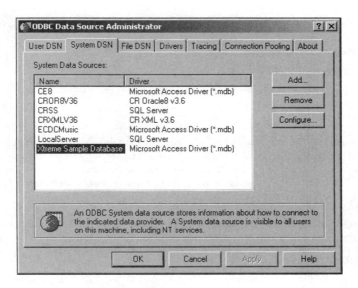

Select the System DSN tab and click on the Add button. This displays a list of drivers for which you want to set up a data source. We are using a Microsoft Access database, so select Microsoft Access Driver (.mdb) and then use the next window to locate the database and give it a name (Xtreme Sample Database), finally selecting OK to finish.

Planning Your Report Design

Before we actually get into the technical report design, we need to spend a little time planning our report to alleviate some of the problems we might face later when we actually sit down and develop the report. Too often as developers we will create reports that we think the user will want, using all of the latest features, bells, and whistles, only to find that the end-user would be happy with something much simpler, and probably easier to read.

Another problem is that a developer will often sit down and crack open the Report Designer without really knowing what the end product will look like, or considering how the end user will use what has been created. What is called for is a bit of planning before we jump right into the technical aspect of designing reports. By planning our report before we get started, we can deliver a report that meets the users' needs and expectations.

If you already have a report design methodology and it works for you, please have a read over this section anyway – you may find a different way of doing things or be able to incorporate some small part of it into what you already do. In any case, there are a number of reports associated with this section available in the downloadable code for this chapter – feel free to modify these reports for your own use.

In a very basic report design methodology, there are four steps to planning a new report:

- ❑ Gather Report Requirements
- ❑ Perform Technical Review
- ❑ Develop Report Prototype
- ❑ Design Report

In most applications, reports are usually tied to a specific function or area of an application. For example, if you have created an application that is used for entering telephone sales orders from customers, chances are there will be a suite of reports tied to that function, showing sales summaries, order totals, etc. The best way to determine what these reports should look like is to actually ask the people that will be using them on a daily basis.

If you are working in a large organization, you will probably have a business analyst who will interview the user, gather their requirements and then communicate these requirements back to you. If you are in a smaller organizer or, if like the rest of us, you are forced to take on a number of roles, you may gather these requirements yourself.

In either case, end-user interviews are the key to targeting a report's content. Organize the interviews with the actual end users (not their supervisors, personal assistants, or others), and ask them to bring along examples of reports they currently use, or would like to use. This is your chance to find out what information they need to better perform their job. Be careful when interviewing, as users will sometimes come up with an arm length long wish list for reports they would like to see.

In the interview, the user should be able to tell you how the report is used and what decisions are made based on this information. If they can't tell you either of these things, either you are interviewing the wrong person or they really don't need the information they have asked for.

Once you have interviewed the end users, you should have a pretty good idea of what reports are required, and how they will be used. From this point, there are many different ways of documenting the user's requirements (such as user requirements statements, or use cases) but the most straightforward method is to create a formal Report Requirements document.

A Report Requirements document will outline what information needs to appear in the report, how the report is used (is it interactive or run in a batch), and the general look and feel of the report. You may also create a mock-up of the report or a rough sketch of what it will look like. With your report requirements in hand, the next step in our method is to perform a technical review of the report's definition.

A good place to start with a technical review is to determine the data source for this report. Most likely the data source will be a relational database, but the data could also reside in spreadsheets, text files, OLAP (OnLine Analytical Processing) data structures, and even non-relational data sources (like Exchange or Outlook folders). Once you have found the data source, you will need to dig a little deeper to determine the exact tables and views that can provide the data required. You may need to develop additional views or stored procedures to consolidate the data prior to developing a report (for speed and ease of use and reuse) and these will need to be documented as well. Again, all of this information is added to your Report Requirements document.

For the next step of the technical review, you will need to investigate whether or not the design of the report is feasible. The user may request twenty columns (when the page will only fit seven landscape) or may have based the design on an existing report or spreadsheet created by hand. Once you are more experienced working with Crystal Reports, you will begin to understand how the tool works and the kind of output that can be achieved. In the meantime, browse through some of the sample reports that ship with the product to get a feel for the types of reports Crystal can produce.

Once you have completed the technical review and you understand where the data for the report resides and you are comfortable that Crystal Reports.NET can deliver the required format, it is then time to create a report prototype from your notes and preliminary sketches. This prototype can be created using Word, Excel, Visio, and so on, but should closely match the report's final layout and design. Again, another important check is to make sure that the layout and design you create can be created with the features and functionality that Crystal Reports.NET has available.

A good way to determine if Crystal Reports.NET can deliver a particular format for data is to find a sample report that shows the data presented in the method you want to use or you could create a small proof-of-concept report with sample data to test the design.

The prototype, combined with a formal Report Requirements document will clearly communicate what the report should look like when it is finished. It also helps gain user acceptance for the design, as they can see what the finished product will look like (even before you have opened the Report Designer). If you are working in a large team, this documentation will communicate the requirements to other report developers, so you don't actually have to brief them on every single report that needs to be developed.

If you are working as a business analyst, application developer, and report developer all-in-one, it can also help you keep on track with the user's requirements and make gaining user acceptance that much easier. Once signed-off by the client, the Report Requirements is a contract, so should it turn out that the report designed isn't what the client wanted, you can point to this document and their signature on it!

Finally, with the documentation and prototype in hand, it is time to actually sit down, open the Report Designer and design your report.

Creating a Crystal Report

In the next few pages, we are going to walk through the steps to create an International Sales report in an existing Windows Application using the Standard Expert – you can open the solution and project that is available in the code download for this example (`C:\CrystalReports\Chapter02\SalesReport_Basic\chapter2.sln`) or create your own.

When creating a report from scratch within Crystal Reports.NET, we have a number of experts that can be used to guide us through the report development process. In this section, we will look at how to use these experts to get started – once you have finished working through the expert, you will have a report you can further develop using the integrated designer. Over time, as the interface becomes familiar, you may choose to start with a blank report and build it up, piece-by-piece, but most developers use the expert to at least get them started.

To start with, create a new Visual Basic .NET project. Select Windows Application from the dialog, call the project SalesReport, and put it in the folder C:\CrystalReports\Chapter02.

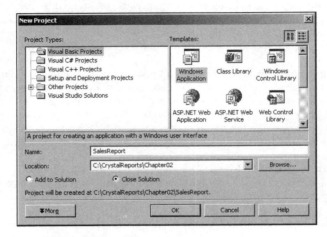

Adding a Report to Your Application

Adding a new report to your application is as simple as selecting Project | Add New Item and selecting Crystal Report from the list of available templates. Enter international_sales.rpt into the name field and click on Open to insert the new report into your application. A separate tab will now appear for the report and allow you to use the integrated Report Designer to create your report, but before you can do this you will see the Crystal Report Gallery window.

The first decision you will need to make about your report is to select how it will be created. In this instance, we are actually going to use one of the Report Experts to walk us through the report design, but there are other options as well, as shown in the following table.

Method	Description
Using the Report Expert	There are a number of different Report Experts available to walk you through step by step to create a report. This is the most popular method even for experienced report developers, as it provides a starting point for further report development.
As a Blank Report	For experienced developers who are familiar with the Report Designer and want to build a report up piece by piece. This is often a good way to produce a report that is leaner, and has fewer overheads built into it. When this is selected the Experts aren't available.
From an Existing Report	If you have an existing report that will serve as the basis for the report you wish to create, you can use this method to import your existing report. Again, when this is selected the Experts aren't available.

Using a Report Expert

If you decide to use a Report Expert, there are seven different experts to choose from. All of the experts share some steps in common – for example, in all of them you will be prompted for the data source for your report, as well as what fields will appear.

As we go through this chapter, we will be looking at all of the major steps involved in creating a report using the experts, but for now here is an overview of the different types of experts available:

- ❑ **Standard** – The Standard Expert is used most often and is the most generic. You can use the Standard Expert to create a columnar report, which include features such as grouping, sorting, and summaries. This expert also includes the ability to add charts, apply a number of pre-defined styles, and filter records, and advanced analysis features like TopN, BottomN (for example, Top 10 or Bottom 10 reports).

- ❑ **Form Letter** – By combining text objects and database fields, Crystal Reports.NET can be used to create form letters and statements. This expert guides you through creating a report and placement of database fields and text within the report.

- ❑ **Form** – To support reports that are designed for a specific paper form, Crystal Reports.NET can use a scanned form or graphic as a guide for your report. Using the Form Expert, you will be able to underlay an image behind your report to correctly place fields on the form. From that point, you can either leave the image in place and print the form and fields on blank paper or delete the image and print the report directly onto your forms.

- ❑ **Cross-Tab** – Cross-tabs within Crystal Reports.NET look similar to a spreadsheet, with columns and rows of summarized data. Using the Cross-Tab expert, you can create a report that will feature a cross-tab object in the report header.

- ❑ **Subreport** – Subreports are reports that are inserted into a main report. Subreports can be unrelated or parameters can be passed between the main and subreports to determine the content to display.

❑ **Mail Label** – Crystal Reports.NET supports multi-column reports and this functionality makes mailing labels possible. It includes a number of mailing labels pre-defined for common label stock from Avery and other suppliers (but only in Letter sizes), or you can create your own custom label size using this expert.

❑ **Drill-Down** – The concept behind drill-down is that you display a summary in your report and users can drill-down into the summary to see the details that make it up.

For this chapter we will look at the Standard Report Expert, so click on OK with Standard selected in the listbox in the Crystal Report Gallery window.

Selecting Your Data Source

The first step in any of the experts is to select your data source. There are five different types of data sources we can use as the basis of our report.

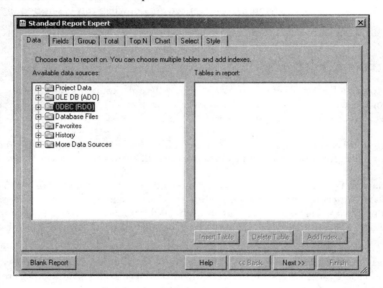

Which of these data sources you select as the basis of your report will depend on your own particular needs and the data sources available to you.

Data Source	Description
Project Data	Crystal Reports.NET can leverage the ADO.NET Framework and report directly from datasets that appear in your application. For more information on how Crystal Reports.NET can be used with ADO.NET data, please see Chapter 6: *Working with .NET Data*.
OLE DB (ADO)	This folder is for data sources that can be accessed through OLE DB, including SQL Server, Oracle, and Microsoft Jet 3.51/4.00 accessible data sources (Access, Excel, Paradox, Dbase, and so on).

Data Source	Description
ODBC (RDO)	This folder is for data sources that can be accessed through an ODBC-compliant driver (which is just about every other data source). In addition to reporting from tables, views, stored procedures, and so on, Crystal Reports.NET will also allow you to enter a SQL command to serve as the basis for your report.
Database Files	This folder includes a number of file-type database formats, including Access, Excel, XML, and Crystal Field Definition files (TTX), as used with previous versions of Crystal Reports and bound reporting.
More Data Sources	These include reporting directly from XML files, Access/Excel through DAO, and Crystal Field Definition Files (TTX).

> **When reporting from an ADO.NET data source, the underlying XML file (with the `.XSD` extension) is used to determine the details of the dataset such as fields, or lengths. Since this XML contains only the definition of the data and not the data itself, you won't be able to browse data from within the Report Designer when using this data source.**

There is also a bug in the first release of Visual Studio .NET – when your report uses an ADO.NET DataSet, the string lengths in the underlying XML schema file are ignored and appear to be 65,534 characters in length. This issue is tracked by Crystal Decisions and should be resolved in future service packs.

To select the table we are going to use in our international sales report, double-click the node for **ODBC (RDO)**, which will open the dialog shown below:

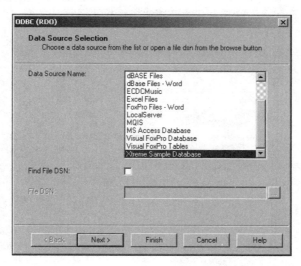

Select the Xtreme Sample Database and click Finish. This data source should now appear in the Data tab of the Report Expert.

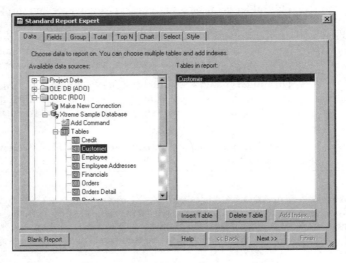

Click the plus icon next to Tables, locate the Customer table, and double-click on it to insert this table into your report.

Multiple Tables

If you select multiple tables to appear in your report, a new tab will appear for Links, allowing you to specify how these tables or views are joined together. By default, Crystal Reports.NET will attempt to make these links for you, based on the primary keys, field lengths, and names. You can clear the links that have been provided for you by clicking the Clear Links button on the right-hand side of the Links dialog (or by highlighting each and clicking the delete button), and re-draw them by dragging one field on top of another.

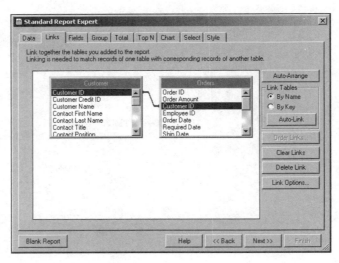

By default, Crystal Reports.NET will join these tables with an `Equal` join, but you can change the join type by right-clicking on top of the link and selecting **Link Options**.... If you have added a second table, delete it now, because we will only use a single table in this example; to do this click on the **Data** tab, select the second table you added from the **Tables in Report** column, and finally click on the **Delete Table** button.

Choosing the Fields For Your Report

Now you have selected the data source for your report, the next step in the Standard Expert is to select the fields that will appear in your report. To do this, click on the **Fields** tab.

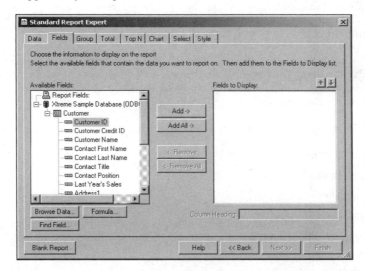

To select a field, highlight the field and then use the arrows to move it from the left-hand list to the right. The fields will be listed using the notation **TableName.FieldName** and if you are unsure of a field's contents or type, you can use the **Browse** button to browse the contents of the field. There is also a **Find** button for finding a particular field in long field lists.

When you look at your report's design a little later, the fields you have selected here will be inserted into the report's detail section and a separate line will be printed for each record in the dataset. You can change the order these fields are inserted using the up and down arrows at the top right-hand corner of the dialog – they are inserted from left to right on your report, from the top of the list of fields that appear here.

For this report, we are inserting:

- ❏ Customer.Customer Name
- ❏ Customer.Contact Last Name
- ❏ Customer.Contact Title
- ❏ Customer.E-mail
- ❏ Customer.Phone

With each field, a corresponding field heading will be added to your report and placed in the page header. You can use the textbox marked Column Heading to change the default heading (usually the field name) or you can edit the headings later in the Report Designer.

Having selected the data source for your report and these five fields, you could click the Finish button to work with your report in the Report Designer, but we are going to push on and have a look at grouping and sorting the data.

Grouping and Sorting

After you have selected the fields that will appear on your report, you can choose which fields will be used for sorting and grouping. Click on the Group tab and use the same concept as before, moving the field from the left-hand list to the right to select it for grouping.

This dialog can be confusing, as developers will select a group field and then preview their report, only to find that the data is sorted, but no group has been inserted. In order to create groups of records, you must specify a field in this dialog *and* in the next dialog we discuss (the Total tab), and select some summary to appear for each group.

The fields we are selecting for the grouping in our report are:

❑   Customer.Country

❑   Customer.Region

❑   Customer.City

You can change the order of the fields you have selected using the up and down arrows in the upper right-hand corner of the dialog, and select a sort order from the drop-down list below.

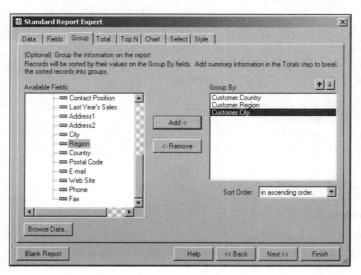

There are four options available for sort order, including:

Sort Order	Description
Ascending	For ordering the data from A-Z, 1-9, etc.
Descending	For ordering the data from Z-A, 9-1, etc.
Original	If your dataset is already sorted, this option will leave the data in its original sort order
Specified	Used for creating your own custom groups and setting some criteria – any records that meet the criteria would belong to the specified group

If you select **in specified order**, a second drop-down list and other items appear in the window.

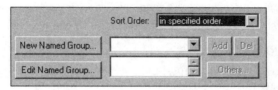

This is called **specified grouping** and allows you to create named groups, and specify some criteria for the group. For example, if you were working with a database field that contained a **Country** field, you could create a new group by clicking on the **New Named Group** button, giving it the name of Asia Pacific, and then specifying the countries that are considered to be in the Asia Pacific group (Australia, New Zealand, and the Philippines, among others).

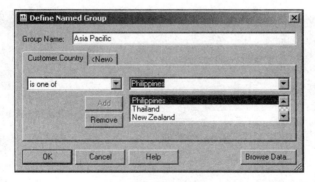

When setting up named groups, you are limited to the standard Crystal record-selection operators (**equal to, not equal to, is one of**, etc.) and can only reference the field you are grouping.

You also have the option of dealing with the other records that fall outside of your grouping criteria by clicking on the **Others** box in the Standard Report Expert window:

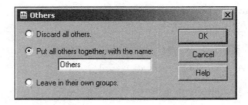

While specified grouping is very useful for re-ordering records, it can be monotonous if you have to use it continually to create the same specified groups in multiple reports. The best practice for specified grouping is to use it only when necessary – if you find you are creating the same groups over and over again, you may want to consider putting this logic into a stored procedure, or creating another lookup table in your database that will determine how your grouping is broken up.

For this example, we are *not* going to use specified grouping, so with your group set as Customer.Country, Customer.Region, and Customer.City in ascending order, the next step is to insert the summaries you want to see within your report.

Working with Simple Summaries

Click on the Total tab in the Standard Report Expert window to add summary information to the report. Summary fields are calculated fields within a Crystal Report, that do not require a formula to be written. Encapsulating the most popular requests for calculations, like sums, and averages, summary fields can be used to rapidly develop reports without a lot of repetitive coding.

To insert a summary field, you will need to select a database field (in this case, Customer.Last Year's Sales) and then choose a summary type from the drop-down list shown below. We have chosen sum, and have also checked the two boxes, Percentage of, and Add Grand Totals.

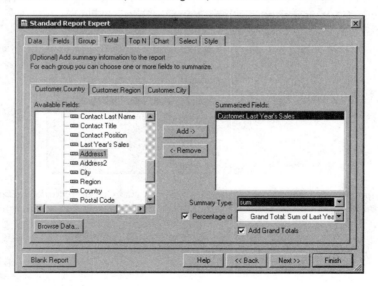

There are over 20 summary operators available for use, but unfortunately the documentation that ships with Crystal Reports.NET does not include a list of them or how they can be used, so a list of the most popular has been included here. Keep in mind that the summary fields available depend on the type of field you have selected, for example, you can't calculate the average of a string field.

Summary Function	Description
Sum	Calculates a sum of all items
Average	Calculates the standard un-weighted average for all items
Maximum	Returns the maximum value
Minimum	Returns the minimum value
Count	Calculates the total number of all items
Sample Variance	Calculates the statistical sample variance of a specific sample of items
Sample Standard Deviation	Calculates the statistical standard deviation of a specific sample of items
Population Variance	Calculates the statistical variance of the entire population of items
Population Standard Deviation	Calculates the statistical standard deviation of the entire population of items
Distinct Count	Calculates the number of distinct items (for instance, if two different instances of "David" appeared in the list, it would only be counted once)
Correlation	Calculates a measure of the relation between two or more items
Covariance	Calculates a measure of the variance between two or more items
Weighted Average	Calculates an average, weighted by the number of times an item appears
Median	Calculates the statistical median of all items
Nth Percentile	Calculates the Nth percentile (where N is pre-defined number)
Nth Largest	Returns the Nth largest item (where N is pre-defined number)
Nth Smallest	Returns the Nth smallest item (where N is pre-defined number)
Mode	Calculates the statistical mode of all items
Nth Most Frequent	Returns the Nth most frequent item (where N is a pre-defined number)

Also available in the formula language are the corresponding functions to these summary fields, so you can also use them in complex formulas with branching and control structures if required. Keep in mind that their use as a summary field will be limited to only a few options or parameters passed to each.

Using Analysis Features

In addition to simple summaries (which we have just looked at) and formulas (which are coming up in Chapter 7), we also have the ability to add a number of analysis features to our report, to help highlight information that may be important or otherwise missed.

On the TopN tab of the Report Expert, we have three options for adding a bit of analysis to our report:

Analysis Type	Description
TopN	Orders your report groups according to a summary field, where you enter a number (*N*) and are presented with the TopN groups, in order from the largest to smallest (for instance, you could create a top 10 report based on last year's sales, to show your best customers). You can also use the options presented to discard the other records or place them in their own group.
BottomN	Will order your report groups according to a summary field, where you enter a number (*N*) and are presented with the BottomN groups (for instance, you could create a bottom 10 report, based on last year's sales to show your worst customers). Similar to TopN, you can use the options presented to group or discard the other records.
Sort All	Will order your report groups according to a summary field, either ascending or descending, or by top or bottom percentage depending on the options you set.

Keep in mind that all of these analysis options will be applied throughout your report, and will apply to any graphs or charts you might insert in the next step of the Report Expert.

Charting and Graphing

For charting and graphing functionality, Crystal Reports.NET relies on a graphing engine created by 3-D graphics. In the Report Experts (as well as the designer itself) you can add a number of different graph types to your report through the Chart page.

To create a chart for your report, select the Chart tab, select a chart type and then select where the data will come from. The most common type of chart is a Group Chart, which requires that both a group and a summary field be inserted into your report. If you would like more information on the different types of graphs, look at section on *Advanced Report Design Techniques* later in this chapter.

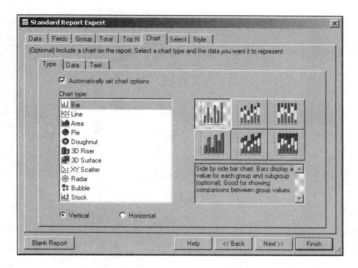

Filtering Your Report

When reporting from a number of different tables, the chances are you don't want to see all of the data in your report. Crystal Reports.NET follows the tradition set in previous versions of the retail product, and has it's own Record Selection Formula that dictates what records are returned to the report, so click on the **Select** tab to use it.

The Record Selection Formula is written using Crystal Reports.NET's own proprietary formula language, which in turn is translated to standard SQL and submitted to the database. When there is a feature that can't be translated to SQL, Crystal retrieves all of the records and uses it's own Report Engine to apply the formula and filter the records.

When working with the **Select** tab in the Report Expert, the options are identical to those you will find in the Select Expert, which is used inside the Report Designer for Record Selection.

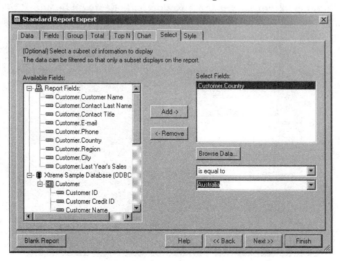

There are a number of basic operators available, including:

❑ Is equal to

❑ Is not equal to

❑ Is less than

❑ Is less than or equal to

❑ Is greater than

❑ Is greater than or equal to

❑ Is one of – for building a list of items, such as Is one of Australia, UK, New Zealand, and is similar to the In operator in SQL

❑ Is between

❑ Is not between

❑ Is like – for wildcard searches where an asterisk represents many characters (for instance, *Zealand), and a question mark represents single characters (????Zealand)

❑ Is starting with – for strings that start with a phrase entered

Remember that this record selection is written to a formula and then translated into the SQL statement – we will look at some more advanced record selection a little later in this chapter and again in Chapter 7, which deals with formulas and logic. For our purposes, we are not going to set any record selection on the report we are creating – we want all of the records to be returned from the sample database, so make sure nothing is in the Select Fields, and move on to the next tab, Style.

Selecting a Report Style

Finally, the last step of the Report Expert involves selecting a particular style for your report and adding a title. There are ten different pre-defined styles to select from and, no, you cannot add your own style to the list! You can also add a report title, in this case International Sales Report, which will be stored in the report file's Summary Information and a Report Title field will be added to your report's design.

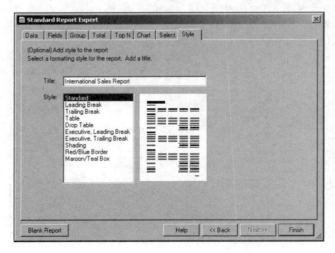

Adding Your Report to a Form

The final step in the Standard Expert is to click the Finish button, which will open your report inside the Report Designer within Visual Studio .NET.

> Make sure that you get into the habit of immediately saving your report by clicking the **Save** or **Save All** icons within the Visual Studio .NET IDE. While the Report Designer does have an undo feature, it is always nice to have a saved copy in case anything should go wrong.

At this point, you probably want to have a look at how your report will appear when it is printed. Running the report will only open a blank form though; unfortunately, the designer does not include an integrated preview so to preview your report, you will need to add the Crystal Reports Viewer to a form, and then specify the Report Source to be the report you have just created.

Open Form1.vb in design mode. Select the form and change the Title in the properties window to International Sales Report, so the user can then see what the report is about if they view the report on a computer. Finally, change the size field so it reads 700,500.

From the Windows Forms section of the Toolbox, drag and drop the CrystalReportViewer onto the form – without this, any reports cannot be seen. If you can't see the Toolbox, click on View | Toolbox to make it appear (the keyboard shortcut is *Ctrl+Alt+X*).

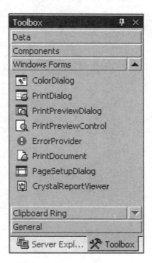

Position the CrystalReportViewer in the top left corner of the form, and drag it's bottom right-hand corner diagonally down, resizing the viewer to fill the whole form. Now when your report is displayed, it is nice and clear. Next, change the anchor property to Top, Bottom, Left, Right so if the form is resized, the CrystalReportViewer, and more importantly, your report inside it, will be resized to match.

From the **Components** section of the Toolbox, drag and drop the **ReportDocument** icon onto the form. This opens up a dialog from which you can choose the report to be opened in the form. Select the report we have just created, displayed as **SalesReport.international_sales**, and click on **OK**.

The `international_sales.rpt` file is now shown in a shaded area at the bottom of the form designer. This shows that the report has been added; and many more reports can be too, using the same method we used here. However, for this example we just want to display the report we have just created, so we will move on.

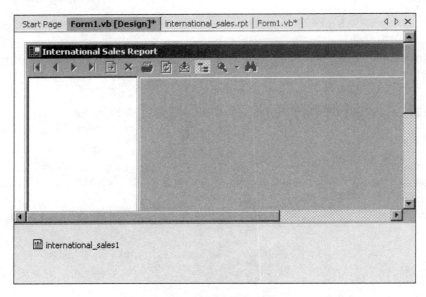

Finally, we want the report to open in the form when it loads, so double-click on the **CrystalReportViewer** to open the code designer. The load procedure will be created because of this action, so all you need to do is tell the form where to find the report. Add the shaded line in the following example to your code:

```
Public Class Form1
    Inherits System.Windows.Forms.Form
    ...
    'Windows Form Designer Generated Code
    ...
    Private Sub CrystalReportViewer1_Load(ByVal sender As System.Object,
                                    ByVal e As System.EventArgs)
                                    Handles CrystalReportViewer1.Load
        CrystalReportViewer1.ReportSource = New international_sales()
    End Sub
End Class
```

That's it! Your basic sales report is complete, and all you have to do is click on the small blue start icon in Visual Studio .NET to see it in action.

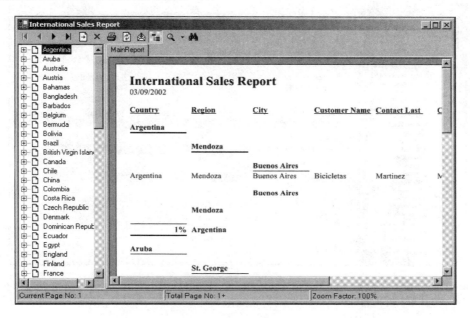

The report is indexed by country, region, and city. Select one of these from the tree-view on the left of the window to jump to that information. As you can see from this example, Crystal Reports.NET can present a huge amount of data in a clear and organized manner.

Now you have stepped through the many stages of the Report Expert, your report should match the `SalesReport_Basic` that is available in the code download. With a basic report using an expert out of the way, it is time to take a look at the Report Designer itself. Make sure you save the Sales Report, as we will use this International Sales Report as the foundation for some later examples.

Working with the Report Design Environment

Regardless of how many times you go through the Report Experts to create reports, you will spend most of your time working with reports in the integrated Report Designer within Visual Studio .NET, shown below. If you have worked with a previous version of Crystal Reports, this interface will seem familiar, but there are subtle differences you'll notice when looking for a specific function or feature.

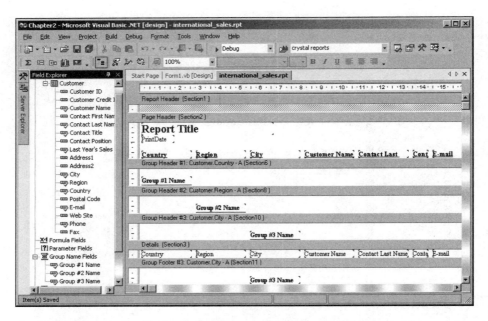

To understand how to work with the designer, we need to take a look at some of the components that make up the Report Designer.

Menus and Toolbars

To start, your familiar Crystal Reports menus and toolbars have gone – the constraints of being embedded in the Visual Studio .NET Framework means that we can't have exclusive control over the menus that appear in the IDE.

Instead, the majority of these options can be found in the toolbars, explorers, or right-click menus within the Report Designer. There are two toolbars available with Crystal Reports.NET, one called Crystal Reports – Main and the other called Crystal Reports – Insert. The main toolbar contains the formatting controls (such as font and size) and the insert toolbar provides the facility to insert summaries, charts, and groups.

For inserting fields into your report, there is a Field Explorer (which used to be invoked by selecting Insert | Field Object in older versions of Crystal Reports). You can drag fields directly from the Field Explorer onto your report.

I mentioned it before, but it is worth repeating here – if you close the Field Explorer, to re-open it again you will need to go to View | Other Windows | Document Outline or press *Ctrl+Alt+T* to view it again.

Setting Default Properties

By default, Crystal Reports.NET will have a number of properties preset. These include the font and formatting for fields in your report, the page size, margins and layout, and so forth.

For more control over the reports you create, you can actually change these default properties. One of the most common scenarios is that Crystal Reports.NET defaults the font to Times New Roman and sets a specific font size for different types of fields. Your standard report template may be in Arial, so you can either spend a considerable amount of time changing the font sizes for the different elements in every report you create, or you can set the defaults and be done with it once and for all – any reports you create from this point onwards will use these settings.

There are two sets of properties associated with Crystal Reports.NET. The first are the default settings, which are written to the local registry and exist for all reports created using that particular machine (there is no easy way to port these settings between two machines unless you get up to some registry wizardry). These options can be found by right-clicking in the Report Designer and selecting **Designer | Default Settings**. Through the default settings, you can control field formatting and fonts, database options and a variety of miscellaneous options grouped together under the different categories.

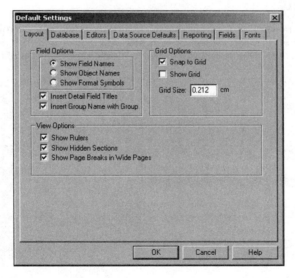

The second type of properties is Report Options, which are specific to the report you are working with. To access the report options, right-click in the Report Designer and select **Report | Report Options**. There are fewer options in this dialog and all are applied only to the report you are working on. Like the default settings, there is not an easy way to share these attributes with other reports. You will find options here for controlling how date-time fields are represented, options for using indexes and sorting, among others.

As for the page and layout attributes of your report, there are two menus that appear when you right-click on your report and select the **Designer** option. **Printer Setup** and **Page Setup** control the orientation, paper size, margins, and so on, and default to the settings of your default printer.

If you are working on a development machine that does not have a printer driver installed or a default printer, you may want to install one (even if you don't have a printer attached or even available) to alleviate possible problems with your report should you need to print in the future. If there is no default printer specified, there is a checkbox in the Printer Setup at the top that is marked No Printer.

It is best practice to develop your report with multiple printers in mind, with a margin appropriate to the printer's unprintable area, and no special features that would be specific to one particular printer (such as oversized paper, or bleed to the edge). This will ensure that your report will print consistently on different types of printers.

Report Design Basics

There are some basic concepts we need to get out of the way before we move on to more advanced topics. We are just going to run through the basics of how a report is put together and the options we have for controlling this framework.

Report Sections

A Crystal Report comprises a number of different sections, as shown in the following screenshot. Each of these sections has a set of properties associated with it as well as a default behavior. For example, the default behavior of the Page Header section is that it will appear on the top of every page of your report.

The sections of your report are clearly marked within the Report Designer by both a section name and number. This number doesn't mean much to us now, but a little later when we want to programmatically control report sections, this notation will come in handy. To view the properties for each of these sections, right-click on your report and select Format Section to open the dialog shown below.

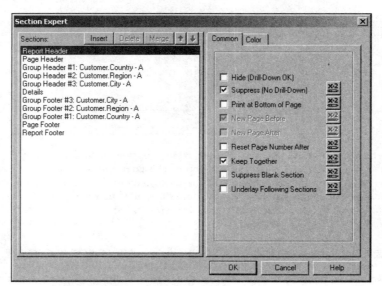

You can choose to suppress a section if you don't want it to appear, or change it's appearance by adjusting the color or size of the section, based on your needs. Here is a rundown of the basic sections that may be contained within a report, as well as their default behavior.

Report Section	Description
Report Header	Appears on the top of the very first page of the report, and is usually suppressed by default. Can be used to indicate the start of a new report or used as a cover sheet.
Report Footer	Appears on the bottom of the very last page of the report, is shown by default, and can be used to summarize the report (number of records, print date, and so on).
Page Header	Appears on the top of each page and can be used for column headings, the report title, page count, among other items.
Page Footer	Appears on the bottom of each page and can be used to display page numbers, print dates, times, and so on.
Group Header	Appears at the head of each group and is usually used to display the group name.
Group Footer	Appears at the end of a group of records and is usually used to display the group name, subtotals, or summaries.
Details Section	One for each record in your report, used to display columns of information, and may be expanded to larger sections of fields, or to create forms.

You can insert multiple sections into your report in a scenario where you might want to have two different page headers, or separate content out for ease of use and design.

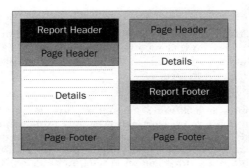

You can control all of these sections through the use of conditional formatting, which we will touch on in Chapter 7, *Formulas and Logic*.

Report Formatting

Given the complex report requirements given to developers, reports can look like anything you can imagine – from a simple invoice to reports that match a preprinted form. To be honest, the majority of time spent developing a report will be in the report formatting. You probably already know where the report's data is coming from, and the record selection you wish to apply – all that remains is putting it together.

There are a number of different levels where formatting can occur – you can apply some attributes by section (such as the background color, or behavior) but the majority of formatting is performed at the object level. Each object within your report will have a unique set of attributes that you can change to control the color, size, font, number, and date formats.

While you can set these for a number of objects at once (by selecting multiple objects with *Ctrl+left-click* or a lasso, sometimes also called a stretch-box), Crystal Reports.NET does not support the concept of grouping or classing objects together, to make setting global properties easier.

If you are using your report with web-based applications, Crystal Reports.NET does allow you to apply attributes from a style sheet to your report. For more information on how this works, check out Chapter 4: *Report Integration for Web-Based Applications*.

Field Objects

Field objects within Crystal Reports.NET contain the majority of your report content. From database fields that display records, to text objects that describe each column, to the summary fields that provide the totals, any report is basically just a collection of field objects (and a little formatting).

There are eight different types of field objects that can be added to your report and they are available from the Field Explorer that is opened by default when you open the Report Designer within .NET (if it's not in view, remember it can be opened by pressing *Ctrl-Alt-T*).

Database Fields

Database fields can be inserted from any of the tables, views, or stored procedures that appear in your report. Database fields are shown on your report using the notation of TableName.FieldName and once a database field has been inserted into your report, a red checkmark will appear beside the field in the Field Explorer to indicate it has been used.

> **If you are trying to insert a field from a stored procedure and you can't see it listed in the Field Explorer to add to your report, this is because by default Crystal Reports.NET will only show you the tables and views within your data source. To display stored procedures, right-click in the Report Designer and from the menu, select Designer | Default Settings and select the Database tab. There you will find a number of checkboxes for the different types of data items you can add to your report, including stored procedures.**

Text Objects

Text objects are used in a report for typing text that will appear in your report (such as the column headings and comments). To insert a text object, right-click on top of your Report Designer in any section, and select Insert | Text Object from the menu. This will insert a text object onto your report in edit mode. You can type text directly into the text object and when you are finished, click anywhere outside the text object to get out of edit mode.

If you want to edit a text object already in place on your report, simply double-click the field to put it back into edit mode. If you have a large amount of text that you need to put into a text object (like an existing form letter), switch to the edit view and right-click directly on top of the text object. In the menu that appears, you will have the option to browse for and import a text file directly into the text object.

You can also format a text object with tab stops, alignment options and even line spacing by right-clicking directly on top of the object and selecting Format from the right-click menu.

Special Fields

Special fields within a Crystal Report are pre-defined fields that serve a specific function within your Report Designer. Examples of these special fields include page numbers, print dates, and data dates. A complete list of these special fields has been included below:

Special Field Name	Description
Print Date	The date when the report was printed
Print Time	The time when the report was printed
Modification Date	The date of the last modification to the report
Modification Time	The time of the last modification to the report
Data Date	The date when the data was read from the database
Data Time	The time when the data was read from the database
Record Number	An internal, sequential record number assigned to all records returned to the report
Page Number	Page number
Group Number	An internal, sequential number assigned to all groups
Total Page Count	The total page count
Report Title	The report title, as saved in the report file's Summary Information
Report Comments	The comments entered in the Summary Information
Record Selection Formula	The Record Selection Formula used by the report
Group Selection Formula	The group selection formula used by the report

Table continued on following page

Special Field Name	Description
File Path and Name	The full path and filename of the report file
File Author	The author of the report from the report file's Summary Information
File Creation Date	The date the report file was created
Page N of M	Where N is the current page and M is the total page count

Summary Fields

Earlier in the chapter, we looked at creating a report using the Standard Expert and one of the tabs in the expert was for Total, where a summary field could be inserted into your report. Summary fields are usually associated with groups or a grand total in your report and can be inserted into your report by right-clicking anywhere within the Report Designer and selecting Insert | Summary from the menu that appears.

At this point, you may also notice that the right-click menu includes an option for Subtotal – (subtotals and summary fields are similar) but whereas a subtotal refers specifically to a sum, a summary field could be a sum, average, or standard deviation.

Formula Fields

Crystal Reports.NET features a rich formula language that has evolved over the years as a powerful way to add complex calculations to reports. Formula fields appear in curly braces and are prefixed by the @ symbol – a formula used within another formula would look like this:

```
{@SalesTax} + {@InvoiceTotal}
```

Formula fields are created using the integrated Formula Editor. To see the editor, right-click on Formula Fields in the Field Explorer, select New, enter a name, and click OK.

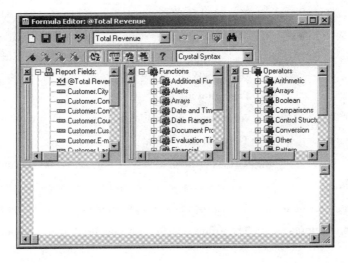

When working with formula fields, you have a choice of two different types of syntax: Crystal syntax or Basic syntax. If you have worked with Crystal Reports before, you will probably be familiar with Crystal syntax. It was the original formula language available with Crystal Reports and is still used for Record Selection Formulas, and conditional formatting.

Basic syntax was introduced to eliminate the need to learn a second formula syntax. The syntax, functions, and control structures are similar to Visual Basic, which many developers are familiar with, and it is easy for developers to create formulas using a language that is familiar to them.

Which language you use depends on what facet of Crystal Reports you are working with. As I mentioned earlier, the record and group selection formulas within Crystal Reports are written using Crystal syntax exclusively, so you are going to have to learn a little bit anyway. For formulas that will appear on your report, you have a choice of using either Crystal or Basic syntax (you can't mix the two in one formula, but you can mix the two different types of formulas in one report). A drop-down list in the Formula Editor controls the syntax and you can switch between the two if required.

Formulas are covered in length in Chapter 7, but keep in mind you may see the Formula Editor appear in other places throughout this book – it is also used to create Record Selection Formulas, and perform conditional formatting among other things.

Parameter Fields

Parameter fields within Crystal Reports.NET are used to prompt the user to enter information when the report is run. Parameters can be used in a number of different ways, from simple data entry (like entering the name of a user to be displayed on the report) to being used with record selection (to filter the content of a report).

Parameter fields are designated using curly braces and are prefixed by a question mark, so a parameter field in use in a formula might look something like this:

```
If {?EnterCountry} = "USA" then "North America"
```

To insert a parameter field into your report, right-click on the Parameter Fields section of the Field Explorer and select New, which will open the following dialog:

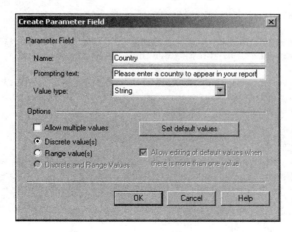

For simple parameters, you will need to give your parameter a name (the question mark prefix will be added for you) and specify some prompting text and a field type for your parameter. By default, parameter fields are set to be strings, but there are actually several different types available including:

- Boolean
- Currency
- Date
- Date Time
- Number
- String
- Time

You will also need to determine what type of values you want to be entered: whether it is a discrete value, or range, among others things.

Once you have created your formula field and inserted it into your report, Crystal Reports.NET will display a default dialog prompting the details just entered, whenever your report is previewed. Most developers find this is a bit too generic for their own use, and prefer to create their own interface with their own forms, including drop-down boxes, and so on, however, if you are not too concerned about how the prompt appears, this is all you need.

The parameter field can now be used just like any other field in your report – you can place it on your report, and use it in formulas. To use a parameter field with record selection, you will first need to create a parameter field to accept the input and then set the record selection to be equal to this parameter field. For example, if you were going to prompt the user for an Invoice Number to reprint an invoice, you would probably want to create a parameter field called `EnterInvoiceId` and set the type to be numeric.

From that point, you would need to alter the record selection to use this parameter field. In this instance, the Record Selection Formula might look something like this:

```
{Orders.InvoiceId} = {?EnterInvoiceId}
```

When the report is refreshed, the user will be prompted to enter an invoice ID, which in turn will be passed to the SQL statement and used to retrieve the records for the report.

An import concept to remember is that the Record Selection Formula must always return a Boolean value – if the value returned is `True`, then the record will be returned to the report. If the value is `False`, it will just move on to the next record.

SQL Expression Fields

In order to make the most of your database server, Crystal Reports.NET allows you to use SQL Expression instead of (or in addition to) Crystal Formulas. Using a SQL Expression field ensures that your calculation will be performed on the database server itself, and you have access to all of the database functions of SQL.

To create a SQL Expression right-click on **SQL Expression Fields** in Field Explorer, select **New**, enter a name, and select **OK**.

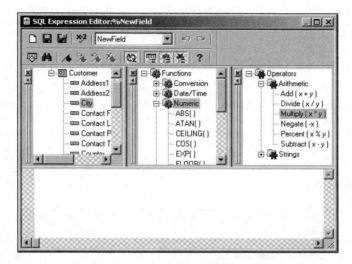

Once you have created a SQL expression field using the SQL Expression Editor, you can drag the field from the Field Explorer onto your report and it will behave just like any other database field.

Unbound Fields

Another definite enhancement to Crystal Reports.NET is the ability to use unbound fields – that is, fields that are not tied to a specific data source. Using unbound fields, you can create a generic report and then programmatically set the content of the fields at run time. This is similar to how Crystal Reports used TTX text files in the past to hold the field structure for a data source, but Crystal Reports.NET points these fields to a `DataSet`.

There are seven different types of unbound fields that you can add to your report:

❑ Boolean

❑ Currency

❑ Date

❑ Date Time

❑ Number

❑ String

❑ Time

When you drag an unbound field onto your report design, it behaves like a placeholder. When we talk about integration for Windows and Web Applications in Chapters 3 and 4, you will learn how to bind data from your project with this field and display the same data in your report. For now, you need to know that until run time, these fields will look and act like formula fields (right down to an @ prefix on each) but they are actually unbound fields that will be used later.

Sorting and Grouping

Earlier in the chapter, we looked at adding sorting and grouping to your report through the Standard Expert. You can also add these features to your report without having to go back into the expert. To start, make sure you understand the difference between what Crystal refers to as sorting and grouping. Sorting in this case usually refers to record-level sorting – for example, if you had a simple listing report with a number of columns, you could sort the values to put them in date order, for example.

Inserting a group is similar, in that the records are re-ordered, but they are also put into their own groups based on a field you have specified. In the example from before, a group could be inserted on a date and each day would have it's own group, with the related records listed as a member of that group. (As a side note, the default grouping option for dates is "by day", but you can also change that to a weekly, monthly, or quarterly interval.)

To add simple record-level sorting to your report, right-click within the Report Designer and from the menu, select Report | Sort Records. A dialog will appear and allow you to select the fields for sorting.

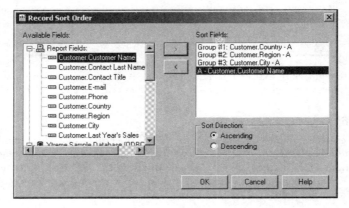

An important note is that groups will always take precedence over record-level sorting, so they will always appear in this dialog first and cannot be removed here. It only makes sense, as you could create a group on one field (like a date) and then within the group, specify a record-level sort on an amount field, for example.

For inserting groups into your report, you can right-click on the report, select Insert | Group, and select a field to serve as the basis for your groups.

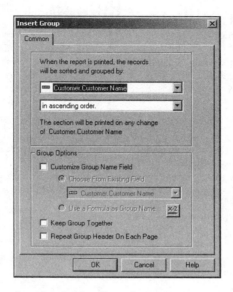

Each distinct record stored within that field will produce a separate group, using the options you have specified in this dialog. A default group name will appear for each group, or you can specify a field or formula for the group name. A common example is where you are grouping on a state abbreviation (for instance, NY) and want to display the full state name (New York). You could either specify another field that contained the full state name, or create an if...then formula to print it for you – although I wouldn't recommend it for this example, as the formula would have to be 50 lines long for every state in the US, let alone the rest of the world!

Record Selection and Filtering

Record selections are important in a report's design, and filtering is used to hone the content in to exactly what the user needs. It used to be that legacy reports would be hundreds of pages long, and users had to flip through them to find the data they needed. With record selection, we can pinpoint the required information and present it to the user in an easy-to-read format.

You have already had a look at record selections with the Standard Expert, and there is not much more to say concerning the record selection operators themselves. The real power of record selection comes with actually getting your hands dirty and writing your own Record Selection Formula. For Crystal Reports.NET users who were not developers, this was always quite difficult, but for developers it opens up a world of possibilities.

When working with the Record Selection Formula in your report, it is important to note that the formula itself has no output. For example, if you were writing a formula to appear on your report, you would actually want some result at the end, whether it is a simple sum or complex statistical calculation.

For the Record Selection Formula, all we want returned is a Boolean variable. When the Record Selection Formula is applied to a record, either a True or False value is returned to us. If the condition is met and a True value is returned, the record is retrieved and will appear in the report. If the value returned is False, the record will be discarded and will not appear in the report.

As far as best practices for Record Selection Formulas are concerned, they can be as long and complex as required, but brevity is recommended.

You should also double-check your Record Selection Formula for any potential bottlenecks when the report is processed. For example, if you were to create a Record Selection Formula to bring back a list of companies where their invoice total was over $10,000, it might look something like this:

```
{@InvoiceTotal} > 10000
```

But when you run your report, you notice that the report takes an extraordinary long time to run. What is happening is that this record selection relies on a formula field ({@InvoiceTotal}) that needs to be calculated before record selection can occur. So in this instance, *every single record* is being retrieved from the database, the InvoiceTotal formula is being calculated and then record selection is being applied locally.

Try to write Record Selection Formulas that take advantage of the data server or platform you are working with and don't be afraid to use a custom SQL statement as the data source for your report if things get too difficult. If you already know SQL, make the most of what you know to create optimized queries from your data and move on to other things.

Advanced Report Design Techniques

With a little bit of basic report design under our belt, we need to have a look at some advanced report design features. These are the features and techniques that can take your report from simple columnar and grouping reports to the more complex analytical reports that turn raw data into valuable information. You may never need to use some of these features, but discussing them now will help us out when we start to look at integrating reports (and their various features) into our applications.

Charting and Graphing

Crystal Reports.NET utilizes a sophisticated graphing engine based on technology from ThreeD Graphics and can create just about any type of chart or graph you can imagine.

Throughout this chapter you have been working on the International Sales report. There are groups for the Country, Region, and City fields in the report, and with all of the summary fields and other content the report runs over multiple pages, making it difficult to visualize the information contained within. In the following pages, we are going to add a chart to the first page of the International Sales report, which will provide the user with an overview of the information displayed.

To begin, open the International Sales report we have been working with (C:\CrystalReports\Chapter02\Chapter02_Basic) in the Report Designer by double-clicking on the report in the Solution Explorer.

To add a chart to this report, right-click on the report and select Insert I Chart, which will open the Chart Expert dialog, shown below:

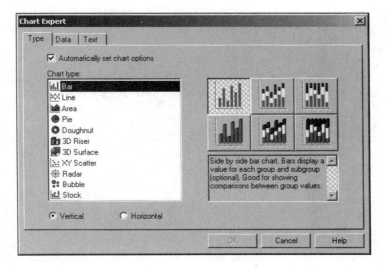

You may have noticed when working with the Standard Expert that there was a tab for Charts – *the same Chart Expert is used in both places.*

There are a number of different templates, including bar charts, pie charts, and 3-D charts, many of which won't be covered in too much detail here. A sample icon of how each will look has been included for you in the Chart Type to the left of the Chart Expert. Please keep in mind that each one of these graph types requires a specific set of information – for example, a pie chart may need only two values passed to it (for the names of the pie slices and their values) while a three-dimensional chart may require three or more values.

When you select a graph type that does not match the data you have available and attempt to exit the Report Expert, a dialog will appear with three options:

- ❏ Continue with Selected Data and Chart Type

- ❏ Change Data or Chart Type Selection (Return to Chart Expert)

- ❏ Let the Expert Choose the Most Appropriate Chart for Data Selected

If you select the first option and choose to ignore the warning message, your chart will be unpredictable at best. The charting engine will attempt to work with the values you have presented, but may present a blank graph or one in which the values are just plain wrong. It is better to use the second or third option to ensure that your graph format matches the data available in your report.

In any case, we know that our report has multiple groupings and summary fields, so we should be fine if we select the Pie Chart with the 3D effect, by clicking the icon for this graph:

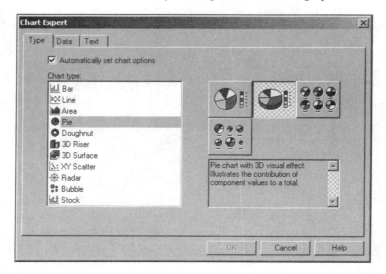

Next, select the type of graph you want to create using the Data tab of the Chart Expert.

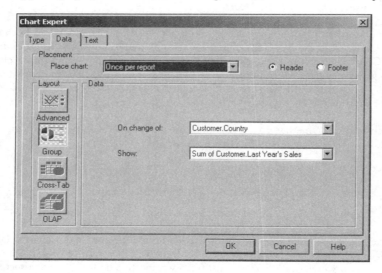

This dialog says there are four different types to choose from (Advanced, Group, Cross-Tab, and OLAP), but OLAP graphs rely on an underlying OLAP grid inserted onto your report, and that feature is not supported in Crystal Reports.NET (at the time of writing, it is supported in the full retail versions of Crystal Reports), so this option will remain permanently grayed out. The Cross-Tab button will also be grayed out if you haven't inserted a Cross-Tab into your report.

Here are the graph types available for use:

❑ Advanced Graphs – Advanced graphs require two fields: an on change of field and a show values field. These are similar to the X and Y fields you would normally use if you were plotting a graph by hand. Just like a manual graph, you can have multiple on change of and show values fields. You can also determine the order for the On change of field and apply TopN/BottomN/Sort All to the same. For the Show field, you can set the summary operator, for example, sum or average, or choose not to summarize the values at all.

❑ Group Graphs – These are based on at least one group and one summary field that appear in your report. Group graphs can be placed at the Report Header/Footer level, or on the Group Header/Footer level, where they will only show the data for that particular group.

❑ Cross-Tab Graphs – These rely on an underlying Cross-Tab grid to provide the required data. These types of graphs can also appear on the Report Header/Footer level or on the Group Header/Footer level with the same filtering of data specifically for that group.

In this case, we have a group and a summary field inserted into our report, so you can select to place the chart Once per report specifying On Change Of Customer.Country, and showing Sum of Customer.Last Year's Sales.

Once you have selected the graph and data type for your report, the only thing left in the Chart Expert is to set the text that will appear on your chart or graph, so select the Text tab. By default, Crystal Reports.NET will automatically enter some text for you or you can override the text and it's formatting if you choose. To enter your own text, uncheck the box beside any of the titles and enter your own title in the textbox provided:

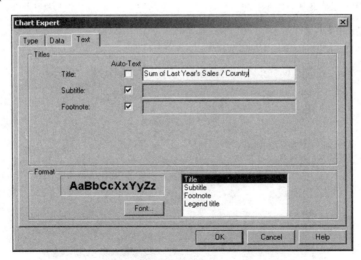

When you click OK to exit the Chart Expert, your Chart will be added to your Report Header. When you see the report in the designer, a pie chart is now displayed in the Report Header. This isn't an accurate drawing of your graph, in fact it is nothing like your graph; it is just a placeholder to show where in the report the graph will be positioned. If you preview the graph in a Windows form, it will look something like the following:

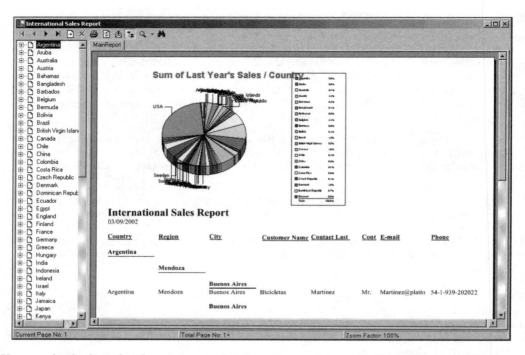

You may be thinking that there is too much information on this graph. Crystal Reports.NET has a TopN function to cut your report down to just the top 10 or top 20 customers, if it makes the graph easier to read. To add TopN analysis to your report, right-click on your report and select **Report | TopN/Sort Group Expert**, which will open the Top N Expert:

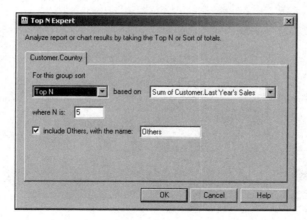

To cut your report down to just the top 5 countries, change the sorting dropdown to TopN sorting on the **Sum of Last Year's Sales** field and enter *5* for the value of N. You will also want to check the box for **include others**, which creates one large group or pie slice with all of the other countries. To see how much this feature can improve a chart, click on OK, and run the report. With the information for all countries displayed, the chart is a huge improvement, compared to our unfiltered output.

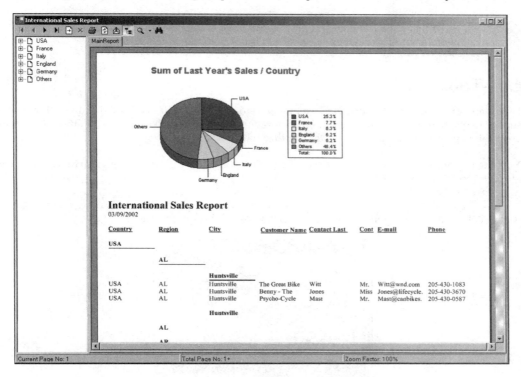

Another option to increase readability would be to make the chart larger. The chart object inserted into your report is just like any other object in that it can be resized to fit your needs; you could even resize the graph to take up the entire first page if that suits the needs of the report.

If you have a graph or chart inserted into your report, you can control the content by right-clicking directly on top of the chart and selecting an option from the menu. The Chart Expert can be used to alter the graph in the way that we have described so far in this section. You may have noticed that the Chart Expert includes an option on the first tab labeled **Automatically Set Chart Options**. If you uncheck this box, another two tabs will appear, allowing you to control other aspects of the report, including the formatting for the graph axes and the general settings (like color, marker size, and so on). Under **Format Chart** are the **Template**, **General**, and **Titles** options, which also allow you to customize the appearance of your chart. The options in all of these menus are context sensitive; for example, you can perform different types of formatting to a pie chart than you can to a bar chart. These options are all relatively simple, so we'll leave it to you to explore the almost endless possibilities.

Unfortunately, if you have used the retail version of Crystal Reports before, you will probably be wondering what happened to the Chart Analyzer, which allowed you to open the graph in another tabbed window. Crystal Reports.NET does not include the full capabilities of the Chart Analyzer, so if you really need to use some of the advanced formatting features for charts and graphs, you are going to have to buy a retail copy of Crystal Reports.

> **Be warned that once you open a report within Crystal Reports.NET, you cannot go back and open it in a previous version, as it is not backwards compatible.**

Cross-Tabs

Cross-tabs within Crystal Reports.NET can be used to display summarized data in rows and columns, similar to a spreadsheet. If you want to create a report with a cross-tab as its main feature, there is a cross-tab expert available that will guide you through the steps to do so.

You can also insert a cross tab into an existing report, which we will walk through here. Create a copy of the International Sales Report we created earlier in this chapter (`C:\CrystalReports\Chapter02\Chapter02_Basic`), and call the directory `Chapter02_CrossTab`. Open the `Chapter2.sln`, and then open `international_sales.rpt`. Right-click on the report, and then select Insert | Cross-Tab from the menu.

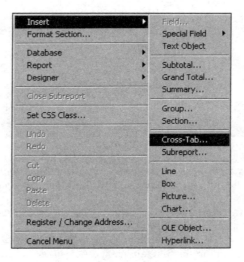

This makes a box appear over your cursor, which you should position over your report, where you want it to appear. Place the cursor over the Group Header #1: Customer.Country – A section, next to the Group #1 Name label. Left-click the mouse, and the following dialog will open. When working with a cross-tab, there are three basic elements: rows, columns, and summarized fields and to start, you will need to select at least one of each using this dialog.

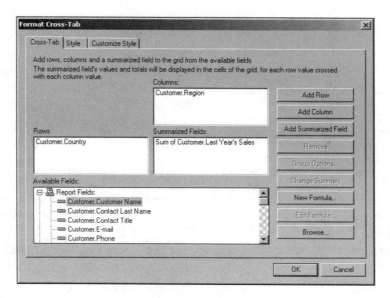

Select Customer.Country for the row, and Customer.Region for the column. Select Customer.Last Year's Sales so it is highlighted, and then click on the Add Summarized Field button, so Sum of Customer.Last Year's Sales appears in the summarized field. Click on OK to create this cross-tab.

In the first section under each country your report now has a summary of the last year's sales by region, so in the screenshot below we have the sales by region for the USA. If you select England in the list to the left of the report, the same cross-tab will appear, with values for the regions in England.

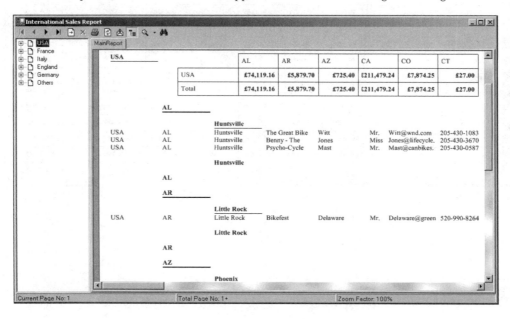

By default, Crystal Reports.NET applies some standard formatting to your cross-tab and draws lines and boxes around the columns and rows. With the use of a style sheet, you can apply a pre-defined style to your cross-tab or simply change individual attributes to suit.

Cross-tabs have come a long way since the early version of Crystal Reports, and now if the data runs off the page, it is continued on the next page and a margin is used so the data is not cut off, eliminating the old problem of taping multiple report pages back together.

The only down side is that there are still some issues with page numbering. If your cross-tab runs across multiple pages, the page number will not work correctly (for instance, if it is three pages across and three down when printed, only the first and every third page will have a number and it will be 1..2..3). Still, those limitations are minor in comparison to the functionality provided.

Another cross-tab report is available in the sample files for Chapter 2, which is called `cross_tab.rpt`. Go to `C:\Crystal Reports\Chapter02\Demo\`, and open and run `Chapter2.sln`. Select **Cross-Tab Report** from the drop-down list in the top-right of the dialog to view the following report:

Employee Sales Summary

Printed   Tuesday, 9 September, 2003

	Davollo	Dodsworth	King	Leverling	Peacock	Suyama	Total
Active Outdoors Crochet Glove	$22,830	$19,755	$62,647	$12,608	$44,810	$24,335	$186,984
Active Outdoors Lycra Glove	$32,055	$39,532	$44,213	$36,371	$64,153	$27,656	$243,980
Descent	$400,063	$405,792	$422,025	$369,674	$364,773	$329,386	$2,291,713
Endorphin	$81,634	$80,021	$71,698	$55,693	$72,341	$88,863	$450,250
Guardian "U" Lock	$9,131	$2,491	$13,409	$250	$963	$255	$26,500
Guardian ATB Lock	$8,621	$17,703	$638	$3,337	$3,299	$22,124	$55,722
Guardian Chain Lock	$5,129	$7,114	$7,507	$3,116	$1,003	$78	$23,947
Guardian Mini Lock	$4,275	$508	$1,329	$3,807	$5,375	$13,326	$28,620
Guardian XL "U" Lock	$6,726	$2,706	$11,179	$2,159	$9,919	$5,376	$38,064
InFlux Crochet Glove	$7,563	$15,555	$8,159	$11,298	$7,063	$21,405	$71,044
InFlux Lycra Glove	$6,091	$13,983	$17,696	$856	$16,415	$19,496	$74,537
Micro Nicros	$8,962	$9,330	$12,210	$17,360	$6,187	$16,492	$70,541
Mini Nicros	$41,679	$21,923	$16,227	$23,156	$13,682	$13,947	$130,613
Mozzie	$132,689	$155,799	$138,859	$118,499	$128,527	$136,799	$811,173
Nicros	$96,820	$86,854	$130,337	$79,175	$84,170	$90,547	$567,903

Subreports

Within Crystal Reports.NET, multiple subreports can be combined into one main report, which allows you to create information-rich reports from multiple sources and display this information side by side.

Both linked and unlinked subreports are available in the code download, in the solution: `C:\CrystalReports\Chapter02\Demo\Chapter2.sln`. Open and run this solution from Visual Studio .NET and choose the report from the drop-down box at the top right of the window.

> **To run the unlinked report, you will need access to the Northwind sample database.**

Subreports come in two varieties – unlinked and linked. Unlinked subreports allow you to insert subreports that are totally unrelated to the main report content. In the example below, a sales graph has been inserted into an Employee Listing report (included in the sample files as `employee_listing_unlinked.rpt`). Both of these reports were developed independently and are from different tables and a different data source.

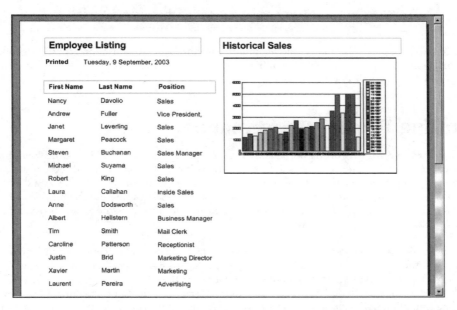

The second type of report is the linked subreport. Linked subreports allow the passing of parameters and variables between the main report and the subreport, which can be used to filter the subreport content. The report shown below has a main report that is the same Employee Listing report, only this time a linked subreport has been inserted showing a commission amount for each employee (included in the sample files as `employee_listing_linked.rpt`). The commission report is a separate report, but is inserted into the details section and linked on the employee ID field.

Employee Listing

Printed on Tuesday, 9 September, 2003

First Name	Last Name	Commision Summary		
Nancy	Davolio	Total Sales: $ 660,756.95	Commision	$ 39,645.42
Andrew	Fuller	Total Sales:	Commision	
Janet	Leverling	Total Sales: $ 649,101.99	Commision	$ 38,946.12
Margaret	Peacock	Total Sales: $ 631,799.77	Commision	$ 37,907.99
Steven	Buchanan	Total Sales:	Commision	
Michael	Suyama	Total Sales: $ 710,401.48	Commision	$ 42,624.09
Robert	King	Total Sales: $ 748,755.94	Commision	$ 44,925.36
Laura	Callahan	Total Sales:	Commision	
Anne	Dodsworth	Total Sales: $ 682,849.21	Commision	$ 40,970.95
Albert	Hellstern	Total Sales:	Commision	
Tim	Smith	Total Sales:	Commision	
Caroline	Patterson	Total Sales:	Commision	
Justin	Brid	Total Sales:	Commision	

For each employee, the subreport is run again and the employee ID is used in record selection on the subreport. When the page is printed, each instance of the subreport is printed next to the corresponding employee, with only their details shown.

Optimizing Report Performance

If you have worked with reporting applications before, there is a usually a bit of time spent on optimizing report performance – users are not happy with reports that run for three minutes, let alone three hours. Over the years, there have been significant enhancements within the Crystal Print Engine itself that have improved performance and cut down on processing time, but the majority of poor report performance does not lie within the Report Designer, but rather in how the report is designed and in the underlying data.

For example, if you have a report that has been developed across an Oracle table that contains 500,000 rows of data, the report is going to take a while to run, regardless of whether you are using Crystal Reports.NET or just submit a SQL Statement from a PL/SQL command prompt. If you believe that a report's performance could be improved, ask your DBA or architect to review the tables, views, and other data impedimenta that you are using in order to verify that you have used the correct primary and foreign keys, and that you have taken the most direct route to join tables in your report.

Following on from that, you also may want to take the SQL that Crystal Reports.NET generates (right-click on your report and select **Database I Show SQL Query**) and paste it into SQL*Plus, Query Analyzer or any other SQL query tool supported by your database platform and see how long it runs. Your DBA could also provide suggestions on ways to improve the SQL statement generated and you can then use the optimized SQL as the basis for your report.

With Crystal Reports.NET itself, there are a couple of options that can help with performance – to view these options, right-click on your report and select Report | Report Options.

There are two options in this dialog that can aid with performance. The first, Use Indexes on Server For Speed, for use with databases that use indexes, will use the index on the database server to sort and retrieve records faster than if the index was not used. The second option, Perform Grouping on Server, for reports that have groups, will push the grouping back to the database server, providing that the details within your report are suppressed (we can't show detailed records in the report, since it actually changes the SQL statement and uses a GROUP BY clause).

Summary

In this chapter, we have looked a simple report methodology and the process behind designing reports and then moved on to actually creating a report using one of the experts that ships with the product. We also had a brief look at some report design concepts and the Report Designer itself, before moving to some more advanced report design topics and finally finishing up with a short overview on optimization.

In summary, this chapter covered:

❑   Planning your report design

❑   Creating a report using an Expert

❑   Working with the report design environment

❑   Report design basics

❑   Advanced report design techniques

❑   Optimizing report performance

With a little bit of basic report design under our belt, we are ready to move to the next chapter, which deals with integrating reports into Windows-based applications.

Professional *Crystal Reports*
for *Visual Studio .NET*

3

Report Integration for Windows-Based Applications

With a bit of basic report design under our belts, it's time to look at actually integrating reports into your Windows-based applications. In the previous chapter, we looked at how to create reports using some of the features within Crystal Reports.NET.

In this chapter, we are going to look at how to integrate and view those same reports from Windows applications, and how to customize our reports at run time using the rich object models provided. We will cover:

- ❏ Determining the correct object model
- ❏ The `CrystalDecisions.Windows.Forms` namespace
- ❏ Using the Crystal Windows Forms Viewer
- ❏ Customizing the Windows Forms Viewer
- ❏ Passing information to the Windows Forms Viewer

Throughout the chapter we will be looking at code examples to illustrate the use of various features and at the end of the chapter, you should be familiar with the majority of report integration concepts and be ready to apply them to your own application development.

Obtaining the Sample Files

All the example reports and code used in this chapter are available for download. The download file can be obtained from www.wrox.com. In the download code for Chapter 3, you will find all of the projects we will work through in this chapter (like the custom viewer shown below), as well as the associated sample reports.

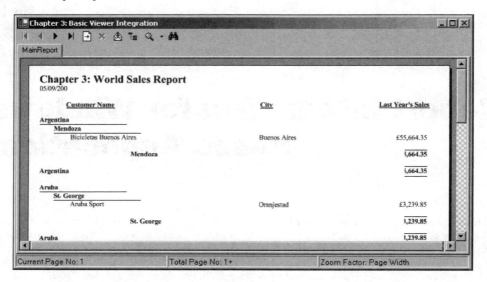

As you go through the chapter, you will be able to actually look at the application we are creating and other examples that illustrate points along the way.

Planning Your Application

Integrating reports is an easy way to add value to your application, and can be an important component of your application's offering. Before we get started on actually integrating Crystal Reports.NET with your Windows application, we need to do a little planning first to make sure the integration goes smoothly.

First, we need to have a report (or suite of reports) to work with – in Chapter 2, we walked through the report planning and design process, so you should have a start on the skills you need to design reports.

Note: If you flipped straight to this chapter or haven't gotten into designing your own reports yet, there are some sample reports located in `C:\program files\Visual Studio.Net\Crystal Reports\Samples\` *that you can use to practice concepts from chapter; alternately there are the sample reports included in the download file as well.*

We need to plan for how those reports will be delivered to users and the Forms that will be required to host them. Crystal Reports.NET uses a feature-rich report viewer that can be inserted onto a Windows Form and used to view reports. The viewer itself has an extensive object model, allowing you to set the source of the report, the appearance of the viewer itself, and what happens when different events fire.

Most applications can utilize a single Windows Form hosting the Crystal Report Viewer and simply pass properties like the report source and viewer settings to this Form. This lends itself to a number of creative solutions for user personalization and settings. You could store viewer settings and preferences in a table or XML file for each user (or group or role) and apply these settings when viewing a report.

In addition, you could also set specific record selection formulas for different groups of users, only allowing them access to the data applicable to them. You could also create a custom user interface allowing users to set and retain parameter settings for future use, or even in order to keep their printing or export preferences, such as frequently used e-mail addresses.

Ultimately, the report integration should be driven by the user's requirements but how these features are delivered is up to you. As you go through the rest of the chapter, think about how the different customization features could be used in your development. If you are not at a point where you can integrate these features into your application, all of the properties, methods, and events are grouped together by function to make it easier to come back and look them up.

Exploring the Development Environment

Visual Studio .NET provides a rich integrated design environment for developing Windows and web applications and there are a number of components and shortcuts to help us integrate Crystal Reports into Windows Applications.

To start with, in the toolbox under the Windows Forms section, you will find the CrystalReportViewer, which we will be working with a little later. When you draw this viewer on a Windows Form, you can set a number of properties and use the viewer to display a preview of your report.

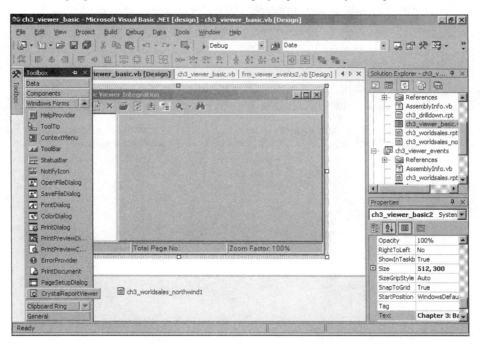

In addition to the CrystalReportViewer, there is also a ReportDocument component available in the components section of the toolbox. We use this component to add strongly-typed and untyped reports to a Form, for use with the viewer mentioned earlier. (Don't be too worried about it at the moment, as we'll cover that a little later in the chapter.)

And finally, the majority of our report integration will take place in the code view of the Form, as shown below.

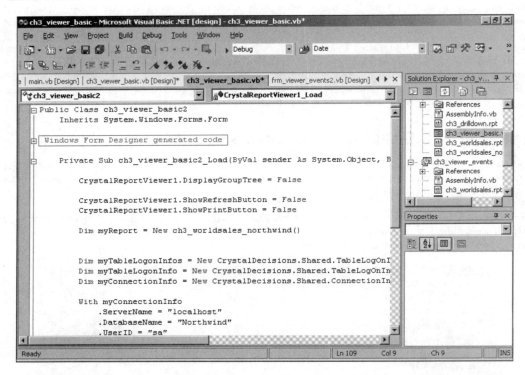

All of the properties, methods, and events related to Crystal Reports object models and integration can be set and modified through this view, as well as through the Properties window.

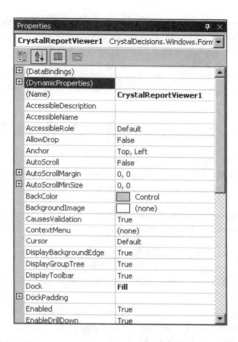

Starting a New Windows Application with VB.NET

To get started with this chapter, we need to create a new Windows Application using Visual Basic.NET. If you want to follow along with the sample code that is available for this chapter, you will find a number of projects within that correspond to the sections in this chapter. If you want to get down and get your hands dirty creating your own project as we go along, then from within Visual Studio select File I New I Project and from Visual Basic Applications, select Windows Applications and specify a name (in the sample code, we have called this project viewer_basic and we have saved it to C:\CrystalReports\Chapter03).

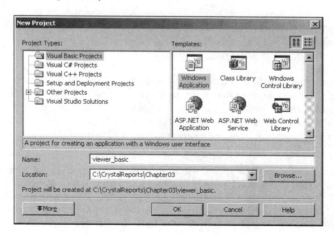

Throughout the chapter, we will be using only one or two Forms to demonstrate different integration features – your own applications will probably have multiple Forms and launch reports from any number of them, but the same concepts can be applied.

Before we actually look at any code, we need to go back to the integration features that you want to incorporate into your application and select the appropriate object model(s).

Determining the Correct Object Model

When working with Windows applications, you have two different object models to choose from, depending on your particular needs. The first, contained within the **Crystal Reports Windows Forms Viewer** object model (`CrystalDecisions.Windows.Forms`), contains all of the functionality required to view a report in the Crystal Reports Windows Forms Viewer and includes the ability to set database logon information, pass parameters and record selection, control the viewer's appearance, and view reports, including reports consumed from an XML Report Web Service.

Using this object model, you can satisfy most basic report integration requirements, but you have no control over the report itself – you won't be able to change the record selection for any subreports that appear in your report, and you won't have access to modify report elements, such as groups, and sorting and formula fields.

> **Note: For more information on working with groups and sorting check out Chapter 2: Getting Started with Crystal Reports.NET.**

You also need to use the **Crystal Reports Engine** object model (`CrystalDecisions.CrystalReports.Engine`) for complete control over your report and the objects and features contained within. Using the Crystal Reports Engine, you are provided with a rich object model that can be used to modify even the smallest elements of your report.

> *Note: You will also need to use this object model if you are using ADO (.Net or "Classic" ADO) as the data source for your report (which is covered in Chapter 6:* Working with .NET Data*).*

It is important to note that the Crystal Reports Engine object model cannot stand alone – it provides no way to view a report and relies on the Crystal Reports Windows Forms Viewer to actually view the report. The functionality covered by the Report Engine is reviewed in Chapter 8, as well as examples of some of the most commonly used features.

Crystal Decisions recommends that you do not overlap these two object models and try to use properties and methods from both at the same time. An example would be where you are setting a parameter field value in the Report Engine object model – you wouldn't want to also try to set a parameter field in the same report using the Crystal Reports Windows Forms Viewer object model. Try to pick an object model based on your requirements and stick with it throughout your application.

> **Note: A good rule of thumb to apply, when making a decision about which object model to use, is that the Report Viewer can be used with simple applications (preview, print, export) where you don't need to change the report's design, or elements within the report. If you need more granular control over the report content, you are going to need to use the Report Engine in conjunction with the Report Viewer.**

Understanding the CrystalDecisions.Windows.Forms Namespace

The `CrystalDecisions.Windows.Forms` namespace consists of a number of classes that provide functionality specific to viewing reports. As you look through the classes below, you can easily map each back to some function within the viewer itself. In the section immediately following, we are going to look at each of these classes in depth and learn what can be done with each.

Class	Description
CrystalReportViewer	Contains the properties, methods, and events relating to the CrystalReportViewer and viewing reports.
DrillEventArgs and DrillSubreportEventArgs	Provides data for the Drill and DrillDownSubreport events on main and subreports. Drill events fire when a user drills down into a group or summary on a particular report or subreport.
ExceptionEventArgs	Provides data for the HandleException event. A HandleException event occurs when there is an error or exception when setting the report properties or viewing the report. It is primarily used for troubleshooting and error messages.
PageNavigateEventArgs	Provides data for the Navigate event. When a user navigates through the pages of a report, the Navigate event fires each time. This can be used to notify the users when they have reached the last page, call custom actions, etc.
SearchEventArgs	Provides data for the Search event. The CrystalReportViewer includes an integrated search function to search for values within a report. The Search event fires when a user searches for a value and could be used to trigger a search of another report or other report descriptions.
ViewerEventArgs	Provides data for the Viewer events. The Viewer event fires when some action has occurred within the viewer itself (for instance, when the report has been loaded) and can be used to launch other actions when the viewer loads.
ZoomEventArgs	Provides data for the ViewZoom event. The ViewZoom event fires when the zoom is changed on the viewer and can be used to suggest the best resolution for a particular report. Also, if you are showing two reports in viewers side-by-side, it can be used to synchronize the zoom factor between the two.

Using the Crystal Report Viewer for Windows Forms

For report files that exist externally to your application (for instance, as a standalone report file, created with either this or a previous version of Crystal Reports) there is not much to creating a simple preview Form for your report.

In this example, we are going to be using the viewer_basic project, which you created earlier. In the project, there should be a default Form1 that we can use. Locate the **CrystalReportViewer** within the toolbox and drag or draw the Report Viewer onto your Form.

Once you have added the Report Viewer to your Form, we now need to set the **ReportSource** property to point to the existing report file. The sample files for this chapter include a sample report (ch3_worldsales.rpt) that we can use. Using the property pages for the Crystal Report Viewer, set the **ReportSource** property to the location of this report file. For instance, if you have put the sample files in your own personal directory, enter the full report file name and path, (C:\CrystalReports\Chapter03\ch3_worldsales.rpt).

You can now run your application and when you preview the Form, your report will be displayed in the Crystal Reports Viewer, as shown below:

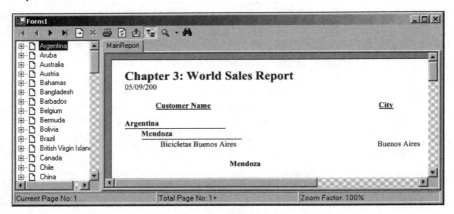

The viewer interacts with the Crystal Reports print engine, runs the report, and displays the results.

From your report preview, you can drill-down into the details, search for a value, print, and export without having to do any additional coding. If you only have one or two reports that you want to integrate into your application and you don't need to customize any features at run time, this may be all you need. But for applications that require a more sophisticated integration with Crystal Reports.NET, you probably need to look at a bit further.

Adding a Report to your Application

Still working in the same solution and project as before, we are going to add a Crystal Report to our application. In the previous walk-through, we looked at referencing a report that was external to our application through setting the file path and name. While this is one method of integrating Crystal Reports, actually adding the report file itself to our project makes it easier to edit and integrate reports into our application.

To add our World Sales report to our project, select **Project | Add Existing Item** which will open the dialog shown below. Change the drop-down list to show **All files** and specify `*.rpt` for the file name to filter the list to show only the available reports.

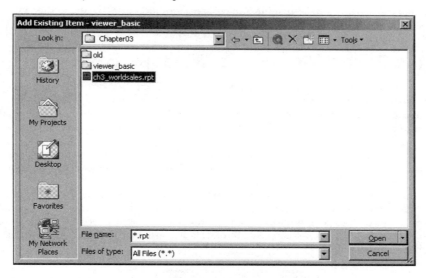

Once you have selected the `ch3_worldsales.rpt` report, click **Open** and this report will be added to your project in the Solution Explorer.

As this report was added to your project, you may have noticed that in addition to the report, another file with the same name as the report (except for a `.vb` extension) is also added, as shown.

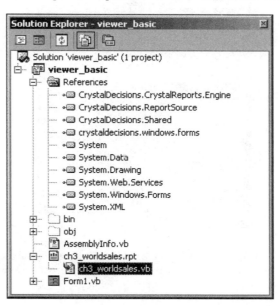

Note:This file is hidden until you select **Show All Files** from the Solution Explorer.

This additional file is the report source file and contains a report class specific to this report called `ReportDocument` that is created automatically for you.

Adding the Report Viewer to a Windows Form

Earlier in the chapter, we quickly dragged the Report Viewer onto a Form and previewed your first report – the good news is that there is not much more involved in adding the Report Viewer to a Form in your application. The Crystal Report Viewer is available from the Windows Forms Toolbox and you can drag it directly onto your Form or draw the viewer on your Form to the size required.

You can easily add the Crystal Report Viewer to an existing Form, to display a report side-by-side with other controls or you could add the report to a new Form to have a separate window for previewing reports.

If you are going to use a separate Form for previewing reports, try changing the **Dock** property of the Crystal Report viewer to **Fill** so it will fill the entire page. To change this property, right-click on the Crystal Report viewer you have dragged or drawn on your Form and select the viewer's properties. From the property page shown below, locate the **Dock** property and use the drop-down list to select the docking for this component.

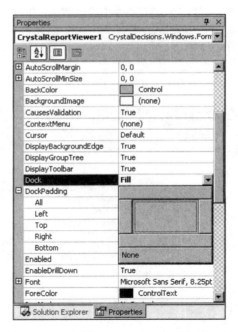

You can also add a margin around the docked viewer by setting the **Dock Padding** properties, which would add blank space around the viewer using the settings and margin you specified.

Binding a Report to the Report Viewer

With the Report Viewer added to your Form, we now need to let the viewer know what report it will be using and this process is called **binding** a report to the viewer. There are four different ways to bind a report to the Crystal Report Viewer:

❑   By report name

❑   By report object

❑   By binding to an untyped report

❑   By binding to strongly-typed report

Binding by Report Name

To bind a report using the report name, all you need to do is set the ReportSource property, either through the property page or through the Form's code. You will want to add this to the Form's Load method, which can be accessed by double-clicking on the Form we are working with. To set the ReportSource property, we need to specify the report file name and path, as shown here:

```
CrystalReportViewer1.ReportSource =
    "C:\\CrystalReports\\Chapter03\\ch3_worldsales.rpt"
```

But since we have already added the report to our application, we could also bind the report by creating a report object, load the report into the object, and bind the object to the Crystal report viewer.

Binding by Report Object

Binding by a report object works slightly differently depending on if you have added the report to your project or if you are referencing it externally. For a report that resides externally to your application, we need to first specify an import of the CrystalDecisions.CrystalReports.Engine, which will allow us to create the object.

In the Solution Explorer, right-click on your project (in our case, viewer_basic) and select **Properties** from the right-click menu to open the dialog shown below, and click on **Imports** in the left-hand pane.

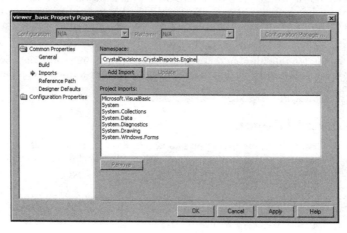

Under the **Common Properties** folder, use the **Imports** option to add the
`CrystalDecisions.CrystalReports.Engine` namespace to your project and click **Apply** and **OK**
to return to your Form.

With this namespace imported, we now need to create the report object as a `ReportDocument`, by
inserting it into the `CrystalReportViewer1_Load` event, as shown:

```
Private Sub CrystalReportViewer1_Load(ByVal sender As System.Object,
    ByVal e As System.EventArgs) Handles CrystalReportViewer1.Load
  Dim myReport = New
      CrystalDecisions.CrystalReports.Engine.ReportDocument()
```

With our object now ready to be used, we can now load the external report file:

```
  myReport.Load("C:\\CrystalReports\\Chapter03\\ch3_worldsales.rpt")
  CrystalReportViewer1.ReportSource = myReport
End Sub
```

If the report you are using has actually been added to your project, a class was automatically generated
for the report, so we could use the class instead to bind the report to the viewer (while the import and
public declaration remain the same):

```
Private Sub CrystalReportViewer1_Load(ByVal sender As System.Object,
    ByVal e As System.EventArgs) Handles CrystalReportViewer1.Load
  Dim myReport As CrystalDecisions.CrystalReports.Engine.ReportDocument
  myReport = New ch3_worldsales()
  CrystalReportViewer1.ReportSource = myReport
End Sub
```

or, if you wanted to eliminate the `myReport` variable, replace that code with the following:

```
  CrystalReportViewer1.ReportSource = New ch3_worldsales()
```

Which method you choose will depend on where the report is physically located and how you wish to
access it. With any of the examples above, you should be able to bind to the report and then run your
application – the Report Viewer should display a preview of your report if you are successful.

> **If you are having trouble binding to a report object, check the report file name and
> path are correct or for a report that has been added to your application, check the
> report name.**

Binding to an Untyped Report

When working with Crystal Reports.NET, you can add individual report files to your project and use
and reference them to print reports from your application. Taking this a step further, you could also use
these reports as components, which is where we start to look at typing.

When integrating reports into an application, we can either use **strongly-typed** reports or **untyped** reports. If you have been working with Visual Studio .NET for any length of time, you have probably heard of strongly-typed objects. A strongly-typed object is predefined with a number of attributes that are specific to that object, giving programmers more structure and a rigorous set of rules to follow, thus making coding easier and the code more consistent.

Within the frame of reference of Crystal Reports.NET, a strongly-typed report can be any report that has been added to your project. What determines the "type" of a report is how it is added and used within your application. When you first add a report to your application, it is considered untyped – the same goes for any external reports that you may reference (such as the report we pointed to earlier, using the file path C:\CrystalReports\Chapter03\ch3_worldsales.rpt).

In the example below, we are going to look at binding to an untyped report. The first step to binding to an untyped report is to add a ReportComponent to the Form we are working with.

To add a report component to your Form, switch to the Layout view of your Form and look in the toolbox under **Components**. In this section, you should see a component labelled ReportDocument. Drag this component onto your Form, which will open the dialog shown below:

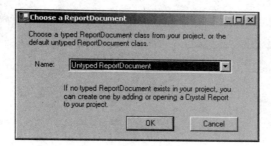

This is the dialog that we use to set whether our report document component is typed or untyped. If you select Untyped ReportDocument, a report component named ReportDocument1 is created and we can then load a report into this component and bind the component to the viewer.

Again, the code to perform the binding will appear in your Form's Form1_Load method and will look something like this:

```
Private Sub Form1_Load(ByVal sender As System.Object, ByVal e As
    System.EventArgs) Handles MyBase.Load
  Dim ReportDocument1 As New ReportDocument()
  ReportDocument1.Load("c:\CrystalReports\Chapter03\ch3_worldsales.rpt")
  CrystalReportViewer1.ReportSource = ReportDocument1
End Sub
```

When your application is run and the Form previewed, the viewer should show a preview the report and allow you to print, export, and perform other functions.

> **If you are experiencing problems binding, check the file name and path of the report you are working with – alternately, if you are binding to a report that exists within your application, check that you have the correct report name.**

Binding to a Strongly-Typed Report

Finally, if you have added a report to your project and then added a ReportDocument component, you can choose to add the report as a strongly-typed report component, which probably has the simplest binding method of all. To create a strongly-typed report document component, drag the ReportDocument component onto your Form.

You will then see the same dialog as before, with a drop-down list of all of the available reports that you have added to your project. Select the existing viewer_basic.ch3_worldsales report to create a strongly-typed report document.

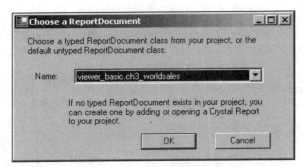

From that point, we just need to set the `ReportSource` property in the Form's `Load` method:

```
Private Sub Form1_Load(ByVal sender As System.Object, ByVal e As
    System.EventArgs) Handles MyBase.Load
  CrystalReportViewer1.ReportSource = ch3_worldsales1
End Sub
```

Here, `ch3_worldsales1` is the name automatically assigned to the ReportDocument component when you added it to your Form.

Regardless of which method you choose to bind your report to the viewer, the result is the same. When you start your application and the Form is loaded, the Crystal Report Viewer will run the report you have set in the `ReportSource` property and display a preview of the same.

Passing Database Logon Info

Most data sources that Crystal Reports can use are secure, requiring a user name, password, and other credentials. When working with the Crystal Report Viewer, we can pass this information through the use of the `TableLogonInfo` collection.

> Note: If your report is based on an unsecured database or file, you don't need to pass any logon information at all to your report.

To understand how the Crystal Reports Viewer works with database credentials, consider that each table in your report is its own unique identity and in turn, its own database credentials. All of these credentials are stored in the `TableLogonInfos` collection, part of the `CrystalDecisions.Shared` namespace, and for each table there is a corresponding `TableLogonInfo` object.

In order to set the database credentials for your report, you will need to loop through all of the tables and set the `ConnectionInfo` properties within `TableLogonInfo` for each. The properties in the `ConnectionInfo` class are:

Property	Description
DatabaseName	Gets or sets the name of the database
Password	Gets or sets the password for logging on to the data source
ServerName	Gets or sets the name of the server or ODBC data source where the database is located
UserID	Gets or sets a user name for logging on to the data source

Since our Xtreme sample data is held within in an unsecured Access database, we are going to use another report in this example. Included with the sample files for this chapter is a copy of the World Sales report (`ch3_worldsales_northwind`) that was created from the Northwind database that ships with SQL Server. You can find this file in the download, through the path `CrystalReports\Chapter03\ch3_worldsales_northwind.rpt`.

We're going to open a new project and add it to our existing one. Click on File | New | Project and select **Windows Application**. Call the project `viewer_database`, saving it to `CrystalReports\Chapter03`. Make sure that the radio button **Add to Solution** is selected as opposed to **Close Solution**:

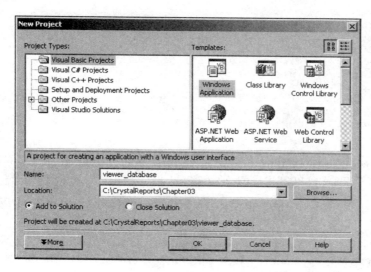

Right-click on the project name, and click **Set As Startup Project**. We're now ready to look at database access.

To add `ch3_worldsales_northwind.rpt` to your project, select **Project | Add new item** and browse for the report where you unzipped the downloaded sample files. Add it to the project and click the **Open** button.

Now drag and drop a **CrystalReportViewer** onto your Form. For the sake of attractiveness, set the **Dock** property to **Fill**.

You will also need to add this report as a component to your Form. Switch to the **Layout** view of your Form and look in the toolbox under **Components**. In this section, you should see a component labeled **ReportDocument**. Drag this component onto your Form.

From the drop-down list, select the `ch3_worldsales_Northwind` report and click **OK**. We are now ready to get on with setting the database credentials for this report.

This report has been written from a single table, `Customer` for which we are setting the `ConnectionInfo`. The name of our server is `localhost`, off of the Northwind database, with `sa` as the user ID, and no password.

Add this code to the `Form1_Load` method:

```
Private Sub Form1_Load(ByVal sender As System.Object, ByVal e As
    System.EventArgs) Handles MyBase.Load
  Dim myReport = New ch3_worldsales_northwind()
  Dim myTableLogonInfos = New CrystalDecisions.Shared.TableLogOnInfos()
  Dim myTableLogonInfo = New CrystalDecisions.Shared.TableLogOnInfo()
  Dim myConnectionInfo = New CrystalDecisions.Shared.ConnectionInfo()

    With myConnectionInfo
      .ServerName = "localhost"
      .DatabaseName = "Northwind"
      .UserID = "sa"
      .Password = ""
    End With

  myTableLogonInfo.ConnectionInfo = myConnectionInfo
  myTableLogonInfo.TableName = "customers"
  myTableLogonInfos.Add(myTableLogonInfo)
  CrystalReportViewer1.LogOnInfo = myTableLogonInfos
  CrystalReportViewer1.ReportSource = myReport
End Sub
```

Make sure that when you are finished setting the `ConnectionInfo` for the table, you specify the table name you are working with prior to using the `Add` method, otherwise you will receive an error message.

Compile and run the example. The report should appear, looking identical to the previous examples.

This is a very simple example, as our report only has one table to worry about. If you have a report that features multiple tables or if you don't know the names of the tables, you could also set up a loop to go through each `report.database.table` in `report.database.tables` and set the `ConnectionInfo` properties for each.

> **Note: In order to get all of the tables in your report and loop through them, you will need to use the Report Engine, which is covered in Chapter 8.**

Setting Report Record Selection

In addition to setting the database credentials for our report, we can also set the record selection formula that is used to filter our report records. The record selection formula within your report is created whenever you use the Select Expert within the Crystal Reports Designer by right-clicking on your report and selecting **Report | Select Expert...**, and then clicking on the table that you wish to see.

This opens up a second dialog box, containing the information on that table. You can choose to hide or show the formula on this box, as shown here:

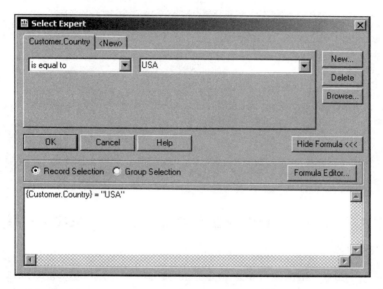

Any selections you make in the Select Expert are translated into a record selection formula written in Crystal Syntax, and displayed in the textbox, as you can see in the case above.

If you click **OK** here, then the next time you run the report it will only return customers in the USA.

For more information on creating formulas and Crystal Syntax, turn over to Chapter 7: Formulas and Logic.

> **You can also edit the record selection formula that is generated by right-clicking on your report in the report designer and selecting Report | Edit Selection Formula | Records.**

When your report is run, this record selection formula is translated into the WHERE clause for the SQL statement that is submitted to the database and the results are returned to Crystal Reports, so while you can't change the SQL statement your report is based on, you can control the records that are returned to the report.

At run time, the `SelectionFormula` property gives us the ability to return or set this value. To return a record selection formula, we would simply request the property as a string, as shown here:

```
CrystalReportViewer1.SelectionFormula.ToString
```

Using the report and viewer we have been working with, we could set the record selection property when the Form loads, before the call to the database, ensuring that only records for customers in the USA are shown:

```
Dim myConnectionInfo = New CrystalDecisions.Shared.ConnectionInfo()
CrystalReportViewer1.SelectionFormula = "{Customer.Country} = 'USA'"
    With myConnectionInfo
        ...
```

Alternately, another way we could use this property is to draw a drop-down list on our Form with all of the different countries in the report and allow the user to select which country they wanted to filter by. When working with record selection, you can come up with some pretty neat ways to deliver one report that could be used for many different types of users.

Speaking of different types of users – the next section deals with how to customize the appearance and layout of the viewer itself. So in addition to showing them only the records they want to see, you could also give them their own custom viewer with which to view the resulting report.

Customizing the Appearance and Layout of the Report Viewer

The `CrystalReportViewer` class contains all of the properties, methods, and events that relate to the viewer itself, its appearance, the methods that are used to make the viewer perform certain actions (like refresh or print a report) and events that can be used to determine when a particular event (such as drill-down or refresh) has occurred. To start learning how to work with the viewer, we are going to start with the basic properties and move on from there.

When previewing your report, you may notice that there is a standard set of icons and layout that appears on your viewer by default, but you can control most of the aspects of the viewer by setting a few simple properties for the Crystal Report Viewer in the Properties window, as shown opposite.

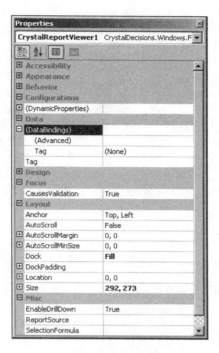

The area at the top of the viewer is the Toolbar, which can be shown or hidden as an entire object, or you can choose to only show certain icons. On the left-hand side is a Group Tree, generated by the grouping that you have inserted into your report. The properties that control these general properties are Boolean and are listed below:

Property	Description
DisplayBackgroundEdge	For showing the off-set edge around your report when previewing
DisplayGroupTree	For showing the group tree on the left-hand side of the viewer
DisplayToolbar	For showing the entire toolbar at the top of the viewer

All of these properties default to True and you cannot change the position of any of these elements – they are fixed in place on the viewer. You can, however, hide the default toolbar and create your own buttons for printing, page navigation, and other functions, and we'll look at that a little later in the chapter.

For the icons within the toolbar, you can also set simple Boolean properties to show or hide a particular icon, as shown below:

- ❑ ShowCloseButton
- ❑ ShowExportButton
- ❑ ShowGotoPageButton
- ❑ ShowGroupTreeButton

❑ ShowPageNavigateButtons

❑ ShowRefreshButton

❑ ShowTextSearchButton

❑ ShowZoomButton

❑ ShowPrintButton

So a typical use of these properties is where you want to give users a view-only preview, with no printing or exporting options and no option to refresh the report. Going back to our original report (ch3_worldsales) we could easily set a few properties before you set your ReportSource property to make this happen.

Double-click anywhere you your Form to open the code view and in the Form's Load method, enter the following:

```
...
End With
        myTableLogonInfo.ConnectionInfo = myConnectionInfo
        myTableLogonInfo.TableName = "customers"
        myTableLogonInfos.Add(myTableLogonInfo)
        CrystalReportViewer1.LogOnInfo = myTableLogonInfos
        CrystalReportViewer1.ReportSource = myReport
        CrystalReportViewer1.DisplayGroupTree = False
        CrystalReportViewer1.ShowExportButton = False
        CrystalReportViewer1.ShowRefreshButton = False
        CrystalReportViewer1.ShowPrintButton = False
        CrystalReportViewer1.ReportSource = New ch3_worldsales_northwind()

    End Sub
```

When the report is previewed, it will appear as shown:

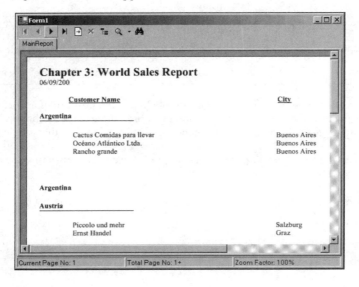

Keep in mind that you can set these properties any time prior to the report preview. You could store individual user or security settings in your application data and then set the appropriate properties prior to viewing the report. This is just one example of where we can customize how a report is presented to the user – the next section on the methods available within the viewer, takes that discussion one step further.

Viewer Methods

When working with the Crystal Report viewer, we have a number of methods available to us, which will allow us to integrate specific viewer functions into our application. As we move through this section, keep in mind that these methods can be used to create your own "look and feel" for the report preview window, as shown below:

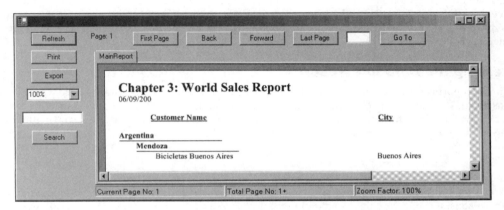

During the course of this section, we will actually be looking at the code behind the custom viewer shown here, so it is probably not a bad idea to start a new project within this chapter's solution file. To create a new project from within Visual Studio select File | New | Project and from Visual Basic Applications, select Windows Applications and specify a name (in the sample code, we have called this project viewer_methods) and location for your project files. Remember to set this project as your startup project.

Once your sample project has been created, add the Crystal Report Viewer to the default Form that is created and copy or add the ch3_worldsales.rpt to your project. Set the ReportSource property to point to this report. We are now ready to get started.

The first thing we need to do to emulate the custom viewer shown earlier is to set the DisplayToolbar and DisplayGroupTree properties to False.

Next, we need to add additional buttons for some of the functions normally associated with the buttons shown on the Viewer Toolbar – the buttons for the next page, previous page, print, export, and so on, using the custom viewer shown above as a guide. We shall walk through each of these in turn below.

The tangible benefit of using the methods described below and your own Form design is that you have more flexibility in how the report appears when viewed and you can match the viewer's user interface to your own application.

Printing a Report

To print a report, there is a simple `PrintReport` method that will invoke a standard Windows printer dialog to select where you would like to print your report, how many copies, and other functions.

To add this code to your custom viewer, drag and drop a button onto your Form, and name it `Print_Button`. Change the **Text** property to `Print`. Double-click the **Print** button you have dropped onto your Form and enter the following code in its `Click` event:

```
CrystalReportViewer1.PrintReport
```

This will open a standard Windows print dialog that will allow you to print your report. If you need to access advanced print options (like printing two pages to separate paper trays) or if you want to control the print process manually, you will need to use the Report Engine to do so, which is covered in Chapter 8.

Refreshing the Data in a Report

When a report is refreshed, it goes back to the database for the most current set of data available and runs again. Drag and drop a button onto the Form, and call it `Refresh_Button`. Change the text to `Refresh`. To refresh from the Crystal Report viewer, you can add the `RefreshReport` method to the **Refresh** button you have created on your custom viewer Form:

```
CrystalReportViewer1.RefreshReport
```

If your report takes a while to run, or if you are concerned about database traffic and load, you may want to consider removing this as an option from your viewer, or even changing the properties of the standard viewer so that the **Refresh** icon does not appear at all, using the syntax `CrystalReportViewer1.ShowRefreshButton = False`.

Exporting a Report

Crystal Reports.NET features a rich export functionality, which is partially exposed in the Crystal Report Viewer. From the viewer, we can call the `ExportReport` method to open a **Save as…** dialog and export your report into one of four formats:

- ❑ Adobe Acrobat (PDF)
- ❑ Microsoft Excel (XLS)
- ❑ Microsoft Word (DOC)
- ❑ Rich-Text Format (RTF)

> **In compatibility testing, the export formats for Microsoft Word and Excel work well with Office 97+ and Rich Text Format can be used by just about any word-processing application (including Word, WordPad, WordPerfect, etc.). For Adobe Acrobat, a version 3.0 or above reader is recommended and the output is consistent across version 3.0 – 5.0.**

So, let's put this functionality into our custom viewer. Drag and drop a button onto the Form once more, this time calling it Export_Button and setting the text to Export. Once again, click on the button to open its code event. Insert the following:

```
CrystalReportViewer1.ExportReport()
```

When the ExportReport method is used, the dialog below will appear and allow you to select an export format from a drop-down list and select where the file is to be saved.

Once the file has been saved, a message box will appear, advising you that the export is complete. You can then use the associated application to open the exported file.

Page Navigation and Zoom

To start with, you probably will want to know what page you're are on at some point. Luckily for us, the Crystal Report Viewer has a simple method called GetCurrentPageNumber that allows us to get the page number of the page we are currently viewing.

In the custom viewer we are working with, we are going to place a label on the Form (we'll call it PageNo_Label) that contains the page number. Initially, we'll set this to Page: 1 using the Text property, but after that, this can be set dynamically using:

```
PageNo_Label.Text = "Page: " &
    CrystalReportViewer1.GetCurrentPageNumber.ToString
```

This method should be called after moving through the report pages, so it should be placed after the code for each of the following buttons (and the Refresh button, of course – do this now).

So, we'll create the following four buttons, and place them on our Form.

Button Name	Button Text Property Value
FirstPage_Button	First Page
BackPage_Button	Back
NextPage_Button	Forward
LastPage_Button	Last Page

In order to navigate through the pages or our report, we have a number of methods that can be called without any additional parameters, as shown below:

- ❑ ShowFirstPage
- ❑ ShowLastPage
- ❑ ShowNextPage
- ❑ ShowPreviousPage

So to put code behind our navigation buttons on our custom Form, (in this case, the **Forward** button) we could use the ShowNextPage method.

```
CrystalReportViewer1.ShowNextPage()
PageNo_Label.Text = "Page: " &
    CrystalReportViewer1.GetCurrentPageNumber.ToString
```

Compile and run this. You should be on page two of the report, and the label should inform you of this. Now populate the remaining buttons with the code, remembering to set the correct method for each button.

These methods do not return a result, so to determine what page you are currently on, we would have to use the GetCurrentPageNumber method immediately after calling the first method, which will return the page you are currently viewing. Unfortunately, we don't have a way to get the total page count, unless you were to use ShowLastPage to go to the last page, use the GetCurrentPageNumber method, and then store the number of the last page in a variable somewhere in your code, but that is a lot of work for one little number.

For navigating to a specific page, ShowNthPage allows us to pass a specific page number to the method, as shown here emulating the functionality of the ShowNextPage method.

```
Dim CurrentPage
CurrentPage = GetCurrentPageNumber
CrystalReportViewer1.ShowNthPage(CurrentPage + 1)
' This will take you to the next page
```

In the custom viewer we are working with, draw a textbox onto the Form, naming it PageNo_TextBox. The point of this textbox is to allow the user to enter a page number and then click the **Go To** button to go to a specific page. Drag and drop a button on the Form next to the textbox, naming the button GoTo_Button and labelling it **Go To**.

Assuming that the textbox you have drawn on your Form is called `PageNo_TextBox`, the following code, placed behind the **Go To** button, checks to see if a page number has been entered. If something has been entered, the `ShowNthPage` method is then called to jump to a specific page.

```
If PageNo_TextBox.Text <> "" Then
  CrystalReportViewer1.ShowNthPage(PageNo_TextBox.Text)
  PageNo_Label.Text = "Page: " &
      CrystalReportViewer1.GetCurrentPageNumber.ToString
  PageNo_TextBox.Text = "  "
Else
  MsgBox("Please enter a page number to jump to",
      MsgBoxStyle.Exclamation, "Please enter a page number")
  PageNo_TextBox.Text = "  "
End If
```

Compile and run, and you should see that this functionality is now implemented.

In addition to page navigation, you also have the ability to choose the zoom factor that is applied to your report. By default, the zoom is set to 100% of the report size unless you specify otherwise. In the example below, we will add a combo box to the Form to allow the user to select a particular zoom factor for viewing.

The name of the combo box is `ComboBox_Zoom`. Assign the **Text** property with the value `100%`, and click on the **Items** property. The String Collection Editor should now open. Enter the following strings, one per line:

❑   25%

❑   50%

❑   Full Size

❑   200%

Now, we move on to the business of selecting and setting a zoom factor based on the index of the item that has been selected. Double-click on the combo box and enter the following code:

```
With CrystalReportViewer1
  Select Case ComboBox_Zoom.SelectedIndex
    Case 0
      .Zoom(25)
    Case 1
      .Zoom(50)
    Case 2
      .Zoom(100)
    Case 3
      .Zoom(200)
  End Select
```

You also may want to consider adding the option to let the user select their own Zoom factor. Keep in mind that 50% is about the lowest resolution at which a report can be read legibly with a 12-point font used in the report itself – if you are concerned about how the report will appear when viewed, you may also set the "minimum zoom" required to view the report as it should appear.

Searching within a Report

Another powerful navigation feature can be found in the `SearchForText` method within Crystal Reports.NET, which will allow you to search for a specific string that appears in your report. In our custom viewer, we will add a textbox (`SearchString_TextBox`) for the user to enter a search string, as well as a **Search** button (`Search_Button`) to kick off this method. Drag both of these items onto the Form, and set their properties appropriately.

The code behind the search button looks like this:

```
If SearchString_TextBox.Text <> "" Then
  CrystalReportViewer1.SearchForText(SearchString_TextBox.Text)
  PageNo_Label.Text = "Page: " &
      CrystalReportViewer1.GetCurrentPageNumber.ToString
  SearchString_TextBox.Text = " "
Else
  MsgBox("Please enter a search string to search for",
      MsgBoxStyle.Exclamation, "Please enter a string to search for...")
  SearchString_TextBox.Text = " "
End If
```

We first check to see if a value is entered and if so, the `SearchForText` method is called, passing the search string that was entered. The Crystal Report Viewer will search the entire report and when the value is found, go directly to the page on which it appears and highlight the value. This method can be called repeatedly to find all of the occurrences of a particular string – each time it finds the string in your report, it will jump to that page and highlight where the value appears.

Using our World Sales report and searching on `Hong Kong` should jump to the first company with a region of `Hong Kong` and highlight the value, as shown below:

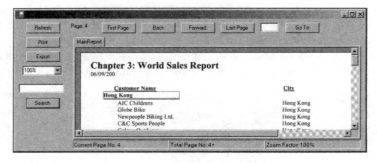

Using Viewer Events

Viewer events provide the ability to track the firing of different events – for instance, when the user navigates through the pages of the report, or when they refresh the report. These events can then be used to fire other code from within your application.

While all of the different events have their own unique properties and methods, they all inherit a common property called `Handled`. This is a Boolean value that is used to determine whether the event was fired and subsequently handled.

In the following section, we will be looking at all of the available events associated with the viewer and their common uses. Again, since this is a new set of functionality contained within the viewer, we are going to create another project to hold all of the code and Forms related to this section.

To create a new project from within Visual Studio select File | New | Project and from Visual Basic Applications, select Windows Applications and specify a name (in the sample code, we have called this project viewer_events) for your project files. Set this as your startup project within the solution.

Once your sample project has been created, add the Crystal Report Viewer to the default Form that is created and copy or add the ch3_worldsales.rpt to your project. Set the ReportSource property to point to this report and let's get coding.

For all of these events, we are going to place the code behind our Form and when a particular event is fired, the code will be run.

Page Navigation Events

For page navigation, the NavigateEventArgs class provides the properties we need to work with the Navigate event, including:

Property	Description
CurrentPageNumber	Returns the current page number
NewPageNumber	Gets or sets the new page number

In the example below, the Navigate event would fire when a user changed the page within the viewer, resulting in a message box that would show the page they are currently on, and the page they are navigating to.

Insert the following subroutine into your Form:

```
Private Sub CrystalReportViewer1_Navigate(ByVal source As Object, ByVal
    MyEvent As CrystalDecisions.Windows.Forms.NavigateEventArgs) Handles
    CrystalReportViewer1.Navigate

  If MyEvent.NewPageNumber <> 1 Then
    MsgBox ("Current page: " & MyEvent.CurrentPageNumber & " New Page: " &
        Event.NewPageNumber)
  End If
End Sub
```

Compile and run with this code. When the Form opens with the report, click on the last page icon. You should see a message box similar to the one below:

This event could be used to determine when the first page was viewed, and pop up another Form with an explanation of the report and its contents, or used to perform a task in the background (like logging page views) while the user is viewing the report.

Refresh Events

The `ReportRefresh` event has no arguments other than the inherited `Handled` property. It can be used to build metrics on how often a report is run or refreshed, and to pass information to users about the report before they launch a refresh, as shown below:

```
Private Sub CrystalReportViewer1_ReportRefresh(ByVal source As Object, ByVal
    MyEvent As CrystalDecisions.Windows.Forms.ViewerEventArgs) Handles
    CrystalReportViewer1.ReportRefresh
      MsgBox ("Please be advised this report takes up to 2 minutes to run.")
End Sub
```

Refresh events are also key to improving application and data performance – if your database is only updated once a day (or once a month) you can keep track of how many times a user attempts to hit the database, and simply remind them with an information box that the data will remain the same during the day, regardless of how many times they hit the refresh button!

Search Events

When a user searches for a report value, either through the standard icon on the toolbar or through your own method call, the `Search` event is fired. The arguments for the `Search` event are:

Property	Description
Direction	Gets or sets the direction in which to search. This can be either Backward or Forward.
PageNumberToBeginSearch	Gets or sets the page number to start searching at.
TextToSearch	Gets or sets the text to search for in the report.

So by using these event arguments, you could keep a record of what values users searched for. An example of getting the text that is being used in the search is included below:

```
Private Sub CrystalReportViewer1_Search(ByVal source As Object, ByVal
    MyEvent As CrystalDecisions.Windows.Forms.SearchEventArgs) Handles
    CrystalReportViewer1.Search
  MsgBox ("You searched for " & event.TextToSearch )
End Sub
```

Viewer Events

The `Load` event is fired whenever the report viewer is initialized from a Windows Form and has no other arguments other than `Handled`. You can use this event to fire other sections of code or launch additional windows for help, or a description of the report, as shown here:

```
Private Sub CrystalReportViewer1_Load(ByVal sender As System.Object, ByVal
    MyEvent As System.EventArgs) Handles CrystalReportViewer1.Load
  MsgBox ("This report shows monthly sales broken down by region")
End Sub
```

Again, you could also use this event for logging as well.

Zoom Events

For those times that the user changes the zoom factor for a particular report, the ViewZoom event fires, and has only one argument in ZoomEventArgs. The NewZoomFactor property will get or set the magnification factor for the viewer, as shown here:

```
Private Sub CrystalReportViewer1_ViewZoom(ByVal source As Object, ByVal
    MyEvent As CrystalDecisions.Windows.Forms.ZoomEventArgs) Handles
    CrystalReportViewer1.ViewZoom

        Select Case MyEvent.NewZoomFactor
            Case "25"
                MsgBox ("You have selected 25%")
            Case "50"
                MsgBox ("You have selected 50%")
            Case "100"
                MsgBox ("You have selected full size")
        End Select
End Sub
```

Drilling into Report Details

If you are working with a report that has groups inserted, you can drill down within the viewer to show the detailed records that make up that group. By default, these details are visible anyway, as shown below:

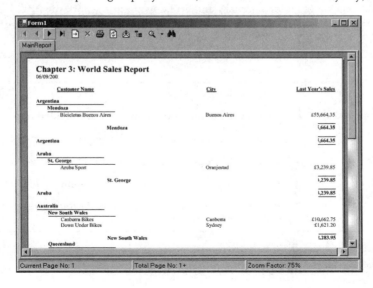

When you drill down into a group, a separate tab is opened within the preview window, showing only the group you have selected. For summary reports, you may want to hide the details and allow users to drill down if they need more information.

This provides an easy way to cut down on report development – instead of multiple reports for different regions, for example, you could create one report and then let the users drill into it and print the section they wanted to see – in the example below, the user has drilled down into Australia, which opens another tab in the viewer and allows them to see the regions within Australia

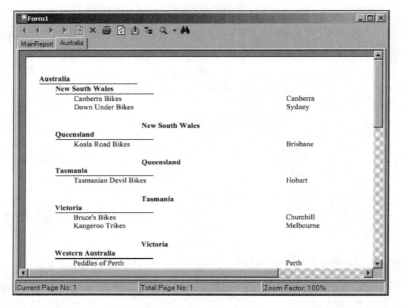

When you double-click a group or summary and drill down into a report, the `Drill` event is fired and can be used to return the name of the group, the level, or other information. There are a number of properties associated with `DrillEventArgs`, including:

Property	Description
CurrentGroupLevel	Returns the group level that was drilled into
CurrentGroupName	Returns the name of the group that was drilled into
CurrentGroupPath	Returns the group number and group level that was drilled into
NewGroupLevel	Returns the target group level that is being drilled into
NewGroupName	Returns the target group name that is being drilled into
NewGroupPath	Returns the target group number and group level that is being drilled into

Note: `CurrentGroupNamePath` *and* `NewGroupNamePath` *are included within* `DrillEventArgs` *but are reserved for future use.*

To see the Drill event in action, you will need to have a report that has at least one group inserted and a section where the details are hidden (not suppressed). In addition, in the Crystal Report Viewer, the EnableDrillDown property must be True. The Drill event will fire whenever you drill down into one of the groups on your report and can be used to determine the group name, and what level has been drilled into, among other things.

Drill events can be used to launch other Forms or processes – for example, when a user drills down on a Country group, you could display a Form giving a background to the country, its currency, and other pertinent information.

The code below demonstrates the Drill event being used to display an information box, containing information on where the user was drilling from and the target they were drilling to.

```
Private Sub CrystalReportViewer1_Drill(ByVal source As Object, ByVal MyEvent
    As CrystalDecisions.Windows.Forms.DrillEventArgs) Handles
    CrystalReportViewer1.Drill

  MsgBox("You drilled into " & MyEvent.NewGroupName() & (Chr(13) & Chr(10)),
      MsgBoxStyle.Information, "Drill Down Event")

End Sub
```

Drilling Down on Subreports

Multiple subreports can be inserted into a main report and provide a way to combing disparate information on a single report. A subreport within a Crystal Report is actually a report in its own right, with its own page numbering, sections, and other information.

There are a number of subreport events that can be used as users drill through a report with subreports, including:

Property	Description
CurrentSubreportName	Returns the name of the subreport that was drilled into
CurrentSubreportPageNumber	Returns the page number that the subreport is on
CurrentSubreportPosition	Returns the location in the viewer where the subreport is
NewSubreportName	Returns the name of subreport that is being drilled into
NewSubreportPageNumber	Returns the page number to drill into the subreport
NewSubreportPosition	Returns the location in the viewer where the subreport is to drill into

Using the properties above, you could determine the name of a report that had been drilled into and then use the same for logging and launching other Forms. Our report does not contain a subreport, but the methods remain the same.

Note: For changing elements of a subreport, we would need to use functionality from the Crystal Report Engine, covered in Chapter 8.

Dealing with Report Exceptions

The `HandleException` event fires whenever you are viewing a report and the viewer encounters any errors or exceptions. This could be caused by a data source not being available, the report file itself being moved to a different location (if external to your application) or any other error that may occur.

There are a number of arguments that are associated with this event, including:

Property	Description
Exception	Returns the exception data for the exception that has occurred
UserData	Returns or sets any type of data that can be used to over-ride what is done in the handling of an exception

The `UserData` property is a generic object that can be used to override the error handling that the viewer would normally do. For example, if your were using an Access database and it had been moved and was no longer available, you could set the `UserData` property to a string containing the location to the `UserData`, and that particular database location would be used.

So, to trap these and other types of errors, you can set up an error handler event and then use the exception to return the error message:

```
Public Sub CrystalReportViewer1_HandleException(ByVal source As Object,
    ByVal MyEvent As CrystalDecisions.Windows.Forms.ExceptionEventArgs)
    Handles CrystalReportViewer1.HandleException

  Dim err As Exception
  err = myEvent.Exception
  MsgBox("An error has occurred with your report:" & (Chr(13) & Chr(10)) &
      err.ToString, MsgBoxStyle.Critical, "Exception Event")
End Sub
```

> **Note: You also may want to consider tying context-sensitive help (where the help topic directly relates to the error message produced) to the error as well, to give the user a more complete description of what the error really means.**

Summary

In this chapter, you have had a look at integrating reports into Windows applications, starting with basic integration with the Crystal Report Viewer for Windows Forms. In terms of ease of use and functionality, the Crystal Report Viewer provides most of the functionality you will need for view-only reporting implementations. In addition to the standard viewer functionality, we also looked at how you could use the properties, methods, and events of the viewer to customize the look and feel or even create your own custom viewer that matches your own application's user interface.

So what is next? For more advanced integration topics and greater control over the report itself, you may want to consider flipping over to Chapter 8 to start learning how the Report Engine can be used to control your report's contents and appearance.

If you also develop web applications, you are probably keen to get into the next chapter, but keep in mind that some of the same concepts we just covered in this chapter (and in Chapter 8 with the Report Engine topics) will also apply to web applications, which we will be looking at next.

Professional **Crystal Reports**
for **Visual Studio .NET**

4

Report Integration for Web-Based Applications

While Windows applications will still continue to be popular for some time to come, the growing trend in application development is for web-based applications.

In this chapter, we are going to look at how to integrate and view reports from within web-based applications created with Visual Studio .NET. In addition, we will look at some of the run-time customizations that can be made to your reports, as well as some issues around web application deployment. This will consist of:

- ❑ Determining the correct Object Model
- ❑ `CrystalDecisions.Web` namespace
- ❑ Using the Crystal Web Forms Viewer
- ❑ Customizing the Crystal Web Forms Viewer
- ❑ Passing information to the Web Forms Viewer

As we go through this chapter, we will be building forms for use in web-based reporting applications, which demonstrate many of the Crystal Reports.NET features that can be used in your own web applications.

Obtaining the Sample Files

All the example reports and code used in this chapter are available for download. The download file can be obtained from www.wrox.com. Once you have downloaded the files, place them in a folder called CrystalReports\Chapter04 on your hard drive.

In Chapter 4, all of the completed projects are included in the downloadable code as well as the reports used throughout the chapter, so you can either browse through the finished projects or create your own projects from scratch using the components provided.

You can use the code as you go through the chapter or cut and paste code samples into your own web application.

Planning Your Application

If you are developing web applications with Visual Studio .NET, chances are you are well acquainted with ASP.NET (and if you aren't, you soon will be!). ASP.NET is not really a language, per se, but rather a set of interrelated technologies and components that come together in one framework to deliver robust web applications. As a developer, you probably already know that the most important part of creating an application is in the planning and design of the application, before the coding actually starts. The integration of Crystal Reports into web applications is no different – a little bit of planning goes a long way.

The first thing we will need to do, before we write a single line of code, is to determine what type of reports we want to deliver in our web application and how they are going to be used. Are they listing or grouped reports? Are they used to check data entry in a form before submitting it? What will the reports look like? Will users want to print the reports from their browser or export to another format such as PDF, RTF, or Excel? All of these questions can help you gather the information you need to design your reports and get a handle on how they are going to be delivered.

> Note: Even if you don't have your own reports to work with, you can still work through this chapter – sample reports are available in `C:\Program Files\Visual Studio .NET\Crystal Reports\Samples\` or in the download files for this chapter.

Once you understand the type of functionality you would like to deliver to the user, you can sit down and start planning how Crystal Reports will be integrated into your web application. Crystal Reports.NET uses a feature-rich report viewer, available out of the box, which can be inserted onto a Web Form and used to view reports. The viewer itself has features that are similar to the Windows form viewer and has an extensive object model, allowing you to set the source of the report, the appearance of the viewer itself, and what happens when different events fire, among other things.

When working with web applications, most users seem to prefer that we pop up an additional window to display reports. This allows them to have the full browser area to view the report and we can pass properties like the report source and viewer settings to this Web Form. This allows us to reuse one "report viewing" form throughout the web application and just set the properties we need each time.

The options for working with reports are endless – based on a user's access rights in your application, you could set a specific record selection formula or allow the user to set and retain parameters they use frequently, or even establish profiles of their favorite reports, so they can run it with all of their settings in place with one click.

Like integrating reporting into Windows applications, the report integration should be driven by the user's requirements, but how these features are delivered is up to you. As you go through the rest of the chapter, think about how the different customization features could be used in your development. If you are not at a point where you can integrate these features into your application, each of the properties, methods, and events are grouped together by function to make it easier to come back and look them up.

A Brief History of Crystal Web Development

When Crystal Reports was first released, the Internet was still in its infancy and Crystal Reports has grown right along beside it. With the introduction of a web component in Crystal Reports 7.0, based on the print engine already in use with its Windows development tools, developers were able to integrate reporting into their own web applications through the use of ASP. This first implementation of web reporting provided a powerful tool for web developers and enabled a whole new class of reporting applications for the web.

It wasn't long before web developers started pushing Crystal Reports on the web to its limit. While version 7.0 of Crystal Reports provided a web engine that was suitable for small workgroup applications of 5-10 users, it lacked the power to handle the first of many large enterprise web applications that were being developed at the time.

A companion product, Seagate Info (formerly Crystal Info) was also introduced utilizing a similar framework, but adding multi-tier processing to the architecture, enabling reports to be processed on a separate machine and then viewed by the user. Unfortunately, customizing the Seagate Info user interface, or creating custom apps that accessed this technology, proved to be cumbersome, so it really didn't take off with developers.

With the release of version 8.0, the reporting technology took another massive leap forward, but some of the same limitations persisted (such as scalability and security) until the advent of Crystal Reports 8.5 and the introduction of Crystal Enterprise 8.5. Leveraging the architecture and code base from Seagate Info, Crystal Enterprise provides a robust application framework that developers can use to create applications that can be scaled from one to ten to ten thousand users and beyond.

So where does that leave you, the Crystal Reports.NET developer? Well, to start, you don't need to buy any additional tools or licenses to integrate reporting into your web applications – Crystal Reports.NET provides all of the tools you need to create web-based workgroup applications.

> Note: To deploy applications beyond a workgroup implementation of 5-10 users to a large number of users you will need to purchase an additional license from Crystal Decisions. Also, if you need to offload processing in a true n-tier application or want to schedule or redistribute reports, you may want to consider moving your application to Crystal Enterprise (covered in Chapter 9).

The other great news is that Crystal Reports.NET builds on the web functionality found in previous products and provides a feature-rich development environment and a rich user experience for viewing reports on the web. If you haven't looked at the Crystal Reports web technology in a while, you are going to be pleasantly surprised.

Exploring the Development Environment

When creating ASP.NET web applications, you don't need a specialized editor to develop the required components – you could just crack open Notepad and create all of the files required yourself. Thankfully, Visual Studio .NET provides a feature-rich development environment that makes things a bit easier when creating ASP.NET applications and there are a number of Crystal-specific components for use in web applications.

To start with, in the toolbox under the Web Forms section, you will find the CrystalReportViewer, which we will be working with a little later. When you drop or draw this viewer on a Web form, as shown below, you can set a number of properties and use the viewer to display a "What-you-see-is-what-you-get" (or WYSIWYG) preview of your report.

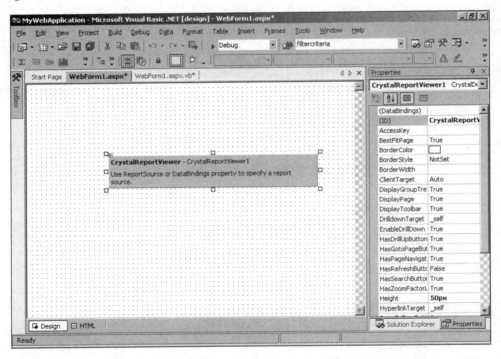

In addition to the CrystalReportViewer, there is also a ReportDocument component available in the Components section of the toolbox. We use this component to add strongly-typed and untyped reports to a form. (If you just opened this book and flipped to this chapter, you may be wondering what a typed report is, don't worry – we'll get to that a little later in the chapter.)

Finally, like most Windows applications, the majority of our report integration will take place in the code view of the form.

Using the object models provided by Crystal Reports.NET, you have almost complete control over the report's appearance and behavior.

Before You Get Started

Before we can actually get into creating web-based applications, you will need to check and see if you have all of the required components installed to run these applications. ASP.NET web applications run on a web server that can either be located on your local machine or on another server that you have access to that has IIS installed.

When you installed Visual Studio .NET, you may have received an error message if you did not have a web server installed on your machine at that time. If you are working on a computer that does not have IIS installed and the required .NET components loaded, you will need to have access to a server that does in order to create the forms and applications demonstrated in this chapter.

For more information on installing the .NET Framework and preparing a web server for application development, check out the Visual Studio .NET Combined Help Collection and search for "Configuring Applications".

Starting a New Web Application with VB.NET

The first thing we need to do to get started is to create a new web application using Visual Basic .NET. Included with the download files for this chapter are a number of projects that are related to the different sections in this chapter. To walk through the examples that follow, you can either create a new solution or open the one that is provided (the same applies to the other projects – you can either follow along or create your own).

To create a new web application, from within Visual Studio, select File | New | Project and from Visual Basic Applications, select ASP.NET Web Application and specify a name (web_viewer_basic) and location for your project files.

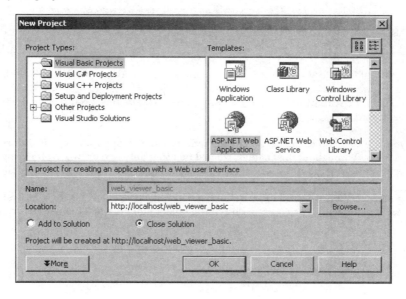

Since you are creating a web application, the location will be a web server that you have access to and the name of your project will actually be used to create a virtual directory on this server. (The good news is that Visual Studio .NET will automatically do this for you if you are building the application from scratch – there is no need to create the folder and virtual directory prior to creating a new project.)

If, however, you choose to use the supplied download code, then you should create a virtual directory (in our case, this is C:\CrystalReports\Chapter04\web_viewer_basic) by selecting Control Panel I Administrative Tools I Internet Information Services, and then right-clicking on Default Web Site. This will open another menu:

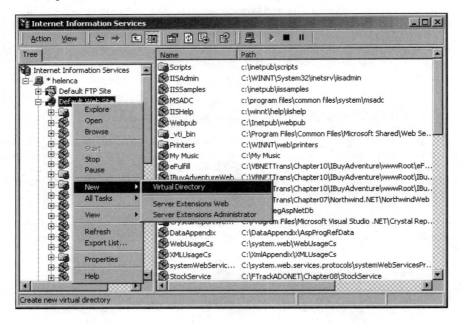

Select New I Virtual Directory and the virtual directory wizard will commence. Assign the new directory the alias web_viewer_basic and set the path to C:\CrystalReports\Chapter04\web_viewer_basic. Make sure both read and write are enabled and finish the wizard.

Either way you choose to do it, the development environment will open with a default form that we will be using in the section. Throughout the chapter, we will be using only one or two Web Forms to demonstrate different integration features, but the same concepts can be applied to your own web applications.

Before you go any further, we need to get some basic architecture decisions for your web application out of the way, starting with a brief discussion of the object models available within Crystal Reports.NET.

Determining the Correct Object Model

When working with web applications, there are two different object models to choose from, each with its own capabilities and strengths. The first, contained within the **Crystal Reports Web Forms Viewer** object model (`CrystalDecisions.web`), contains all of the functionality required to view a report in the Crystal Reports Web Forms Viewer, including the ability to set database logon information, pass parameters and record selection, control the viewer's appearance, and view reports, including reports consumed from an XML Report Web Service.

Using the `CrystalDecisions.Web` object model, you are covered for most basic report integration requirements, but you have no control over the report itself at run time – you won't be able to change the record selection for any subreports that appear in your report and you won't have access to modify report elements, like groups and sorting, or formula fields.

For complete control over the report and its content, you need to use the **Crystal Reports Engine** object model (`CrystalDecisions.CrystalReports.Engine`) in conjunction with the viewer object model. This will allow you complete control over your report and the objects and features contained within. Using the Crystal Reports Engine means that you have a rich object model that can be used to modify even the tiniest elements of your report.

> *Note: You will also need to use the Report Engine object model if you are using ADO (.NET or "Classic" ADO) as the data source for your report (which is covered in Chapter 6:* Working with .NET Data*).*

It is important to note that the Crystal Reports Engine object model cannot stand alone – it provides no way to view a report and relies on the Crystal Reports Web (or Windows) Forms Viewer to actually view the report.

Crystal Decisions recommends that you do not overlap the two object models and try to use properties and methods from both at the same time. An example would be where you are setting a parameter field value in the Report Engine object model – you wouldn't want to also try to set a parameter field in the same report using the Crystal Reports Windows Forms Viewer object model. Try to pick an object model based on your requirements and (as I recommended in the last chapter with the Windows Forms Viewer) stick with it!

Understanding the CrystalDecisions.Web Namespace

The `CrystalDecisions.Web` namespace contains all of the classes that relate to functions available within the Web Forms Viewer itself. The following table illustrates the different classes that are available, as well as their use in web applications.

Class	Description
`CrystalReportViewer`	Contains the properties, methods, and events relating to the `CrystalReportViewer` and viewing reports. Note: some properties of this class are inherited from `CrystalReportViewerBase`.

Table continued on following page

Class	Description
CrystalReportViewerBase	Contains properties for setting the target browser edition, database logon information, etc.
DrillEventArgs	Provides data for the Drill event on main reports and subreports. Drill events fire when a user drills down into a group or summary on a particular main report or subreport.
DrillSubreportEventArgs	Provides data for the DrillDownSubreport event on main reports and subreports. Drill events fire when a user drills down into a group or summary on a particular main report or subreport.
ExceptionEventArgs	Provides data for the HandleException event. HandleException events occur when there is an error or exception when setting report properties or viewing the report. Primarily used for troubleshooting and error messages.
NavigateEventArgs	Provides data for the Navigate event. When a user navigates through the pages of a report, the Navigate event fires each time. This can be used to notify the users when they have reached the last page, to call custom actions, etc.
SearchEventArgs	Provides data for the Search event. The CrystalReportViewer includes an integrated search function to search for values within a report. The Search event fires when a user searches for a value and could be used to trigger a search of another report or other report descriptions, etc.
ViewerEventArgs	Provides data for the Viewer event. The Viewer event fires when some action has occurred within the viewer itself and can be used to launch other actions when the viewer loads, etc.
ZoomEventArgs	Provides data for the ViewZoom event. The ViewZoom event fires when the zoom is changed on the viewer and can be used to suggest the best resolution for a particular report (100%, 200%, etc.), or if you are showing two reports in viewers side by side, to synchronize the zoom factor between the two (so the magnification on both reports stays the same – if you change one to 200%, the other view changes as well).

Using the Crystal Report Viewer for Web Forms

For report files that live externally to your application (for instance, as a standalone report file, created with either this or a previous version of Crystal Reports) there is not much to creating a simple preview form for your report. We are going to walk through that process in the following section.

Earlier we created a new project called web_viewer_basic and within that project there should be a default Web Form (WebForm1.aspx) that was created when you created the project. To start, we need to drag or draw the Crystal Report Viewer onto our Web Form:

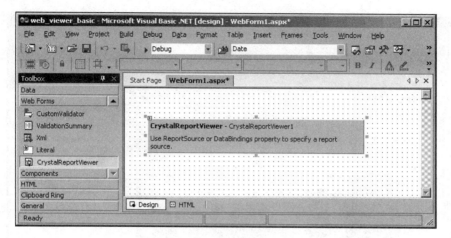

From that point, we need to set the ReportSource property to let the viewer know where to get the report from. To access this property, locate the Properties window for the Crystal Report Viewer and open the (DataBindings) property, by clicking on the ellipse at the side, to show the dialog that appears below:

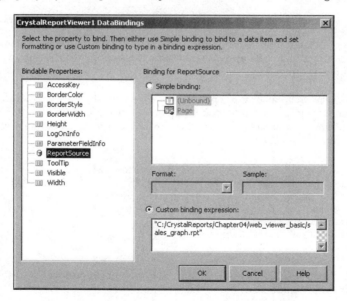

Click on the ReportSource property and click on the radio button to select Custom Binding Expression. In this example, we are going to assume that you have unzipped the download files for this chapter to your hard drive in a folder called CrystalReports\Chapter04 – included in these files is a Sales Graph report (sales_graph.rpt) that we will be using through this walkthrough.

Once you have entered the name and path for your report, click **OK** to accept your changes and return to the form we were working with. The report will now be displayed in a "Preview" mode in the form designer, as shown here:

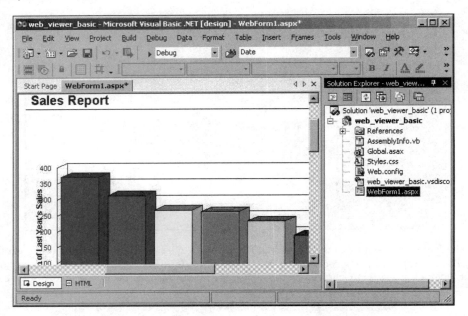

If we were working with a Windows form, this would be all that is required to actually preview a report. Since Web Forms work a little differently, there is an extra step involved before we can run our application and preview our report.

Double-click anywhere on your form to open the code view for the form and locate the section of code marked **Web Form Designer generated code**. Expand this section to find the `Page_Init` function and add a line of code immediately after the `InitializeComponent()` call to bind your report to the viewer when the page is initialized:

```
Private Sub Page_Init(ByVal sender As System.Object, ByVal e As
    System.EventArgs) Handles MyBase.Init
    'CODEGEN: This method call is required by the Web Form Designer
    'Do not modify it using the code editor.
    InitializeComponent()
    CrystalReportViewer1.DataBind()
End Sub
```

Whenever you run your application and preview the form, your report will be displayed in the Crystal Report Viewer, as shown next:

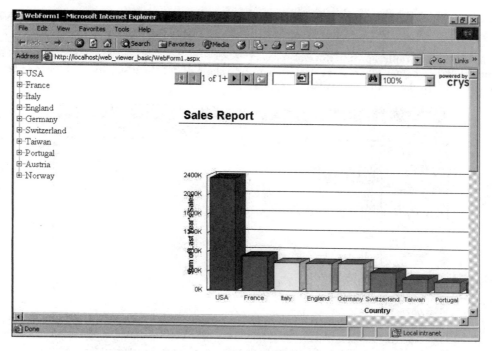

The viewer interacts with the Crystal Reports print engine, runs the report, and displays the results. From your report preview, you can drill-down into the details or search for a value, without having to do any additional coding.

If you only have one or two reports that you want to integrate into a view-only application and you don't need to customize any features at run time, this may be all you need. But for applications that required a more sophisticated integration with Crystal Reports.NET, you probably need to look a bit further.

In the following sections, we are going to walk through adding a report to your application, binding the report to the Crystal Report Viewer, and customizing the viewer.

Adding a Report to Your Application

To add a new report to your application, you have two choices – you can either use an existing report that you have created (using this or a previous version of Crystal Reports), or you can use the Report Designer integrated within Visual Studio .NET to create a report from scratch. For our purposes, we are going to add an existing report to our next sample application (for more information on creating reports from scratch, check out Chapter 2: *Getting Started with Crystal Reports*.)

In this example, we will add the Sales Graph report to web_viewer_basic2. Whereas the approach in our first example favors publication of a report that will always be found by the same path, but is subject to regular updates, this option favors a report that is not likely to change and so can be incorporated into the application, allowing us to alter its features, or even build it from the ground up. This is also relevant to whether we are using strongly typed or untyped reports, as we discussed in the last chapter.

Once again, you have the choice of building the project or using the code provided – but remember that if you use the code provided, you must create a virtual directory for it in IIS on your machine.

To add our Sales Graph report to this new project, select Project | Add Existing Item, which will open the dialog shown below. Change the drop-down list to show All files and specify *.rpt for the file name to filter the list to show only the available reports.

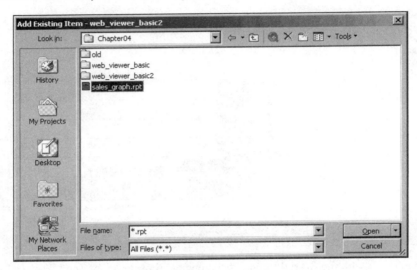

Once you have selected the Sales_Graph.rpt report, click Open and this report will be added to your project in the Solution Explorer.

Once you have added your report to your project, it will appear in the Solutions Explorer and you can view the design of the report using the Report Designer and access its properties through its **Properties** page.

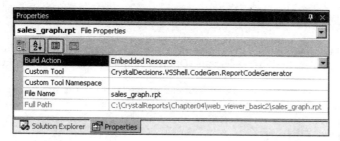

Adding the Report Viewer to a Web Form

You can add the Crystal Report Viewer from the Web Forms Toolbox and drag or draw the viewer onto your form – unlike the Crystal Report Viewer for Windows forms, the Web Forms Viewer does not provide a view of how the viewer will appear on your page until you actually bind a report to it, at design or run time.

In fact, we'll do this now for `web_viewer_basic2`. Just drag a **CrystalReportViewer** over from the Toolbox and place it on the Web Form. Don't bother setting a report source for it yet, as we are about to look at different methods for binding the report to the viewer.

The Crystal Report Viewer can be used on existing forms to display a report side by side with other controls, or you could add the report to a new form to have a separate window for previewing reports.

Binding a Report to the Report Viewer

With the Report Viewer added to your form, we now need to bind a report to the viewer itself. As we saw in Chapter 3 for Windows-based applications, there are five different ways to bind a report to the Crystal Report Viewer:

- ❑ By report name
- ❑ By report object
- ❑ By binding to an untyped report
- ❑ By binding to strongly-typed report
- ❑ By binding to strongly-typed cached report

Binding by Report Name

To bind a report using the report name, as we did in our first example, all you need to do is set the `ReportSource` property, either through the **Data Bindings** properties for the report or through the form's code, as shown here:

```
CrystalReportViewer1.ReportSource =
"C:\CrystalReports\Chapter04\web_viewer_basic\sales_graph.rpt"
```

Then in the Page_Init event of your form, you would need to add a single line of code to call the DataBind method immediately after the InitializeComponent() call, as shown here:

```
CrystalReportViewer1.DataBind()
```

If you prefer to set the initial report source using the property pages, you will need to open the **Properties** page for the report viewer, and then select the **(DataBindings)** property as we did in the first example.

But since we have added the report to our application, we could also bind the report by creating a report object, loading the report into the object, and binding the object to the Crystal Report Viewer.

Binding by Report Object

Binding by a report object works slightly differently depending on if you have added the report to your project, or if you are referencing it externally. For a report that resides external to your application, you need to first specify an import of the CrystalDecisions.CrystalReports.Engine, which will allow you to create the object.

If this is not already present, we shall add it. In the Solution Explorer, right-click on your project title and select **Properties** from the right-click menu to open the dialog shown below.

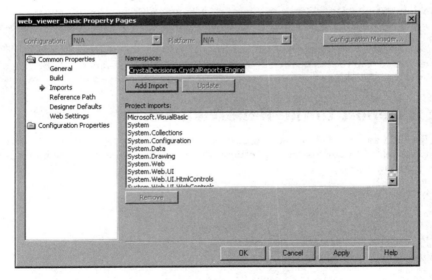

Under the **Common Properties** folder, use the **Imports** option to add the CrystalDecisions.CrystalReports.Engine namespace to your project and click **OK** to return to your form.

With this namespace imported, we now need to create the report object as a ReportDocument in the form's Declarations section, as shown:

```
Dim myReport as New ReportDocument()
```

With our object now ready to be used, we can now load the external report file by placing the following code under the **Page_Init** event:

```
...
InitializeComponent()
myReport.Load("C:\CrystalReports\Chapter04\sales_graph.rpt")
CrystalReportViewer1.ReportSource = myReport
```

If the report you are using has actually been added to your project (as ours was above), a class was automatically generated for the report, so we could use the class instead to bind the report to the viewer (while the `import` and `Public` declaration remain the same):

```
...
InitializeComponent()
myReport = New sales_graph()
CrystalReportViewer1.ReportSource = myReport
```

or, if you wanted to eliminate the `myReport` variable:

```
CrystalReportViewer1.ReportSource = New sales_graph()
```

Which method you choose will depend on where the report is physically located and how you wish to access it.

Binding to an Untyped Report

When working with Crystal Reports.NET, you can add individual report files to your project and use and reference them to view reports from your application. Taking this a step further, you could also use these reports as components, which is where we start looking at typing.

When integrating reports into an application, we can either use strongly-typed reports or untyped reports. If you have been working with Visual Studio .NET for any length of time, you have probably heard of strongly-typed objects. A strongly-typed object is predefined with a number of attributes that are specific to that object, giving programmers more structure and a rigorous set of rules to follow, whereas an untyped report does not have this structure or rules applied to it, making it more difficult to work with.

Within the frame of reference of Crystal Reports.NET, a strongly-typed report can be any report that has been added to your project. When you add a report to a project, you will notice that in addition to the report, another file (with a `.vb` extension) is also added, as shown overleaf:

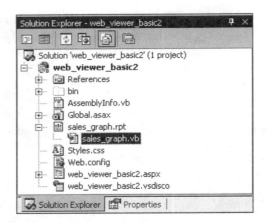

Note: This file is hidden until you select Show All Files from the Solution Explorer.

This additional file is the report source file and contains a report class specific to each report, called `ReportDocument`, which is derived from the `ReportClass` class and is created automatically for you.

An example of an untyped report would be a report that is stored externally to your project. For instance, you could view a report by setting an external reference (as in our first example, where we set the ReportSource property in the (DataBindings) to `"C:\CrystalReports\Chapter04\web_viewer_basic\sales_graph.rpt"`.

We'll just have a brief look at how we do this. Create a virtual directory called `web_viewer_untyped` pointing at `C:\CrystalReports\Chapter04\web_viewer_untyped` (if this is where you have downloaded the source code to) or alternatively build it from scratch.

To add a report component to your application, switch to the Layout view of your form and look in the toolbox under Components. In this section, you should see a component labeled ReportDocument. Drag this component onto your form, which will open the dialog shown below:

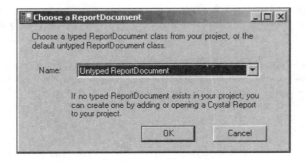

It is using this dialog that we set whether our ReportDocument component is typed or untyped. If you select Untyped ReportDocument, then we are not really accomplishing much new here. Drag a new `CrystalReportViewer` onto the Web Form, and then load a report into ReportDocument1 and bind the component to the viewer.

```
...
InitializeComponent()
Dim ReportDocument1 As New ReportDocument()
ReportDocument1.Load("C:\CrystalReports\Chapter04\sales_graph.rpt")
CrystalReportViewer1.ReportSource = ReportDocument1
```

Binding to a Strongly-Typed Report

Finally, you can choose to add a strongly-typed report component, which probably has the simplest binding method of all. First of all, add the report that you wish to bind to your project. In our case, this will be sales_graph.rpt. To create a strongly-typed **ReportDocument** component, drag the **ReportDocument** component onto your Web Form. (The code for this Web Form is available in the code download for the chapter as web_viewer_stronglytyped.)

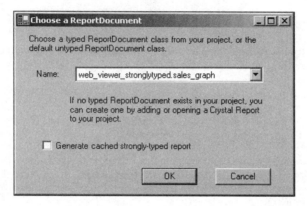

You will then see the same dialog before, with a drop-down list of all of the available reports that are in your project. Select an existing report to create a strongly-typed **ReportDocument**. Now, insert the CrystalDecisions.CrystalReports.Engine namespace into the project using the **Properties** page as we did previously, drag on a CrystalReportViewer, and we're set. From that point, we just need to set the **ReportSource** property in the Page_Init event once more:

```
CrystalReportViewer1.ReportSource = sales_graph1
```

(Where sales_graph1 is the name automatically assigned to the **ReportDocument** component when you added it to your form.)

Binding to a Strongly-Typed Cached Report

Another option for strongly-typed reports is the ability to use ASP.NET caching with your report. When you added your report to your application, you may have noticed that there was a checkbox for **Generate cached strongly-typed report**. Report caching is based on the underlying ASP.NET caching model and provides an easy way to improve your application's performance.

When a report is cached, the subsequent Web Form that is used to view the report will load faster when accessed by different users. To add a report to your Web Form as a cached report, select this option as you add a strongly-typed report to your application from the dialog shown overleaf:

129

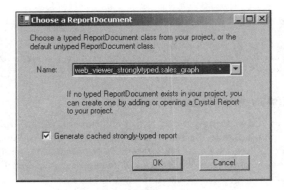

You will see that your report file will be inserted as `cached_sales_graph1` and an additional object will be inserted into the Web Form's source file.

You could then bind to this particular cached report just as you would to any other strongly-typed report, but with a different name:

```
CrystalReportViewer1.ReportSource = cached_sales_graph1
```

When multiple users visit the same report, they will actually be looking at a cached copy and not hitting the database in real time. (To ensure this is true, the viewer by default does not have a refresh button showing.)

So regardless of which method you choose to bind your report to the viewer, the result is the same. For ease of use and functionality provided, the easiest method is going to be to stick with strongly-typed reports, because in the long run the structure and coding standards will mean you can create reporting applications quickly, in a consistent manner.

After binding, you can run your application and when the form is loaded the Crystal Report Viewer will run the report you have set in the **ReportSource** property and display a preview of it. But before we can move on to customizing the viewer, we need to look at working with secured databases.

Note: Before we finish up with viewer basics and binding, keep in mind that reports that were created from a secure data source may require a user name and password. Turn back to Chapter 3 to the section titled "*Passing Database Logon Info*" to review the use of the `LogonInfo` collection – it behaves in the same way for either the web or Windows form viewers and the same goes for the record selection formula – it can be returned or set using the `SelectionFormula` property, and its use is also described in Chapter 3.

Customizing the Appearance and Layout of the Report Viewer

The `CrystalReportViewer` class contains all of the properties, methods, and events that relate to the viewer itself; its appearance, methods that are used to make the viewer perform certain actions (such as refresh or go to the next page), and events that can be used to determine when a particular event (such as drill-down or refresh) has occurred. To start learning how to work with the viewer, we are going to start with the basic properties and move on from there.

To get started, we need to create a new project to work in – from within Visual Studio, select File | New | Project and from Visual Basic Applications, select ASP.NET Web Application and specify a name and location for your project files.

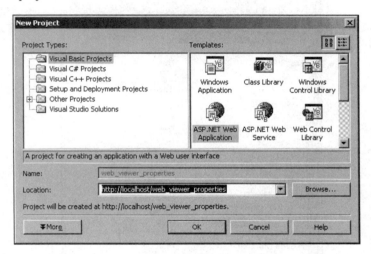

In the sample files, we have called this project (web_viewer_properties). Once you have selected a name for your project and clicked OK, the development environment will open with a default form that we will be using in the section. Alternatively, you can create a virtual directory for this project using the sample code provided.

We also need to add a report to work with in this section, so select Project | Add Existing Item and select product_listing_bytype.rpt. Add this to your project, insert the CrystalDecisions.CrystalReports.Engine namespace, drag across a ReportDocument and place this on the form (selecting product_listing_bytype.rpt out of the options on the dialog box), and then insert the CrystalReportViewer and set the binding to this report in the Page_Init event:

```
CrystalReportViewer1.ReportSource = product_listing_bytype1
```

You are now ready to get started!

When you were working through the earlier example, binding to a viewer and previewing your report, you may have noticed that there is a standard set of icons and layout that appears by default on the CrystalReportViewer. You can control most of the aspects of the viewer and toolbar by setting a few simple properties, as shown overleaf.

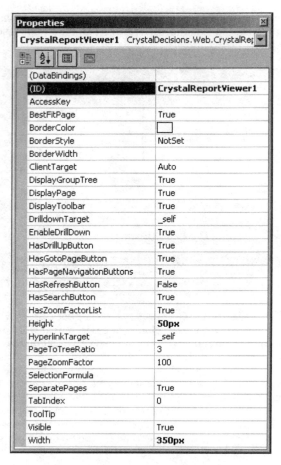

The area at the top of the viewer is the toolbar, which can be shown or hidden as an entire object or you can choose to only show certain icons. On the left-hand side is a Group Tree, generated by the grouping that you have inserted into your report. The properties that control these general properties are Boolean and are listed below:

Property	Description
BestFitPage	For showing the report as-is or with scroll-bars
DisplayGroupTree	For showing the group tree on the left-hand side of the viewer
DisplayPage	For showing the page view
DisplayToolbar	For showing the entire toolbar at the top of the viewer
SeperatePages	For displaying a report in separate pages or one long page

All of these properties default to `True` and you cannot change the position of any of these elements – they are fixed in place on the viewer. You can, however, hide all of these icons and create your own buttons for printing, page navigation, and so on.

For the icons within the toolbar, you can also set simple Boolean properties to show or hide a particular icon, as shown below:

- ❑   `HasDrillUpButton`
- ❑   `HasGotoPageButton`
- ❑   `HasLevelUpButton`
- ❑   `HasPageNavigationButtons`
- ❑   `HasRefreshButton`
- ❑   `HasSearchButton`
- ❑   `HasZoomFactorList`

So a typical use of these properties is where you want to give users a preview of the report with the ability to refresh the data shown. You could easily set a few properties before you set your `ReportSource` property to make this happen:

```
CrystalReportViewer1.HasRefreshButton = true
```

When the report is previewed, it will appear as shown:

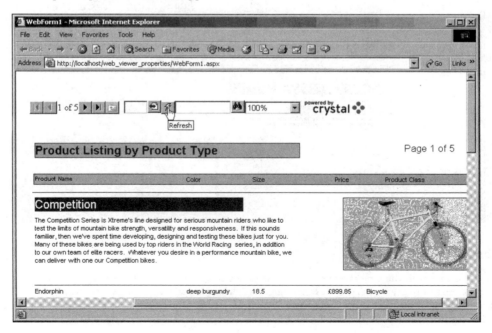

In addition to simple Boolean properties, there are also a couple of other properties that can be set to control the appearance and behavior of the viewer, including:

Property	Description
PageToTreeRatio	For setting the ratio between the group tree and the rest of the page – larger numbers mean a larger report page, with a smaller group tree
PageZoomFactor	The initial zoom factor for the report when viewed

So if we wanted to change the PageToTreeRatio and zoom factor so that the report was presented a little bit better on the page, we could add the following code to be evaluated when the page was loaded:

```
CrystalReportViewer1.PageToTreeRatio = 7
CrystalReportViewer1.PageZoomFactor = 80
```

Our previewed Web Form would look like this:

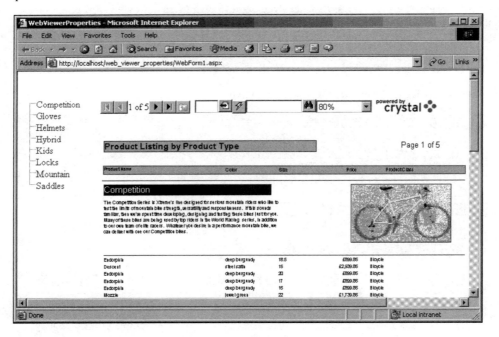

Viewer Methods

When working with the CrystalReportViewer, we have a number of methods available to us, which will allow us to integrate specific viewer functions into our application. As we move through this section, keep in mind that these methods can be used to create your own "look and feel" for the report preview window.

Create a new Web Form, which we'll call `web_viewer_methods`. Again, the code for this application is included with the download code. Drag a **CrystalReportViewer** onto this form. Include the report `product_listing_bytype.rpt` in your project (in the download code, the path is `CrystalReports/Chapter04/product_listing_bytype.rpt`). Drag a **ReportDocument** component from the Toolbox onto your form, and when the dialog box opens up, select **web_viewer_methods.product_listing_bytype** from the drop-down box. Click **OK**.

Now we add some code to tie our report to the application. In the `Page_Init` event in the designer generated code, once again add:

```
CrystalReportViewer1.DataBind()
```

Now all that remains is to set the `ReportSource` property in the `Page_Load` sub:

```
CrystalReportViewer1.ReportSource = product_listing_bytype1
```

Compile and run this. Now, we're all set to customize our viewer.

In this example, we are actually going to walk through building a custom viewer. The first thing we need to do is set the **DisplayToolbar** property and the **DisplayGroupTree** property to `False` in the Properties pane for the viewer, and add some additional buttons and textboxes to our Web Form using the screen shot earlier as a guide, which we will walk through below.

As we walk through this example, we are going to add the code behind these buttons and this form using the methods described below and learn how to match the viewer user interface to your own application.

Setting Browser Rendering

The `CrystalReportViewerBase` class provides a number of key properties, one of which is the `ClientTarget`. The `ClientTarget` property is a string and determines how the Crystal Report Viewer will render the report.

These strings are:

- ❑   `ie4` – for Internet Explorer 4.0
- ❑   `ie5` – for Internet Explorer 5.0
- ❑   `uplevel` – for most other web browsers
- ❑   `downlevel` – for very basic web browsers

A web browser is considered `uplevel` if it can support the following minimum requirements:

- ❑   ECMAScript (JScript, JavaScript) version 1.2.
- ❑   HTML version 4.0
- ❑   The Microsoft Document Object Model (MSDOM)
- ❑   Cascading style sheets (CSS)

Browsers that fall into the `downlevel` category include those browsers that only provide support for HTML version 3.2.

So, to set the browser version you are targeting, you could set the `ClientTarget` property for your form like this, under the `Page_Load` subroutine:

```
CrystalReportViewer1.ClientTarget = "ie4"
```

There is also an `Auto` value, which is the default setting and automatically selects the best rendering option based on the browser type. Unless you are writing an application for a specific browser or compatibility level, leaving this property set to `Auto` will provide the best viewing experience for the browser you are using.

> For more information on detecting the browser type your web application is using, see the topic *"Detecting Browser Types in Web Forms"* in the Visual Studio .NET combined help collection.

Refreshing the Data in a Report

When a report is refreshed, it goes back to the database for the most current set of data available and runs the report again. On our custom web viewer, you should have a **Refresh** button, so pull a **Button** control onto the Web Form and rename it `Refresh_Button` in the **ID** property in the Properties pane. Change the **text** property to `Refresh`.

Now, click on the `Refresh_Button` on your form to open the code for it. We can add some code behind this button to refresh the report using the `RefreshReport` method as shown below:

```
Private Sub Refresh_Button_Click(ByVal sender As System.Object, ByVal e
    As System.EventArgs) Handles Refresh_Button.Click
    CrystalReportViewer1.RefreshReport()
End Sub
```

Compile and run the application. The button should now be present on your form. Click on it. This will cause the report to return to the database and read the records again. Use this functionality with caution – if a report has a large SQL query to perform before it can return the first page, you may experience performance problems.

Page Navigation and Zoom

Now we are going to insert some buttons across the top of our Web Form in the same way we did with the **Refresh** button, with the following names and text values:

Button Name (ID Property Value)	Text Property Value
FirstPage_Button	First
Back_Button	Back
Forward_Button	Forward
LastPage_Button	Last

We access these properties, once again, through the Properties pane in Visual Studio .NET.

For page navigation using the buttons we have drawn on our custom form, we have a number of methods that can be called without any additional parameters, as shown below:

- ❑ ShowFirstPage
- ❑ ShowPreviousPage
- ❑ ShowNextPage
- ❑ ShowLastPage

These methods do not return a result, and unlike the Windows Forms Viewer, the Web Form Viewer does not have a GetCurrentPageNumber method, which would have returned an integer representing the page you are currently viewing.

To add these methods to the page navigation buttons, double-click the appropriate buttons on your Web Form and enter the code behind, as shown:

```
CrystalReportViewer1.ShowNextPage()
```

Do this for the other three buttons, including the appropriate method for each. Compile the project and test these buttons.

In addition to page navigation, you also have the ability to choose the zoom factor that is applied to your report. By default, the zoom is set to 100% of the report size unless you specify otherwise.

In our custom viewer, you should have a drop-down list for the zoom factor. To create our own zoom factor functionality, drag a drop-down list onto the form. Open the properties for your drop-down list (in our example, we have named the drop-down list ZoomList).

In the properties for your drop-down list, locate and open the Items property, which should open the dialog shown here:

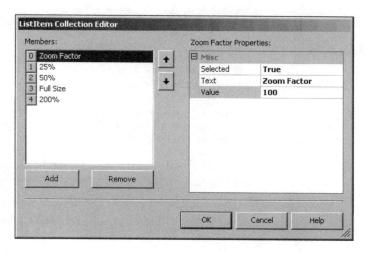

Using this dialog, we are going to create the items that will appear in our drop-down list and specify the corresponding values that will be passed to the form when an item is selected. Use the Add button to add items and make sure that the values correspond to the text you have entered (for instance, Full Size = 100, 50% = 50, and so on).

Once you have entered all of the values, click OK to accept these changes and return to your form's design. To use the Zoom method, double-click your drop-down box and add the following code:

```
CrystalReportViewer1.Zoom(DropDownList1.SelectedItem.Value)
```

This is simply calling the Zoom method using the item the user selects from your drop-down box. When you run your application and preview your custom viewer, you should be able to select your own zoom factor, and have it appear in the browser by pressing the Refresh button, as shown here:

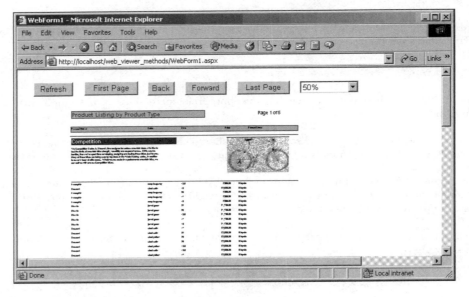

Searching within a Report

Another powerful navigation feature can be found in the SearchForText method within Crystal Reports.NET, which will allow you to search for a specific string that appears in your report.

On our custom viewer, we are going to create a textbox and a button labeled Search. We are going to use this textbox to enter some search string and when the user clicks the Search button, we are going to use the SearchForText method to find the search string within our report.

To start, we will call our textbox TextBox_SearchString and our Search button Search_Button. Add these to the design view of our Web Form, remembering to replace the Text property for the button with Search.

To use the SearchForText method, double-click the Search button and add the following code behind:

```
Private Sub Search_Button_Click(ByVal sender As System.Object, ByVal e As
    System.EventArgs) Handles Search_Button.Click
    If TextBox_SearchString.Text <> "" Then
        CrystalReportViewer1.SearchForText(TextBox_SearchString.Text, _
        CrystalDecisions.[Shared].SearchDirection.Forward)
    End If
    TextBox_SearchString.Text = " "
End Sub
```

The Crystal Report Viewer will search the entire report and when the value is found, go directly to the page on which it appears (the last line of code above is just to clear the textbox for the next search) This method can be called repeatedly to find all of the occurrences of a particular string – each time it finds the string in your report (in our example below, we searched for Youth Helmet), it will jump to that page, as shown below:

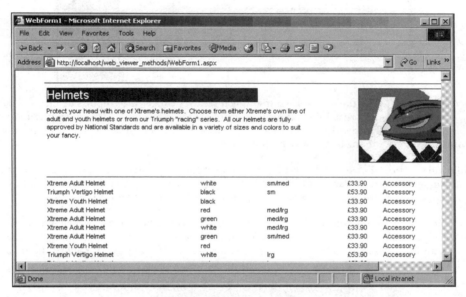

> You may have noticed that this method is slightly different between the Windows and web viewers for Crystal Reports: with both types of Forms Viewer, you can pass the additional parameter of **Search Direction** for searching forwards or backwards through your report. However, in addition, this method in Windows will highlight the found value. The web version does not have this capability.

Printing Your Report

Now, if you have already done some report integration with Windows applications, you may have noticed that the Web Forms Viewer is missing one very important icon – the Print button. When a Crystal Report is viewed on the web, it is actually rendered in static HTML 3.2 or HTML 4.0, with all of the report elements represented in HTML code and syntax.

This makes things difficult when it comes time to print your report – in a case where you were just using the plain old viewer with little or no modification, imagine if you were to click on the print button from your browser to print your report. Here is a preview of what your printed report would look like:

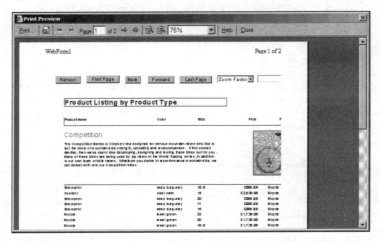

It is not very pretty to say the least – if your application uses single-page reports or discrete parts of a report, you may be happy with this, but for the rest of us, there has to be a better solution. So in answer to this limitation in HTML and the way reports are presented in a browser window, we have to come up with some creative solutions to actually print our report to a printer.

The following sections detail the different ways a report can be printed from the Web, as well as some of the advantages and drawbacks of each method. Since we are looking at new functionality within Crystal Reports.NET, we are going to create a new project specifically for this section.

From within Visual Studio, select File | New | Project and from Visual Basic Applications, select ASP.NET Web Application and call this new application web_viewer_print. This application is included with the download code. To use the downloaded version a virtual directory should again be created for it in its downloaded location.

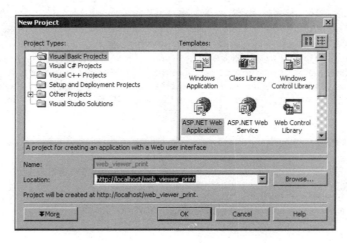

Once you have clicked **OK**, the development environment will open with the default form that we will be using in the section.

We also need to add a report to work with in this section, so select **Project | Add Existing Item**. Change the drop-down list to show **All Files** and specify `*.rpt` for the file name to filter the list to show only the available reports. The `web_printing_report.rpt` file is in the code download path `CrystalReports\Chapter04\web_printing_report.rpt`.

Once you have selected the `web_printing_report.rpt` report, click **Open** and this report will be added to your project in the Solution Explorer – we will be looking at the different methods for printing this report in the following sections.

Now, simply drag a **ReportDocument** component onto the form, which should offer you `web_viewer_printing.web_printing_report` as first choice in the drop-down box. Select it and drag a **CrystalReportViewer** onto the Web Form. Now, to bind the `ReportDocument` component to the viewer, merely enter the following code in the Web Form's `Page_Init` event, as we have done more than once in this chapter:

```
CrystalReportViewer1.ReportSource = New web_printing_report()
```

Compile and run the application to check that everything is working. We are now ready to start looking at printing this report.

Printing from the Browser

The simplest method for printing a report is to print directly from the browser. You have already seen how well this works, but there are some tricks that we can use to improve the way the report prints if we are forced to use this method.

First of all, you can disable the **DisplayGroupTree** property if the report is likely to be printed. Do this by setting it to **False** in the Properties window, or you could do this programmatically by inserting the following code into the `Page_Load` event:

```
CrystalReportViewer1.DisplayGroupTree = False
```

The viewer object model provides a property called `SeperatePages` that by default is set to `True`, meaning that the report is chunked up into individual HTML pages based on the report pagination.

When this property is set to `False`, the report itself becomes one long page, which can then be printed just like any other web page. You can set this property through the property page of the Crystal Report Viewer, as shown here:

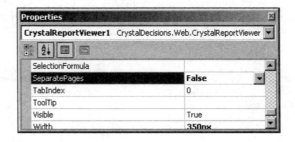

or you can also set this option programmatically:

```
CrystalReportViewer1.SeparatePages = False
```

Another trick is to actually turn off the toolbar and all of the icons so that the output on the page is close to what you would like to see when the report is printed.

```
CrystalReportViewer1.DisplayToolbar = False
```

So with the toolbar turned off and our report showing as one long page, you can then print your report and have a somewhat-decent output as shown here in a preview from Internet Explorer:

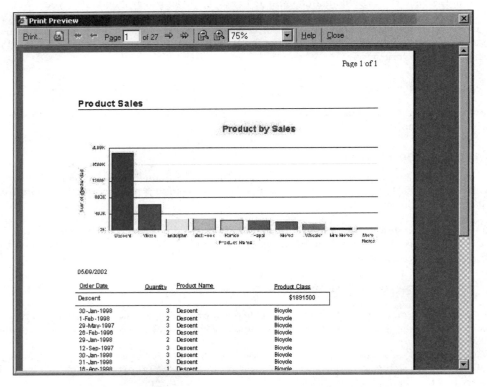

The only problem is that this method does not take advantage of any of the neat formatting features for page headers and footers, as the browser just thinks this is one big page to be printed. In addition, the column headings are only printed on the first page, so it is difficult to read the report as you move through the pages.

> Note: This method is only recommended for reports with a small number of pages (1-20) as the entire report is concatenated into one long page, which may take a while to render on screen or print.

However, with that said, printing from the browser is the easiest method of printing your report from the web, even with its limitations. For report developers who have put a lot of time and effort into their report design and want that report to be seen and printed by the users (and look good!) we need to look at another solution.

Printing from the Adobe Acrobat Plug-In

Crystal Reports.NET supports many export formats, and one of the more popular ones is Adobe's Portable Document Format or PDF. Using the export functionality within Crystal Reports.NET and a copy of Adobe Acrobat Reader (or the plug-in) installed on the client machine, reports can be printed from the web.

This is one of the methods recommended by Crystal Decisions for printing your reports in a presentation-quality format, and it actually developed the workaround used in this section to help developers who were used to the way Crystal Reports normally operates and were frustrated by not having that print button.

The first thing we need to do is create a new Web form that will contain our instructions. We will call this form `AcrobatPrinter.aspx`, and create it by right-clicking on the project name, and selecting **Add | Add New Item**. We will then select **Web Form** and name it as above. Right-click on it and select **Set as Start Page**.

Draw or drag a button onto the Web form and call it `PDF_Button`, and label it **Export via PDF**.

Now we need to do some setup to utilize the Crystal Reports Engine (covered in Chapter 8) and set some options available from the `CrystalDecisions.Shared` namespace.

So, we are going to put some code behind our export button to dimension variables for the export options that we want to use, and also for the specific options for exporting to a disk file. Click on the button in the designer, and insert the following code:

```
Private Sub PDF_Button_Click(ByVal sender As System.Object, ByVal e As _
    System.EventArgs) Handles PDF_Button.Click
  Dim myExportOptions As CrystalDecisions.Shared.ExportOptions
  Dim myDiskFileDestinationOptions As _
    CrystalDecisions.Shared.DiskFileDestinationOptions
```

Next, we are going to create a variable to hold the name of the file that we are going to be exporting to, as well as creating a new instance of a Sales Report that has already been added both to the project and to this form, through the `ReportDocument` component.

```
  Dim myExportFile As String
  Dim myReport As New web_printing_report()
```

For our next order of business, we need to set a temporary location for the output file – this can be anywhere on your server – and we are going to build a unique file name using the session ID from the ASP.NET session and tacking the PDF extension on the end, so the file association will work correctly when we go to view this file in our browser.

```
myExportFile = "C:\CrystalReports\Chapter04\PDF " & _
    Session.SessionID.ToString & ".pdf"
```

Now, for the meat of the matter – actually setting the destination options to export your report to a PDF file and write it to the disk.

```
myDiskFileDestinationOptions = New
    CrystalDecisions.Shared.DiskFileDestinationOptions()
myDiskFileDestinationOptions.DiskFileName = myExportFile
myExportOptions = myReport.ExportOptions
  With myExportOptions
    .DestinationOptions = myDiskFileDestinationOptions
    .ExportDestinationType = .ExportDestinationType.DiskFile
    .ExportFormatType = .ExportFormatType.PortableDocFormat
  End With
```

Then, we call the Export method to export our report:

```
myReport.Export()
```

But we are not done yet! We need to take the exported PDF file that has been generated and output it to the browser so the user can view it using the Acrobat Plug-In or standalone viewer. To do that, we are going to use some simple response statements to return the file to the browser:

```
Response.ClearContent()
Response.ClearHeaders()
Response.ContentType = "application/pdf"
Response.WriteFile(myExportFile)
Response.Flush()
Response.Close()
```

Finally, once we have delivered the file to the user, we need to clean up after ourselves and remove the file from the server altogether.

```
System.IO.File.Delete(myExportFile)
End Sub
```

So when all of this code is put together behind our export button and our application is run, the user can click the button and preview and print the report from Adobe Acrobat, with the page numbering and other features in place, as shown here:

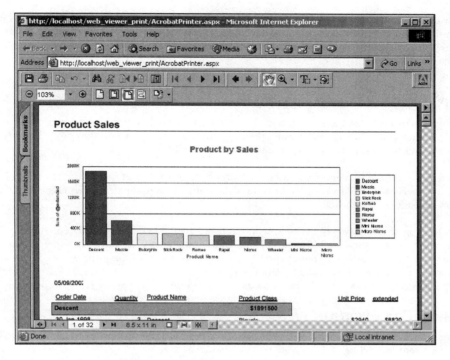

Printing from other Export Formats

In addition to Adobe Acrobat format, you can also print to other supported export formats such as Excel, Word, or others, by changing the file extension, the MIME type, and the `ExportFormatType` property in the code above. There are a number of different destinations that are supported, including:

Name	Description	MIME Type
Excel	To export to a Microsoft Excel file	`application/vnd.ms-xls`
HTML32	To export to an HTML file compatible with HTML v3.2	`application/html`
HTML40	To export to an HTML file compatible with HTML v4.0	`application/html`
PortableDocFormat	To export to PDF (Acrobat) format	`application/pdf`
RichText	To export to an RTF file for use with Microsoft Word, WordPerfect, and so on	`application/rtf`
WordForWindows	To export to a Microsoft Word file	`application/msword`

If you want to export to Word, the RTF export actually provides a better export format. To open the RTF on the client side using Word (instead of the application associated with the RTF file extension), leave the `ExportFormatType` property set to `RichText` but change the MIME type to be `application/msword`.

Using Viewer Events

Viewer events provide the ability to track when different events are fired from the browser – for instance, when the user navigates through the pages of the report or when they refresh the report. These events can then be used to fire other code within your application.

While all of the different events have their own unique properties and methods, they all inherit a common property called `Handled` that is a Boolean value used to determine whether the event was fired and subsequently handled.

In the following section, we will be looking at all of the available events associated with the viewer and their common use – if you would like to try out some of the events listed below, open the custom viewer we were working with earlier in the chapter (`WebForm1.aspx` from the project `web_viewer_properties`) and add a label to your form (call it `Event_Label`) – we'll use this label to notify the user when an event is fired. Clear its **Text** property. Now we are ready to begin.

Page Navigation Events

For page navigation, the `NavigateEventArgs` class provides the properties we need to work with the `Navigate` event, including:

Property	Description
CurrentPageNumber	Returns the current page number
NewPageNumber	Gets or sets the new page number

In the example below, the `Navigate` event would fire when a user changed the page within the viewer, resulting in a label that would show the page they are coming from and the page they are navigating to.

Insert the following subroutine into your Web Form code:

```
Private Sub CrystalReportViewer1_Navigate(ByVal source As Object, ByVal
    MyEvent As CrystalDecisions.Web.NavigateEventArgs) Handles
    CrystalReportViewer1.Navigate

  If MyEvent.NewPageNumber <> 1 Then
    Event_Label.Text = "Current page: " & MyEvent.CurrentPageNumber & _
    " New Page: " & MyEvent.NewPageNumber
  End If
End Sub
```

So, as the user navigates through the pages, this information is shown and can be used in your application. Compile and run this code to see this happen.

Refresh Events

The `ReportRefresh` event has no arguments other than the inherited `Handled` property. It can be used to build metrics on how often a report is run or refreshed, and to pass information to users about the report before they launch a refresh, as shown below:

```
Private Sub CrystalReportViewer1_ReportRefresh(ByVal source As Object,
    ByVal MyEvent As CrystalDecisions.Web.ViewerEventArgs) Handles
    CrystalReportViewer1.ReportRefresh
  Event_Label.Text = "Please be advised this report takes up to 2 minutes
        to run."
End Sub
```

Insert this subroutine into your Web Form code, in the same way as we did above. Compile and run. The message should now appear in the label when you hit **Refresh**.

Search Events

When a user searches for a report value, either through the standard icon on the toolbar or through your own method call, the `Search` event is fired. The arguments for the `Search` event are:

Property	Description
Direction	Gets or sets the direction in which to search. This can be either Backward or Forward.
PageNumberToBeginSearch	Gets or sets the page number to start searching at.
TextToSearch	Gets or sets the text to search for in the report.

So by using these event arguments, you could keep a record of what values users searched for or offer a "Top Ten" search facility to let them search using the ten most requested search strings. An example of getting the text that is being used in the search is included below – insert this subroutine into your code, build and run it:

```
Private Sub CrystalReportViewer1_Search(ByVal source As Object, ByVal
    MyEvent As CrystalDecisions.Web.SearchEventArgs) Handles
    CrystalReportViewer1.Search
  Event_Label.Text = "You searched for " & MyEvent.TextToSearch
End Sub
```

Zoom Events

When the user changes the zoom factor for a particular report, the `ViewZoom` event fires, and has only one argument, `ZoomEventArgs`. The `NewZoomFactor` property will get or set the magnification factor for the viewer, as shown here:

```
Private Sub CrystalReportViewer1_ViewZoom(ByVal source As Object, ByVal
    MyEvent As CrystalDecisions.Web.ZoomEventArgs) Handles
    CrystalReportViewer1.ViewZoom
```

```
Select Case MyEvent.NewZoomFactor
   Case "25"
      Event_Label.Text = "You have selected 25%"
   Case "50"
      Event_Label.Text = "You have selected 50%"
   Case "100"
      Event_Label.Text = "You have selected full size"
   End Select
End Sub
```

> **Note:** For further customization of your report and control of your report's features and functionality, you may want to turn to Chapter 8 to learn how to work with the Crystal Reports Engine, which provides control over your report at run time.

Summary

By now you know how to integrate reporting into both your Windows and web applications, with this chapter focusing on the latter. You should be able to pick the right object model for the functionality you want to provide to your users, as well as work with all of the properties, methods, and events contained within those models.

For our next trick, we are going to look at extending Crystal Reports through the use of XML Report Web Services, which is the topic of Chapter 5.

Professional **Crystal Reports**
for **Visual Studio .NET**

5

Creating XML Report Web Services

In the previous chapters, we had a look at how to integrate reports into Windows and Web-based applications, but now we need to learn how to leverage those skills and work with XML Report Web Services.

In this chapter, we will be looking at:

- ❑ An XML report Web Services overview
- ❑ Creating XML report Web Services
- ❑ Consuming XML report Web Services
- ❑ Deploying applications that use XML report Web Services

At the end of this chapter, you will be able to identify what an XML Report Web Service is and understand how it can be used in your application. You should also be able to create a Report Service from an existing Crystal Report and utilize the service with the Crystal Windows or Web Viewer to view the report.

Obtaining the Sample Files

All the example reports and code used in this chapter are available for download. The download file can be obtained from www.wrox.com.

There is a compiled Web Service that is included in the download files, including all of the examples shown throughout the chapter. However, it is simpler to create Web Services as opposed to setting up pre-compiled code, though an installer is included with the download code. Therefore, we recommend that you build your own according to the instructions in this chapter.

XML Report Web Services Overview

In the past, there have been a number of different methods for sharing information between different companies or organizations. Over the years a number of standards and standard file formats have emerged, but each had its own unique strengths and weaknesses. EDI, for instance was created to exchange data between companies (usually for purchasing or other supply-chain related use) but the EDI format was exacting and cumbersome for developers to use in their applications.

If you have worked as a developer for long, chances are you have made your own ad hoc attempt at information exchange – through extracts, data interchange, database replication, and synchronization. While these methods may provide information to the people who need it, it is very time-consuming trying to impose some standards on these processes and the information itself.

Even when information was successfully shared between organizations, it was then a question of "What do we do with it now?" Often, another database instance would have to be created, transformation and loading routines developed and finally, another suite of reports would have to be created, resulting in duplication of effort between whoever owned the data and the organization they were sharing it with.

With the introduction of XML Web Services with Visual Studio .NET and in particular, XML Report Web Services provided by Crystal Reports.NET, some of these information sharing and integration problems can be solved.

In its most simple terms, an XML Web Service is a piece of code that provides a specific function (or set of functions) that can be shared between different development environments and applications. The fact that these services are based on common standards, like XML, SOAP, and HTML means that this technology can be leveraged across a number of different applications or uses.

Using an XML Web Service, you could encapsulate a snippet of code to process credit card transactions, for example, and compile this code to a Web Service. From that point, any number of different applications on different platforms, local and remote, could use that same Web Service and the functionality it provides.

The same concept applies to reports you may have developed – through the use of **XML Report Web Services,** a developer can create a feature-rich report that can be compiled and used (and reused) by information consumers and application developers without losing any of the inherent formatting or features.

What Are XML Report Web Services?

The simplest definition of an XML Report Web Service is that it is a report file that has been published as a web service, which can be consumed and viewed on any number of different platforms (including Windows and Web-based applications created with Visual Studio .NET or other tools).

During the publishing process, Visual Studio examines your report file, its content, the layout of the report, and which features are used when creating a Report Web Service from your report file. Visual Studio will create a DLL file and then take all of the attributes, including the data types for the fields you have selected, parameters, and resulting data types, and generate an XML file to describe these attributes.

When the Report Web Service is used or consumed, another special type of XML file is created, called a Web Service Description Language (.wsdl) file, as shown below.

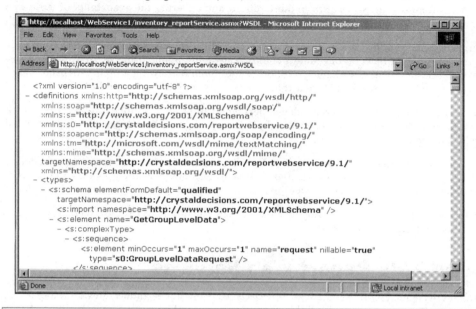

This particular web service ships with the sample code for this chapter and is built from the inventory report (`inventory_report.rpt`) also included in the sample files.

This file is written using Web Services Description Language, or WSDL. For applications and users that will access this Report Web Service, this file documents how they can interact with the service itself.

Normally, if you were an application developer creating a web service from scratch, you would develop most of these components yourself using the tools available within Visual Studio .NET and the .NET Framework. With XML Report Web Services, Crystal Reports does most of the work for you.

Note: If you are interested in creating other types of web services from scratch, find a copy of Professional ASP.NET 1.0 *(either in book form or available on www.wroxbase.com) and check out Chapter 19: Exposing Web Services. This chapter also provides some good background information on web services and the different protocols used with them. You also may want to check out other titles from Wrox Press that specifically deal with Web Services, such as* Professional ASP.NET Web Services *and* Professional XML Web Services.

How Would I Use an XML Report Web Service?

The most common scenario for using an XML Report Web Service is when you need to share a report or its content with another department or organization. One example of when this type of web service would be useful is managing the supply chain and inventory between a vendor and their customer.

To keep customers in the loop, a vendor could create a number of Crystal Reports that display all of the required information for backorders, shipped orders, and item availability. The vendor could then create XML Report Web Services from these reports and advertise the availability of these web services to their customers.

For larger customers who already have an intranet or other vehicle for display the content from these web services, their application developers could create a few simple pages to view the reports served up by the web services. Instead of having a report sent to them or viewing a report snapshot, they would actually have access to live data in their report, served directly from the vendor's data.

For smaller customers who don't have developers who can provide an interface to these web services, the vendor may choose to create their own application that gives these types of customer access to the reports available in the web services.

In either scenario, there is tremendous value to both the vendor and their customer – information is provided in real time, with no additional effort required to update a data mart, or produce and send reports or extracts. All of the manual effort required to deliver this type of solution in the past is no longer required.

In the following sections, we are going to walk through creating XML Report Web Services and applications that can consume them.

Creating XML Report Web Services

The process of creating XML Report Web Services is relatively simple and features a number of shortcuts to help cut down on development time. Unlike the process you would use to create web services from scratch, there is no custom coding required to publish an existing Crystal Report file to a XML Report Web Service.

Creating Basic Report Web Services

To get started with this chapter, we need to create a new Windows Application using Visual Basic. NET. If you want to follow along with the sample code that is available for this chapter, you can open the solutions file (Chapter5.sln) and you will find a number of projects within that correspond to the sections in this chapter. To create your own project as we go along, create a new project from within Visual Studio by selecting File | New | Project and from Visual Basic Applications, select ASP.NET Web Service and specify a name (in the sample code, we have called this project WebService1) and location on your web server for your project files.

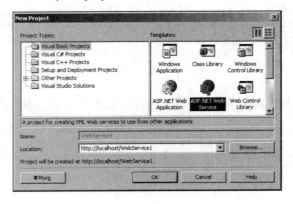

In this example, we are going to create a Report Web Service from the inventory report (`inventory_report.rpt`), one of the reports included with the code samples (in our installation we have downloaded this to `C:\CrystalReports\Chapter05\inventory_report.rpt`; you may wish to alter this depending on your own installation).

To add this report to your web service, select Add | Existing Item and browse to where you have unzipped your code files and select the `inventory_report.rpt`

Once you have added this report to your project, it should appear in the resources and you can edit the report design and content as required. For now, we'll leave the content as-is until we start looking at some of the more advanced features.

With the report added, simply right-click on the report itself in the Project Explorer and from the right-click menu, select Publish as web service as shown below:

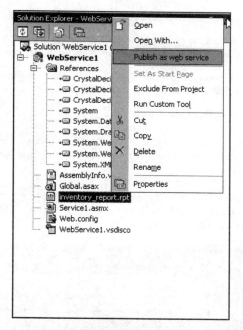

This will in turn generate an ASMX file that will also appear in the Project Explorer. There is also a source file generated for your Report Web Service, but by default it is hidden. To show the source file, select the option for Show All Files in the solution explorer and you should see all three files, as shown in the screenshot overleaf.

Remember to compile `inventory_reportService.asmx` before you attempt to run it. You can do this by selecting Build from your menu or hitting *F5* on your keyboard.

Note: Be sure that the report you are publishing as a Web Service does not have a comment as the first line of the record selection formula, as the selection formula will be ignored.

To edit your record selection formula, open the report in the Report Designer, right-click on the report and select Report | Edit Selection Formula | Record *and remove or move the first line.*

This issue has been tracked and will hopefully be fixed in future releases.

For Report Web Services created using Visual Basic, the Web Service file will have the extension .vb tacked on the end. You can alter this source file to add additional functionality, launch other web services, and perform other functions.

With your report published as a Web Service, you should be able to right-click directly on the corresponding .asmx file and select View in Browser from the right-click menu to display a list of valid operations for your web service, as shown below:

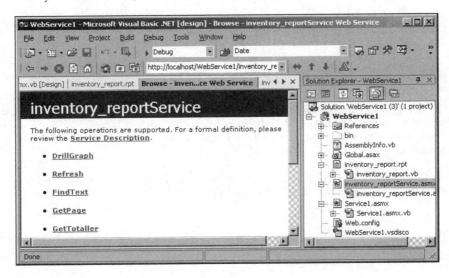

Creating XML Report Web Services

The URL for your web service in this example is:

```
http://localhost/WebService1/inventory_reportService.asmx
```

but if our report name had a space in it for example "Inventory Report" the space would be encoded and the URL would look like this:

```
http://localhost/WebService1/Inventory%20ReportService.asmx
```

> **Note: A good practice for Report Web Services is to ensure that the name of your report does not have any spaces in it – in this instance renaming the report to remove the space or replace it with an underscore would probably be easier than remembering to put in the spaces or correct encoding when calling your Report Web Service.**

To toggle the formal definition, select the link for Service Description to display the XML document shown here:

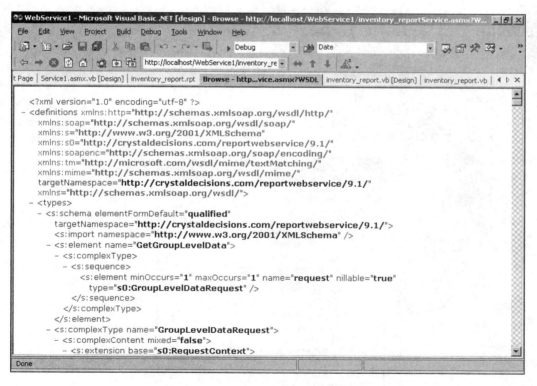

When we look at consuming XML Report Web Services a little later in this chapter, we will look at some of these methods and their use.

Creating Report Web Services with Multiple Reports

If you have multiple reports that you would like to publish as XML Report Web Services, you can place all of these report files into a web service project by following the same procedure as a single report file.

Simply add each report from the Project | Add Existing Item menu and then right-click on each and select Publish as Web Service. To view the Report Web Service for a specific report, just reference the name of the correct .asmx file associated with that report – again, remember to compile them before trying to view them.

For example if you were to add a report named sales_graph.rpt to the project we have been working with and publish it as a web service, the URL reference would be:

```
http://localhost/WebService1/sales_graphService.asmx
```

This is an easy way to keep related reports and services together and can serve as the basis for a naming and hierarchy structure for your Report Web Services.

Utilizing the Generic Report Web Service

In addition to creating individual Report Web Services for each report you wish to publish as a Web Service, Crystal Reports.NET also includes a generic Web Report Service, which supports what are known as Server Reports.

Server Reports are Crystal Report files that can be accessed through a generic Report Web Service (ServerFileReportService.asmx) and are available for use from the Server Explorer within the Visual Studio .NET IDE, as shown below:

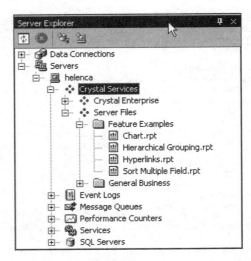

When working with the generic Report Web Service, there is no need to publish each report individually, but there are a couple of properties that you will need to set when viewing your reports using this method.

To view a report through the generic Report Web Service, you will need to specify the Web Service URL that points to the generic Report Web Service, which in turn, accesses the report specified in the `ReportPath` property. With the `ReportPath`, you don't actually need to put the full path of the report because this property references a root directory that is specified in an XML filed called `crystalserverfile.config`, shown below, which can be found in `C:\Program Files\Microsoft Visual Studio.NET\Crystal Reports\Config` on the server.

> **Note: This file also controls what reports you will see in the IDE under the Server Files node of the Crystal Services branch of your server.**

When you first install Crystal Reports.NET, the `RootDirectory` tag within the file refers to the sample reports that ship with the product, so when you browse the **Server Files** node of the Server Explorer within the Visual Studio IDE, you are actually starting at the `C:\Program Files\Microsoft Visual Studio.NET\Crystal Reports\Samples\Reports` directory. The URL to access this Web Service is:

```
http://localhost/crystalreportwebformviewer/ServerFileReportService.asmx
```

If you don't see any reports underneath the **Server Files** node, check to see if you have the Web Services component of Crystal Reports.NET installed. If you took all of the defaults on the Visual Studio .NET installation, you wouldn't have this option installed, as shown below.

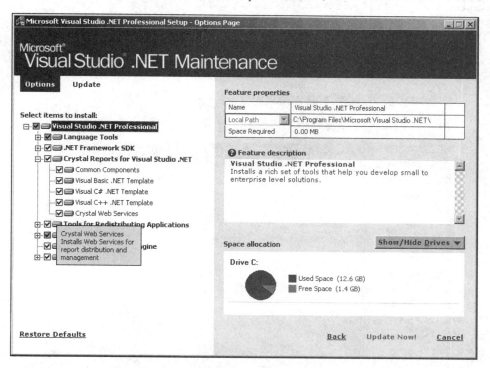

You will need to re-run the setup wizard to add this component before you can use the generic Report Web Service. If you believe you have installed the component and still don't see the `crystalserverfile.config`, you can create another using the XML code below, replacing the location in the `<RootDirectory>` tag with the location of your reports.

```xml
<?xml version="1.0" encoding="utf-8"?>
<ServerFileConfig
xmlns:xsd="http://www.w3.org/2001/XMLSchema"
xmlns:xsi="http://www.w3.org/2001/XMLSchema-instance">
<RootDirectory>C:\Program Files\Microsoft Visual Studio
.NET\Crystal Reports\Samples\Reports</RootDirectory>
</ServerFileConfig>
```

You may also experience problems if the generic report web service does not have write permissions to the folder specified in the `crystalserverfile.config` document. One workaround is to grant the ASPNET account read and write access to the `C:\program files\Microsoft Visual Studio.NET\Crystal Reports\` directory or simply edit the `crystalserverfile.config` file and point it to a directory where the correct permissions have been set.

Again, this is another issue that has been tracked by Crystal Decisions and should be fixed in future releases.

Consuming XML Report Web Services

When consuming XML Report Web Services, the `.asmx` file associated with the service provides the entry point for consumption. When you request this `.asmx` file without any additional parameters or strings attached, the service will display a default help page like the one shown below, listing all of the methods that are available for the service.

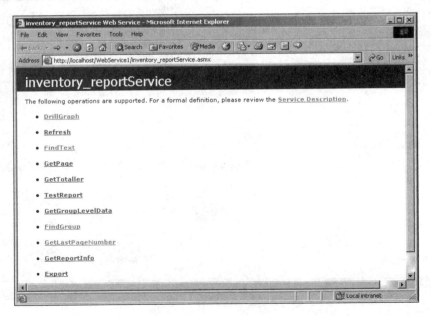

From the listing of methods, you can drill down for further information about their use. In addition, you can invoke methods that support using the HTTP-POST protocol – with Report Web Services, the only method that supports the POST protocol is the Test Report method shown below.

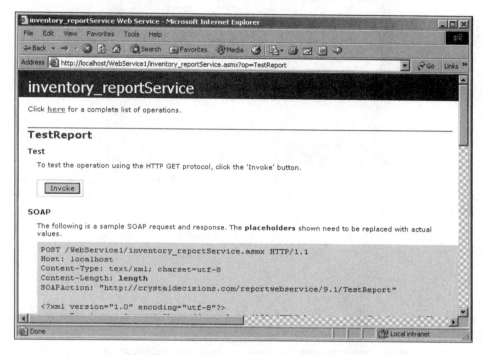

When you invoke this method, the result should be a summary of the report information, including the title of the report and the file name.

External Report Web Service

The first method we are going to look at for consuming an XML Report Web Service from an application uses a direct URL call to the Report Web Service from the Crystal Windows or Web Report Viewer. To use this method you would need to first have created your Web Service and noted the location and URL of the ASMX file, which we have already done.

Next, we need to create a project from within Visual Studio by selecting File | New | Project and from Visual Basic Applications, select Windows Application and specify a name (in the sample code, we have called this project consumer) and location for your project files.

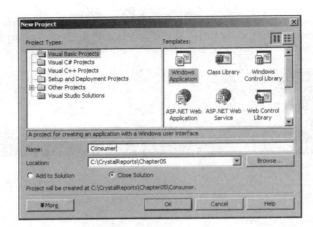

Whenever you create a new project, a default form is added and to that form we need to add the Crystal Report Viewer. You can drag or draw the viewer onto your form and set any additional properties, methods, and events required. Here we have set the **Dock** property to Fill.

To bind the Crystal Report Viewer to your Report Web Service, you will need to set the ReportSource property in the New event (as shown below using the URL from our earlier example):

```
CrystalReportViewer1.ReportSource =
"http://localhost/webservice1/inventory_reportService.asmx"
```

With the ReportSource property set, you can treat this just like any other report, setting properties for the viewer and previewing the report, which is shown below:

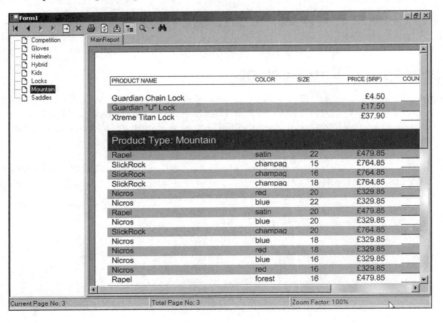

Internal Report Web Service

An internal report Web Service refers to a Web Service that has been added to your project as a reference. This method is sometimes also called the "Proxy Method", because every application that consumes a web service has to have a way to communicate with the service when the application is running. Adding a reference to your Report Web Service creates a Proxy Class that in turn can communicate with the service and create a local copy.

To add the XML Report Web Service to your Web or Windows application, select Project | Add Web Reference to open the dialog shown below.

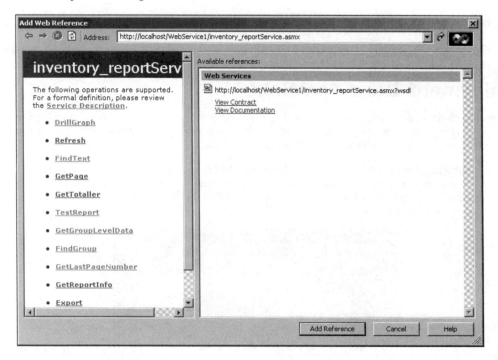

Using this dialog, enter the complete URL of your Report Web Service and click OK, and this will add this reference to your project in the Project Explorer under Web References.

To bind an internal report web service to the Windows Crystal Report viewer, you will again need to set the report source, only this time using the reference you have added instead of a URL. For example:

```
CrystalReportViewer1.ReportSource = New localhost.inventory_reportService()
```

From that point, all of the techniques you learned in Chapters 3 and 4 can be applied to the Report Viewer to customize how your report is presented.

Generic Report Web Service

To consume a report served through the generic Report Web Service, you will need to add the report from the Server Explorer to your project. In the Server Explorer dialog, under the node marked Crystal Services, navigate to the Server Files branch, where you should be able to see all of the available reports that are within the path specified in your `ServerFiles.Config` file.

To add a report to your project, simply drag and drop the report onto a Windows or Web form. From that point, you can add the appropriate Crystal Report Viewer to your form and bind the report to the viewer, as shown here:

```
CrystalReportViewer1.ReportSource = serverFileReport1
```

All of the properties, methods, and events available in the Crystal Report Viewer can be used from this point.

Deployment Considerations

Report Web Services are deployed on a web server and can be consumed by developers and users within your organization or externally based on where you deploy the service itself and what access users have to the location you have selected.

When deploying Report Web Services, we have two deployment options – the first is the easiest and involves copying your project to the web server for deployment. To use this method, you will need to open the project where your Report Web Service resides and select Project | Copy Project, which will open the dialog shown below:

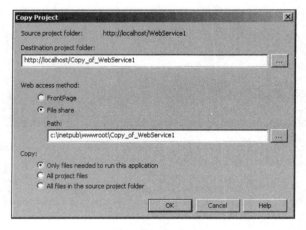

You will need to specify a folder location for your project, as well as a web access method. If you select the FrontPage method, you must have the Front Page Extensions installed and configured on the server where you want to deploy your Report Web Service. Choose the File Share method if you have direct access to the server and just want to copy the files over.

At the bottom of the dialog, you will also need to select what files you want copied across to the web server. You have three choices:

❑ **Copy files needed to run this application** – will copy across all of the built output files and any files where the `BuildAction` property is set to `Content`.

❑ **All project files** – will copy across everything, including the output and source files, etc.

❑ **All Files in the source project folder** – will copy across all files within the folder, regardless of whether they are included in the project or not.

The second method of deploying a Report Web Service involves creating a web setup project that can be used to deploy your service on a local or remote web server. To create a new web setup project, select **New | Project** and from the folder marked **Setup and Deployment Projects**, select the icon for **Web Setup Project** and make sure you click the radio button for **Add to Solution** (instead of **Close Solution**).

We will call this project WebServiceSetup.

A new tab called **File System** will open – right-click on the **Web Application Folder** and select **Add | Project Output**. From the dialog that appears below, select **Content Files, Primary output,** and **Debug Symbols** all at once using *Ctrl*-click or *Shift*-click.

With these components added, save your project and select **Build WebServiceSetup** to create a Windows Installer Package (MSI) that will install your Report Web Service. If you are deploying this to a server that does not have Visual Studio .NET or the .NET Framework installed, you will need to install that first before you install and deploy your Report Web Service.

Summary

In this chapter, we had a look at XML Report Web Services and how they can be used to improve the exchange of information between organizations, cut down on development time and extend simple reporting applications. We found that from the Visual Studio IDE, it is only a few clicks to add a report and publish as a Web Service.

With an XML Report Web Service created, the second half of the chapter focused on actually consuming and deploying XML Report Web Services. With that under our belt, it is time to take a look at working with .NET data.

Professional *Crystal Reports* for *Visual Studio .NET*

6

Working with .NET Data

In the previous chapters, we focused on report integration and web services, but we need to go back and have a look at what lies underneath those reports – the data your report is based on and how Crystal Reports.NET uses this data.

In this chapter, we will be looking at the way Crystal Reports.NET works with different data sources and how it interacts with ADO.NET. This will include:

- ❑ Understanding data access
- ❑ Working with data sources
- ❑ Creating SQL commands and expressions
- ❑ Working with ADO.NET

At the end of this chapter, you will have an understanding of how Crystal Reports.NET interacts with different data sources, the options for working with these data sources, and using ADO.NET as a data source for your report development.

The Sample Files

In the download files for Chapter 6 (C:\CrystalReports\Chapter06\), you will find all of the data sets and reports used in this chapter:

- ❑ Employee_Profile_Basic – This version is used as the starting point in two examples in this chapter
- ❑ Employee_Profile_Table – The same as the basic version with a second table added to the report

- ❑ Employee_Profile_SQLExp – The same as the basic version with a SQL Expression added to the report

- ❑ SQLCommand – A report based on a Virtual Table created from a SQL command, discussed in *Defining Virtual Tables*, later in this chapter

- ❑ Reporting_App_Dataset – An application that only contains a dataset.

- ❑ Reporting_App_ViewData – An application that displays an ADO.NET dataset

- ❑ Reporting_App – A report that takes its data from an ADO.NET dataset

If you have problems running these examples please read the sections in this chapter relating to the examples.

Data Access with Crystal Reports.NET

Traditionally, Crystal Reports has accessed data through two different methods – native connections and ODBC connections. A native connection to a data source was accomplished through a set of specialized DLL files and executables that were specific to your data source. Over the years, Crystal Reports has teamed up with databases, applications and other vendors to create a number of native drivers, for PC or file-type databases (Access, or Dbase), relational databases, and ERP (Enterprise Resource Planning) systems.

The second data access method is through the ODBC (Open Database Connectivity) layer, providing a common interface for interrogating relational databases. Regardless of where the data resides, ODBC provides a reliable, stable platform that can be used to develop drivers and data access methods.

With the integration of Crystal Reports into Visual Studio .NET, the native and ODBC drivers that were included with previous versions of Crystal Reports are no longer provided for use, and data sources are now accessed through one of the following methods:

Data Source	Description
Project Data	Crystal Reports can leverage the ADO.NET Framework and report directly from the datasets that appear in your application.
OLEDB (ADO)	For data sources that can be accessed through OLEDB, including SQL Server, Oracle, and Microsoft Jet 3.51/4.00-accessible data sources (Access, Excel, Paradox, Dbase)
ODBC (RDO)	For data sources that can be accessed through an ODBC-compliant driver (which is just about every other data source). In addition to reporting from tables, views, and stored procedures, Crystal Reports.NET will also allow you to enter a SQL command to serve as the basis for your report (See Working with SQL Commands and Expressions later in this chapter).
Database Files	Includes a number of file-type database formats, including Access, Excel, XML, and Crystal Field Definition files (TTX), as used with previous versions of Crystal Reports and bound reporting.
More Data Sources	Anything else supported.

To help both new and existing report developers, the following section walks through the different types of data you may want to integrate into your reporting application.

Database Files

Previous versions of Crystal Reports could use a direct, native connection to create reports using the information in file-type databases, including Dbase/Xbase, Paradox, and FoxPro, among others.

Through this direct connection, Crystal Reports extracted data without having to submit a SQL statement against a database server. With the ease of use and improved performance, there was also a price. When working with these types of databases, the only join available between two or more tables was a left-outer join, meaning all of the information from the left-hand table will be read first, and any matching items from the right-hand table will also be shown.

As mentioned earlier, these native drivers (and the limitations that came with them) are not included with Crystal Reports.NET, apart from the direct drivers for Excel and Access. In order to create reports from these data sources, we have a number of options:

❑ Use an ODBC connection – using a compatible ODBC driver to access your data source

❑ Use an ADO.NET dataset – create a dataset from your data source

❑ Create a custom data provider – for developers who have a specific data file format, you can create a custom data provider for your data source

For more information on creating your own Custom Data Provider, check out the MSDN article at http://msdn.microsoft.com/msdnmag/issues/01/12/DataProv/toc.asp.

> One type of native connection that is still supported is the direct connection to Microsoft Access databases and Excel spreadsheets. Both of these file types can be used as the data source for your report without having to use ODBC.

Relational Databases

By far, the most popular data access method is through a native or ODBC connection to a relational database. The retail version of Crystal Reports that you would buy in a store ships native drivers for the most popular RDBMS, including DB/2, Informix, Oracle, Sybase, among others. Most of these native drivers require that the standard database client be installed and configured before they can be used.

Again, these drivers are not available with Crystal Reports.NET, so you will need to look at connecting to these data sources through the following methods:

❑ Use an ODBC connection – uses a compatible ODBC driver to access your data source.

❑ Use an OLEDB connection – uses a compatible OLEDB provider to access your data source. Providers are available for SQL Server, Oracle, ODBC Drivers, and Jet 4.0, among others.

❑ Use an ADO.NET dataset – creates a dataset from your data source.

❑ Utilize a custom data provider – currently, there is a custom data provider available for SQL Server and an Oracle provider in beta (available from the MSDN site), that allow you direct access to the database.

OLAP Data

OLAP data (sometimes called multidimensional data) can be accessed and used in your application through OLEDB for OLAP, a standard interface for accessing OLAP data but unfortunately Crystal Reports.NET does not support OLAP reporting in this version. If you do have an existing report that shows an OLAP grid, this area will be blanked out when you first import your report.

Crystal Dictionaries, Queries, and Info Views

With previous retail versions of Crystal Reports, there were two separate tools designed to make report development easier. The first, Crystal Query, could be used to create Crystal-specific QRY files that contained SQL queries. You could then use these query files as the data source for your report.

The second tool, Crystal Dictionaries, was used to create dictionaries (DC5, DCT) that served as a meta-data layer between your report and the database itself. Using a Crystal Dictionary, you could take care of all of the linking and joins for the user, re-organize and alias fields and tables, and add help text and data for browsing, among other things.

Unfortunately, none of these file formats is supported as a data source for reports within Crystal Reports.NET. If you do have an existing report that uses any of these data sources, you will receive an error message and will be unable to use the report. If you wanted to create a report with similar features, you would need to base your report on the underlying database.

If you do need to work with complex SQL queries, Crystal Reports.NET provides the ability to use SQL Commands as the basis for your report, effectively cutting out the need to use Crystal Query files. For creating a metadata layer between the end user and the database itself, there is not currently any way to work around this, other than using various third-party metadata providers.

Other Data Sources

Crystal Reports in the past has included a number of drivers for non-traditional data sources, including SalesLogix Act!, Microsoft Exchange, Microsoft Logs, and more. Most of these data sources have had their own unique setup and configuration requirements, as they do not fit in to the standard data source categories that can be accessed through a native or ODBC driver.

Since the drivers for these data sources are not included with Crystal Reports.NET, you will need to find an alternative method of accessing this data, using a data provider.

So, in summary, Crystal Reports.NET supports the following data sources:

- ❑ Any database with an ODBC driver
- ❑ Any database with an OLEDB Provider
- ❑ Microsoft Access databases
- ❑ Microsoft Excel workbooks
- ❑ ADO.NET datasets
- ❑ Legacy recordsets (Classic ADO, CDO, DAO, RDO – which covers just about everything else)

Now that you understand the different ways Crystal Reports.NET can access data, we need to take a look at actually working with these data sources from within your report.

Working with Data Sources

When working with data within the Report Designer, most of the options and functionality relating to databases and tables can be found in the **Database** menu found under the main menu by right-clicking in your report.

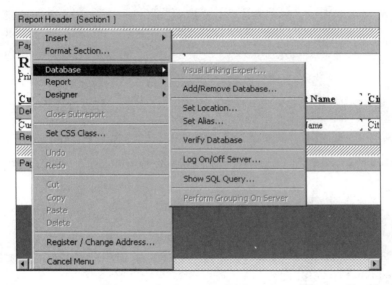

In the following sections, we are going to look at some of the most common tasks when working with data in our reports.

Setting Database Options

Crystal Reports.NET has a number of options that are specific to working with data sources and can be set once for the design environment. To see these settings, open any report, right-click, and select **Designer | Default Settings | Database**, which will open the dialog shown overleaf:

You can select the database objects you wish to show when creating a Crystal Report, including:

❑ Tables

❑ Views

❑ System Tables

❑ Synonyms

❑ Stored Procedures

> **This is where most developers get tripped up when working with stored procedures. They won't appear as an available data source when you connect to your server UNTIL you turn the Show... Stored Procedure setting on.**

You can also set a filter for database objects, using the **Table name LIKE** and **Owner LIKE** textboxes. Use the (%) symbol for multiple characters and the underscore (_) to indicate a single character. If you were looking for all objects owned by user DMCAMIS, the **Owner LIKE** text would be DMCAMIS%.

With the options in the middle of the dialog, select whether to list the tables and fields by their **Name**, **Description**, or **Both**, and use the checkboxes beside these options to sort table and field names alphabetically.

Finally, in the bottom of the dialog, under **Advanced Options**, select from the following:

❑ **Use Indexes or Server for Speed** – Use existing database indexes or the database server itself for processing where a performance improvement could be gained.

❑ **Perform Grouping on Server** – If you have created a summary report with none of the details showing and no drill-down capabilities, you can push the grouping of that report back to the server. This improves performance, because Crystal Reports.NET doesn't have to get all the records and do the grouping itself. A GROUP BY clause will be inserted into the SQL that Crystal Reports generated.

❑ **Database Server is Case Insensitive** – By default, Crystal Reports.NET is case sensitive, meaning {Customer.Country}="ca" and {Customer.Country}="CA" would return different data sets. This setting eliminates that case sensitivity for SQL databases.

❑ **Select Distinct Data for Browsing** – When browsing for data from pull-down or browse dialogs, this ensures that only a distinct recordset (no duplicates) is returned.

Since some of these changes relate directly to the database you are working with, you may need to log off and log back on for them to take effect.

Adding a Database or Table to a Report

When designing a report, you will need to add additional databases or tables from time to time as the need arises. In the sample reports included with this chapter, there is an Employee Profile (Employee_Profile_Basic) that lists employee names, birth dates, and hire dates. It does not list the employee's city – that information is held within another table that we are going to add to the report.

To start with, open Employee_Profile_Basic in Visual Studio .NET by double-clicking on the solution (.sln) file within that folder. Double-click on employee_profile.rpt to open it in the Report Designer. Look at the four fields that are displayed in the report, and then look in the Field Explorer (View | Other Windows | Document Outline) where you will see the Employee table under Database Fields:

We want to add the City to the report, but it isn't available from this table, so we are going to have to add the table that it is in. Right-click anywhere within the report, and select **Database | Add/Remove Database**, to open the Database Expert dialog, which you can then use to add additional data structures to the report.

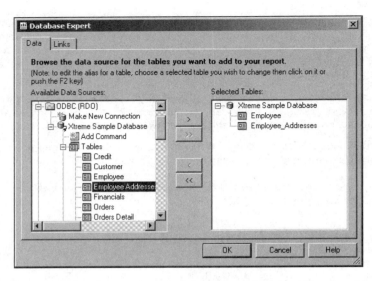

Locate the Xtreme Sample Database and expand the node to find the table you wish to add, in this case, Employee_Addresses. Select the table name and click on the arrow icon to add it to the right window, which indicates that it has been added to your report. You can add further databases or tables here. When you have finished, select the Links tab, which allows you to specify the relationships between these tables.

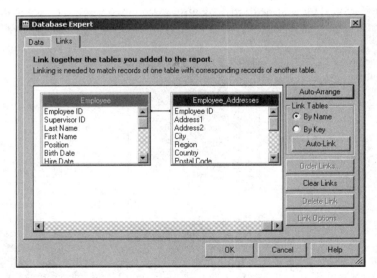

You may need to draw the link(s) to indicate the relationship between the new tables you have added to the tables currently in your report. On this occasion, the link between Employee and Employee_Addresses was automatically generated. By clicking on the link, and then on Link Options, we can set the options for the join types that these links represent (detailed in the next section). When you have finished, click OK to exit the Database Expert and return to your report design.

The first thing you should look for is your new table in the Field Explorer:

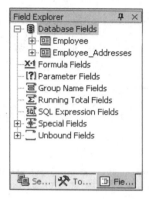

If you expand the `Employee_Address` table you can now add some extra items to the report that you couldn't see before, for example, `Country`, `Postal Code`, and of course, `City`.

Drag `City` from the Field Explorer to the **Details** section of your report, and position a label directly above it in the **Page Header**. You have now successfully added another table to your report, and to prove this you should be able to see a field from this new table in your report. Click on the **Start** button in Visual Studio .NET to open your new report, which should look something like the following:

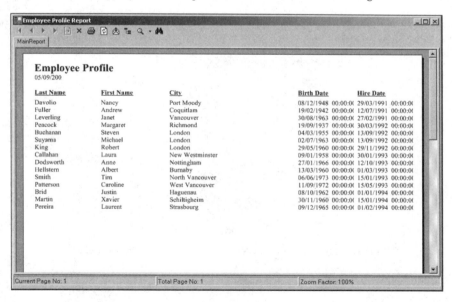

This report should now be similar to `Employee_Report_Table` that is saved in the `Chapter06` folder of the code download.

You may want to adjust the linking in the Visual Linking Expert, or check the database schema for more information on how the tables should be joined together, which is described in the next section.

Using the Visual Linking Expert

Relational databases are usually split into a number of different tables – these tables can be joined back together to create complex queries. In Crystal Reports.NET, these joins are created by using the Visual Linking Expert to visually draw a line between two key fields and setting options on these links to indicate join types.

In addition to specifying database linking when you first add a data source to your report you can also invoke the Visual Linking Expert at any time by right-clicking on your report and selecting **Database |** **Visual Linking Expert** from the right-click menu that appears (this is the same dialog that you used a moment ago to set up the links).

Using the dialog, you can draw links between the databases and tables in your report to indicate the relationship between each. To draw a line between two fields, imitate dragging the first field and dropping it on top of the second. You will know you have the field positioned correctly when your cursor turns into the shortcut icon.

If you make a mistake, you can remove a link by clicking on the line to highlight it and pressing the delete key, or to clear all links, use the button of the same name on the right-hand side of the expert.

> **Our earlier example was very simple – in the Visual Linking Expert you can create multiple links between tables if your database schema requires them.**

By default, Crystal Reports will join two SQL tables with an `Equal` join. To change the default join type, right-click directly on the line drawn between the two tables and select **Link Options** from the menu.

Using the **Link Options** dialog, select a join type for this link from the list below:

❑ Inner Join

❑ Left Outer Join

❑ Right Outer Join

❑ Full Outer Join

You can also select an operator to work with the join type you have selected, including:

Operator	Description
=	Equal To
>	Greater Than
>=	Greater Than or Equal To
<	Less Than
<=	Less Than or Equal To
!=	Not Equal To

*At any point you can click the **Auto-Arrange** button to arrange the Visual Linking Expert layout for readability, but sometimes you will get better results if you position the tables yourself.*

If it's still open from the last example, take a look at `employee_profile.rpt` in Crystal Reports.NET. The report has been created from the `Employee` and `Employee_Addresses` tables. To see the SQL that Crystal Reports.NET has generated, right-click on the report, and select **Database | Show SQL Query**:

```
SELECT `Employee`.`Last Name`, `Employee`.`First Name`, `Employee`.`Birth Date`,
`Employee`.`Hire Date`, `Employee_Addresses`.`City`
FROM   `Employee` `Employee` INNER JOIN `Employee Addresses` `Employee_Addresses`
ON `Employee`.`Employee ID`=`Employee_Addresses`.`Employee ID`
```

The fields you select in your report control the contents of the `SELECT` statement, but it is the links that control the `FROM` clause. When working with multiple tables or a large database, your database administrator should be able to give you some guidance on how the tables should be arranged and joined together.

If you find working with links in Crystal Reports.NET difficult, you can always use a SQL command as the data source for your report, and perform any joins in the SQL statement you write.

Verifying Database Structures Used in Your Report

As your database structures evolve and change, Crystal Reports you have created from these structures may no longer work due to differing field names and types. To ensure that the changes made in the database are reflected and accounted for in your existing reports, you will need to verify the database that they were created on by selecting **Database | Verify Database** from the main right-click menu.

If you have databases or tables in your report that are not used, you may receive the message **Verify files in report that are not used?** Click **Yes** to proceed.

At this point, Crystal Reports.NET will run through the data structures in your report and verify that nothing has changed. If all of the data structures are unchanged, **The database is up to date** will be displayed on your screen.

If anything has changed in the data structures, you will receive a message informing you of this, and that Crystal Reports.NET is proceeding to fix the report:

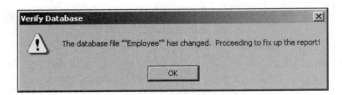

If Crystal Reports.NET finds simple changes, like a database field has been extended, or a decimal place changed, it will simply update its version of the data structures and display the message The database is up to date.

If Crystal Reports.NET finds a major change (like a field name missing, or a changed field type) it will open a Map Fields dialog. A list of unmapped fields will appear in the upper left-hand corner of this dialog. These are fields that are currently in your report that Crystal Reports.NET could not find when it attempted to verify the underlying data structure. To resolve any mismatched fields, select a field out of the dialog with Report Fields at the top, locate its counterpart in the list on the right-hand side, and click Map.

> *If the type of the field has changed as well as the name, uncheck the Match Type option to show all fields.*

When you have finished mapping all of the fields that were not found in the verification of the data structures, you can return to your report design and Crystal Reports.NET will use these mapped values in place of the missing fields.

Changing a Database Location

Another handy feature is the ability to change the location of the database that your report uses. For example, you can design a report on your test database, and then later point it to a production version. To change the location of the database in your report, right-click and select Database | Set Location and from the dialog shown, select the database or table you want to point to.

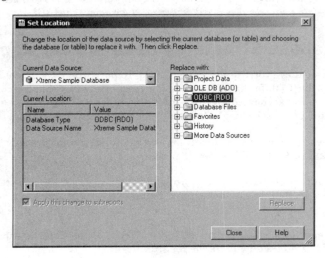

Using the Data Explorer tree on the right, locate the data source and database or table you wish to change the location to, highlight, and click the Replace button.

If you are using multiple databases or tables in your report and subreports, there is a checkbox in the bottom left-hand corner with the option of Apply this change to subreports. Turning this option on will change the database location for all other subreports as well.

If the data structures are different between the old database or table and the database in the new location you have selected, the Map Fields dialog will appear, and you must map any unfound fields in your report to fields in the new database structure.

Setting a Database Alias

Aliases are used when you need to reference a table in a report more than once. A common example would be where you had an employee table with a supervisor ID that was also the employee ID of the supervisor. To get Crystal Reports.NET to reference the same table, you would need to add it to the report a second time, and give it an alias like EmployeeSupervisor.

To set a database alias, open the Database Expert by selecting Database | Add/Remove Database. In the window on the left, find and then double-click on the database or table you want to apply the alias to, and the following dialog will open.

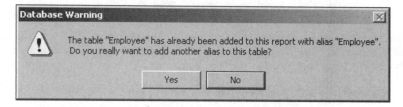

Select Yes, and enter the new alias for the database in the Alias Name dialog.

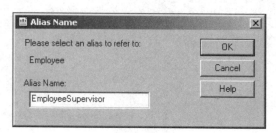

You will see your new alias in the right-hand window of the Database Expert, with the alias you specified in the previous dialog. You can edit this name by selecting the table in the Selected Tables window, and pressing *F2*.

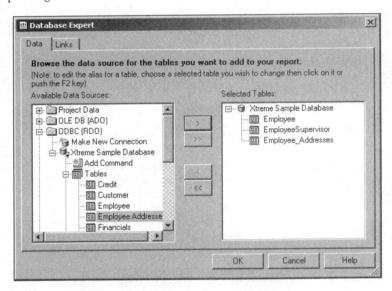

This will only change the alias of the data source within Crystal Reports.NET and will not touch the underlying SQL statement. Selecting OK will accept this and present you with the Visual Link Designer, which you can use to change the links between the different tables as we described earlier in this chapter.

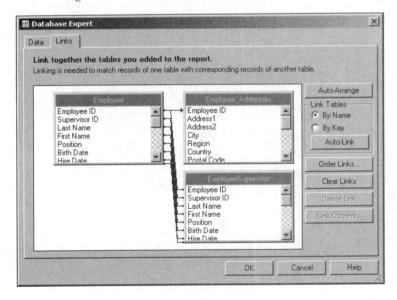

Working with SQL Commands and Expressions

New with this release of Crystal Reports, is the functionality to use custom SQL commands as the data source for your report. Using this method, you can create a *virtual table* that contains all of the fields you want to use in your report. This functionality offers a flexible alternative to using Crystal Reports' own database and linking functionality, and can help you reuse the investment you have made in other report tools, or existing SQL statements. To summarize, SQL commands are the basis of a report.

SQL Expressions are used within a report, to create new values to display; for example, projected sales figures can be generated by applying a mathematical expression to the previous year's sales.

Defining Virtual Tables

To see this feature in action, create a new Visual Basic .NET Windows Application within Visual Studio .NET called SQLCommand. (This project is available in the code download at the location C:\CrystalReports\Chapter06\SQLCommand.) Select **Project | Add New Item** and then choose Crystal Report from the available templates. Call the file sql_command.rpt, and click on **Open**. We will first step through the setup of a basic report again.

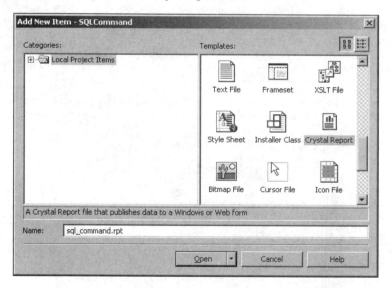

This will open the Crystal Report Gallery and allow you to select an expert to help you get started. In this example, we are going to select the Standard Report Expert, but SQL commands can be used with any of the experts listed.

The first step of the Standard Report Expert is selecting the data source for your report – double-click the node for **ODBC (RDO)** and select Xtreme Sample Database as our sample data source. This will open the dialog overleaf where you can double-click on **Add Command** to do just that.

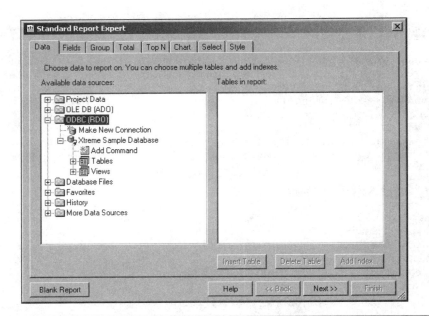

> When adding an additional data source to an existing report using **Database |
> Add/Remove Database**, the option to add a SQL command is also available.

When you select Add Command, another dialog will open and allow you to enter a SQL statement to
serve as the data source for your report. Enter SELECT * from Customer in the window.

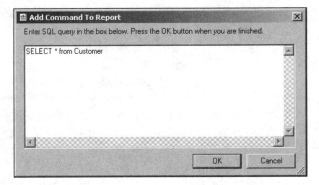

Click on **OK**, and Crystal Reports will treat the results of this query as a virtual table. You can now use
the fields you have specified in your select statement in your report.

Click **Next** to move on to the Fields tab, and where you would normally see a table to select data from,
you will see your command. It behaves just like a table in this dialog, so click on the + to expand the
command, and you will see the results of your SQL command, in this case the Customer table.

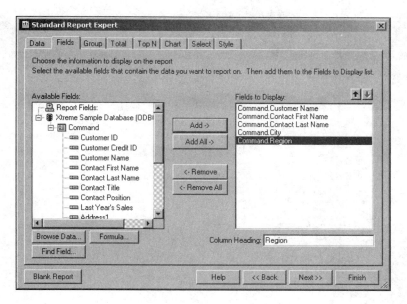

Now select the fields you want to see on your report, which in this case are:

- ❏ Customer Name
- ❏ Contact First Name
- ❏ Contact Last Name
- ❏ City
- ❏ Region

That's all you need to do to make a basic report based on a SQL command, so click on Finish to generate the report, and your Report Designer should show these fields in the Details section of sql_command.rpt. You know how to preview your report now, but here is a reminder of the basic steps:

- ❏ Drag the CrystalReportViewer (under Windows Forms in the Toolbox) to Form1.vb
- ❏ Drag ReportDocument (under Components in the Toolbox) to Form1.vb
- ❏ Double-click on the CrystalReportViewer that sits on your form to generate the procedure that loads your report when you run the report
- ❏ Insert the following code in the procedure:

```
CrystalReportViewer1.ReportSource = New sql_command()
```

When you run your report, it should look something like the report in the following screenshot, and you now know how to create a report based on a Virtual Table created from a SQL command.

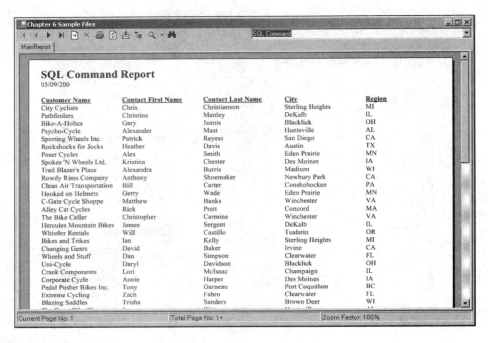

Troubleshooting SQL Commands

After you have worked with SQL commands in Crystal Reports.NET, you will realize that the error messages returned aren't always the most informative. A lot of the problem with this has to do with the error messages that are returned from the database, as opposed to Crystal's own error handling and messaging.

In an effort to keep errors down to a minimum, take the following points into consideration:

❑ The dialog to enter a SQL statement has no syntax checker or editing tools. To ensure your SQL statement will work, test it first in your own SQL query tool (SQL*PLUS, Query Analyzer, Microsoft Query).

❑ The SQL statement that you enter must include a SELECT statement and return a result set, and cannot contain any data-definition or manipulation commands.

Creating SQL Expressions

One way to improve report processing in Crystal Reports.NET is to use SQL expressions in your report instead of formulas written in Crystal Reports. These SQL expressions are passed back to the database and all of their processing occurs there. To understand how to use SQL expressions in a report, open Employee_Profile_Basic from the code download.

Open employee_profile.rpt in the form designer, locate the section of the Field Explorer marked SQL Expression Fields, and right-click directly on the section. From the right-click menu, select New... and enter a name for your SQL expression.

In this case we are going to create a SQL Expression called New Salary that will show the effect of a 6% increase on the employee's Salary. Once you have given your SQL expression a name and clicked OK, the SQL Expression Editor will open, which you can use to create a SQL expression using the available fields, functions, and operators shown.

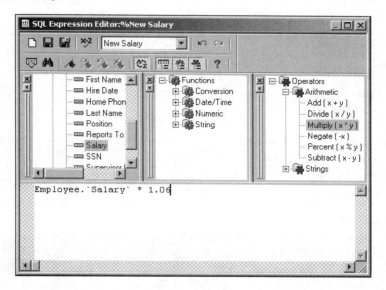

If the SQL Expression Editor looks familiar, this is because it is really the Crystal Reports Formula Editor in a different guise. The standard functions and operators have been replaced with SQL functions and operators.

The SQL Expression Editor is not that flash on features, but does include a syntax checker. Enter your expression by double-clicking on the field you want to work with (Salary), then do the same for the multiply operator, and finally enter *1.06* to represent the 6% increase in salary. To check the syntax of your expression, click the X+2 button located in the toolbar, and you will hopefully see the following dialog:

When you have finished editing the SQL expression, click on the Save and Close icon in the upper left-hand corner to exit.

Sometimes when the syntax checker passes your expression, complex expressions may still fail when executed, because unfortunately the checker doesn't know everything; however, it will point out any basic errors or typos.

> **Only use the functions and operators supported by your database. If in doubt, consult with your database administrator on the correct usage of syntax.**

Your SQL Expression should now appear in the list in the Field Explorer and you can drag and drop this field onto your report. The field should appear just like any other field shown on your report, showing that the SQL expression itself has been added.

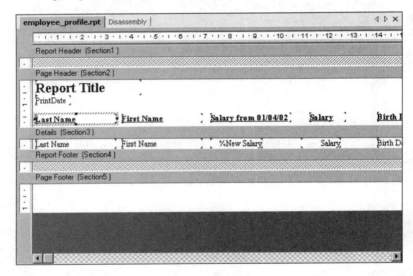

You can see that the SQL expression can be identified as a % character precedes the name, New Salary.

When your report runs or is previewed, this calculation will occur on the database server and the results are returned to your report, just like any other database field. This report you have created is the same as Employee_Profile_SQLExp, which is available in the code download for this book.

Working with ADO.NET

ADO.NET is a new data interface standard introduced with the .NET Framework that provides access to many different types of data, including SQL Server, OLE-DB-compliant data sources, and XML. Using ADO.NET, all of the data access and manipulation is handled by a number of individual components that work together to select from, insert into, and update data sources.

When working with ADO.NET, the resulting data can be stored in a special structure called a dataset, which can be used by the application itself and as the data source for a Crystal Report.

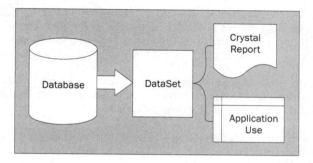

A dataset is a disconnected, in-memory data collection. Applications use ADO.NET to populate the `DataSet` object, which you can then write to, search, copy from, and so on. To run reports that show this list of information, we don't actually need to go back to the database again as the information is held within the dataset.

We can design the report based on the structure of this dataset, and when the report is run, we point the report to this data, which is used to preview and print the report. This provides a definite performance advantage and represents best practice for writing reports that use application data. In the following sections, we are going to briefly cover how to create an ADO.NET dataset and then use it as the data source for a report.

An ADO.NET Dataset

To create an ADO.NET dataset, we need to use the ADO.NET Dataset Designer. To invoke the Designer, create a new Windows Application called `Reporting_App`. Select **Project** | **Add New Item** and select **DataSet** from the list of available templates.

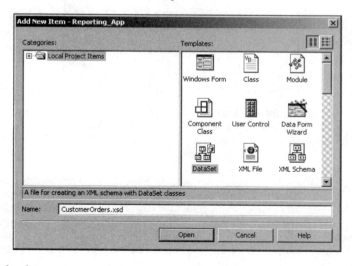

Set the name of the dataset to `CustomerOrders.xsd`, and then click on **open** to see the Dataset Designer with a blank view. You should notice that in the Solution Explorer the `CustomerOrders` dataset that you have just created has appeared.

To start building your dataset, you will need to specify where the underlying data comes from. On the left-hand side of the Visual Studio .NET IDE, locate the Server Explorer and find the section marked Data Connections. This toolbar contains all of the data sources that can be accessed, including the Northwind database that we will use in this example (*accessing this database is discussed earlier in Chapter 3*).

If your data source is not listed, right-click on Data Connections and select Add Connection from the right-click menu. To set up a new Data Connection, you will need to specify a provider and the appropriate server name and credentials for your data source.

The Northwind database that we want to use should be available. The tables and fields within the data source should appear below its node.

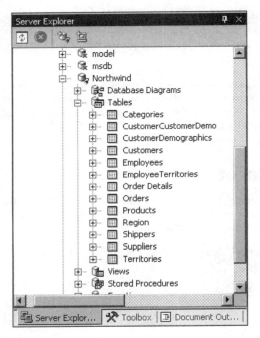

To build a **dataset**, you can simply drag-and-drop the required tables from your database connection onto the dataset design surface and specify the relationships and keys between the data sources. In our example, we are going to use the Customers and Orders tables from the Northwind database, so add these tables.

The relationship between the two tables is on the CustomerID, so to create this link you can click and drag from the CustomerID in the Orders table to the CustomerID in the Customers table. This action opens the Edit Relation dialog (also opened by right-clicking on an existing link, and selecting Edit Relation), in which you select the parent and child elements from the two drop-down lists. Our parent element should be set to Customers, our child element should be set to Orders, the key should be CustomerOrdersKey1, and both of the key fields should be set to CustomerID.

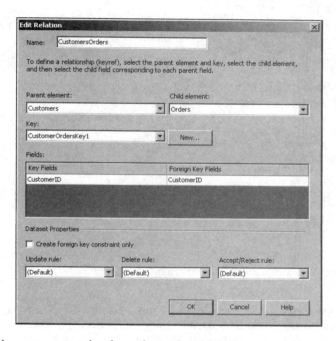

Select OK to see the customers and orders relationship. Make sure that CustomerID and OrderID are the only key fields in each of the tables, because we want the tables in the dataset to match the tables in the Northwind database.

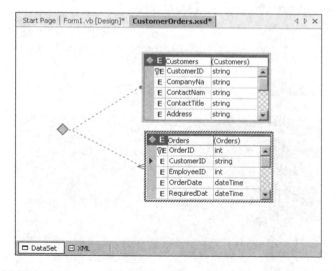

You can view the XML that describes this relationship and data by clicking on the XML tab at the bottom left of the dataset design window. You can check that your relationship has been entered correctly, by comparing the three fields that can be found at the bottom of your XML schema with these three fields here – they should match:

```
                </xs:element>
            </xs:choice>
        </xs:complexType>
        <xs:unique name="CustomerOrdersKey1" msdata:PrimaryKey="true">
            <xs:selector xpath=".//mstns:Customers" />
            <xs:field xpath="mstns:CustomerID" />
        </xs:unique>
        <xs:unique name="CustomerOrdersKey2" msdata:PrimaryKey="true">
            <xs:selector xpath=".//mstns:Orders" />
            <xs:field xpath="mstns:OrderID" />
        </xs:unique>
        <xs:keyref name="CustomersOrders" refer="CustomerOrdersKey1">
            <xs:selector xpath=".//mstns:Orders" />
            <xs:field xpath="mstns:CustomerID" />
        </xs:keyref>
    </xs:element>
</xs:schema>
```

You can manually edit the XML, although it is much easier to stay within the bounds of the development environment, and edit the dataset using the properties window. Information on creating complex datasets is available in *Fast Track ADO.NET* (1-86100-760-4) from Wrox Press.

Now you have finished creating your dataset, select Build Solution from the Build menu to build your dataset and generate the database object for this dataset. Create a copy of this project so we can use this dataset in a report that we will build later in this chapter. We will now go on to display this dataset in a DataGrid on a Windows form.

Viewing the Contents of a Dataset

Open Form1.vb in design mode, and from the Windows Forms section of the Toolbox, drag a DataGrid to the form. Just for presentation, add a label to the top of the form saying The CustomerOrders Dataset.

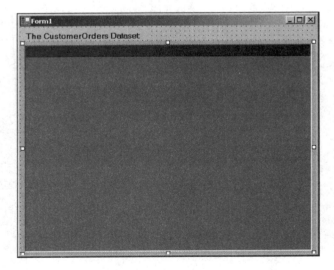

Next add an **OleDbDataAdapter** to the form by dragging and dropping one from the **Data** section of the Toolbox. This action opens the **Data Adapter Configuration Wizard** that will help you step through the process of setting up your data adapter. The first thing you will have to do is select your data connection. Make sure this is the same as the data source you built your dataset from, in this case, the Northwind database.

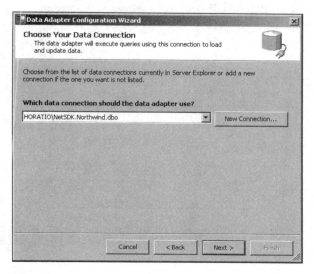

If it is not the default enter the details for your Northwind Database. Click on **New Connection** to open the Data Link Properties window. Enter the location of your SQL Server and the security settings, and select Northwind from the list of available databases. Test the connection, and if all is good, click on **OK** to continue setting up the **OleDbDataAdapter**.

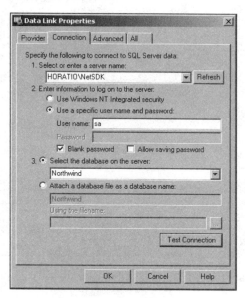

The next dialog allows you to choose a query type, to decide how the data adapter will query the database. We will use SQL statements for this purpose, so select Use SQL statements. Click on Next to get to the Generate the SQL Statements dialog, and then click on Query Builder to generate your statement. This opens the Query Builder, and in front of it, the Add Table dialog:

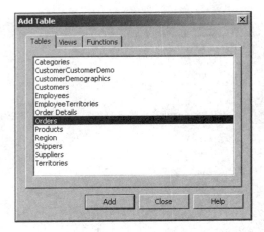

Add the Customers and Orders tables that make up our dataset, and click on Close, and the SQL query will start to be built. Then simply check the (All Columns) boxes in both of the tables to complete our query:

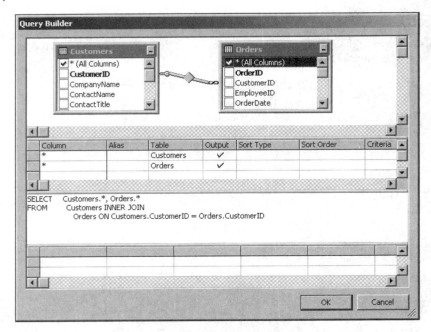

Click on OK and then Finish, to complete configuration of the data adapter.

Now the data source has been defined, double-click on the form (not in `DataGrid1`) to open up the code designer for `Form1.vb`. This action creates a procedure called `Form1_load`, which fires when the form is loaded. Insert the following code into this procedure:

```
Private Sub Form1_Load(ByVal sender As System.Object,
                       ByVal e As System.EventArgs) Handles MyBase.Load
    Dim CustomerOrders As New DataSet()
    OleDbDataAdapter1.Fill(CustomerOrders)
    DataGrid1.SetDataBinding(CustomerOrders, "Customers")
End Sub
```

This code will use the data adapter we have just set up to fill the dataset with information from the `Customers` table in the Northwind Database, and display it in `DataGrid1`.

Working with ADO.NET requires two namespaces: `System.Data`, and since we are using OLEDB, the `System.Data.OleDb` namespace as well. Add the imports statements to the top of `Form1.vb`.

```
Imports System.Data
Imports System.Data.OleDb

Public Class Form1
    Inherits System.Windows.Forms.Form
```

Run the code and your application should open, and display the dataset it has been loaded with, providing you with access to data from the `CustomerOrders` dataset:

The application you have created should be the same as `Reporting_App_ViewData`, which is available in the code download. Now we will go on to using the dataset as the data source for a report.

Creating a Report from an ADO.NET Dataset

The CustomerOrders dataset for the database object we have built will be populated when the application is started. When designing a report based on this dataset, we cannot browse the content of any of the fields as the dataset hasn't been populated at this point, but if you do have any questions about what type of content the fields could contain, view the database to find out, or use a viewing application like the one we have just built.

To create a report based on an ADO.NET dataset, start by opening the copy you made of Reporting_App at the end of the section *An ADO.NET Dataset*. Select Project | Add New Item, and select Crystal Report from the list of available templates. Call the report adonet_sample.rpt, click on Open, and the familiar Crystal Report Gallery will open with options for creating your report.

Again, we are going to use the Standard Report Expert, although you could use any other expert you wish to get started. Since we are using the Standard Report Expert, the first step is to select the data for our report. The Data Explorer contains a folder, for adding Project Data.

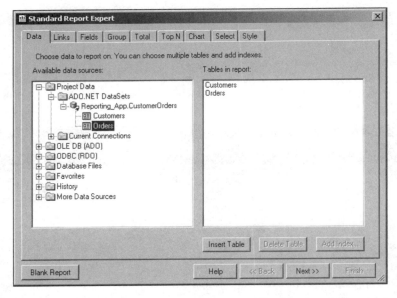

All of the dataset objects that were generated during the build will be listed here, in the format of Project.datasetName (for example, Reporting_App.CustomerOrders). Simply add the tables from the dataset to your report, to gain access to all of the fields within the dataset.

You can then use these tables and fields in your report development just like using any other source, with one catch. When Crystal Reports.NET looks at the fields in your dataset, it ignores the length that the string actually is, and instead thinks that all of the string fields are the maximum length (65,534 characters).

This shouldn't affect you unless your are using any formulas that use the length or other string functions dependent on the length, in which case you will need to use the trim function before you attempt to get the length of a string (not the best solution if you have leading or trailing spaces in your string).

This issue has been tracked by Crystal Decisions, and should be fixed in future releases of the product.

Click the Fields tab to select the fields that will appear in your report. Choose CompanyName, City, and Region from the Customers table. Then select OrderDate and ShippedDate from the Orders table.

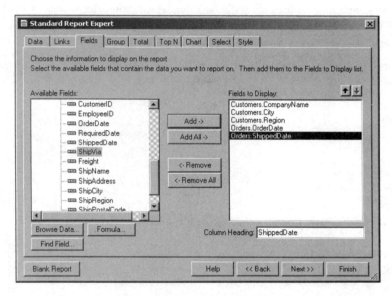

Select Finish to create the report from your ADO.NET dataset. Now you can simply save the report and integrate it into your application. The section below outlines how to use this type of report with the Windows Report Viewer, and provides a brief note of how to use it with the Web Report Viewer.

Viewing Reports Containing an ADO.NET Dataset

If you were to set the ReportSource property for the Windows Report Viewer to your newly created report based on ADO.NET, and previewed it exactly the same as you would a normal report, nothing would appear. By default, the ADO.NET dataset we have used does not contain any data.

To continue from our previous example, where we created a report from the dataset based on the Customers and Orders tables, we are going to look at the code required to integrate this report (based on an ADO.NET dataset) into a Windows Application.

To start with, we need a form to host the Crystal Reports Viewer. From your project, open Form1.vb, and drag the CrystalReportViewer from the Toolbox to the form. Next, add the report as you normally would, by dragging ReportDocument from the Components section of the Toolbox, and selecting our new report, adonet_sample.rpt.

Next we have to add an OleDbDataApdapter just as we did in the data viewer project earlier. This involves dragging the control onto our form, and stepping through the Data Adapter Configuration Wizard, which in brief comprises (look back to the *Viewing the Contents of a Dataset* section if you need a guide through these steps):

❑ Choosing your data connection – if it isn't the default, enter the details for your Northwind Database.

❑ Choosing a query type – we will use SQL statements

❑ Generating the SQL Statements – click on the Query Builder button, and use the Add Tables dialog to add the Customers and Orders tables as we did before. Select (All Columns), and check the SQL generated is as follows:

```
SELECT
    Customers.*,
    Orders.*
FROM
    Customers
INNER JOIN
    Orders
ON
    Customers.CustomerID = Orders.CustomerID
```

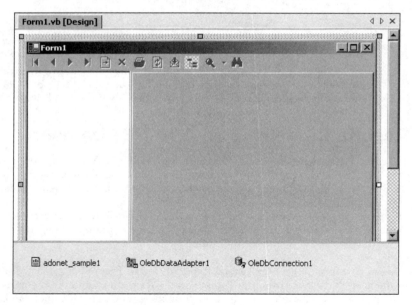

Notice how OleDbConnection1 has also appeared on the report next to OleDbDataApdapter1. This is generated from the connection information that you provided the Data Adapter Configuration Wizard with.

With the form now set up to access the dataset, we need to look at some code. Add the same namespaces as we did to view the dataset earlier in this chapter. In addition, since we will be printing a report based on this data, we need to add the `CrystalDecisions.CrystalReports.Engine` namespace to the code behind this form, as shown here:

```
Imports System.Data
Imports System.Data.OleDb
Imports CrystalDecisions.CrystalReports.Engine

Public Class Form1
    Inherits System.Windows.Forms.Form
```

Next we need to add variables to dimension the connection, the data adapter, and the dataset, and get the form ready to accept data. We will connect to the Northwind database using `OleDbConnection1` (as seen on the form designer), and submit a SQL query that will return a result set, filling the `Customers` table, and then the `Orders` table in the dataset. To do this, double-click on the **CrystalReportViewer** in the form designer to generate the `CrystalReportViewer1_Load` procedure. Then insert the following code:

```
Private Sub CrystalReportViewer1_Load(ByVal sender As System.Object,
                           ByVal e As System.EventArgs)
                           Handles CrystalReportViewer1.Load

    Dim myDataSet = New CustomerOrders()

    Dim sqlString As String = "Select * from Customers"
    OleDbDataAdapter1 = New OleDbDataAdapter(sqlString, OleDbConnection1)
    OleDbDataAdapter1.Fill(myDataSet, "Customers")

    sqlString = "Select * from Orders"
    OleDbDataAdapter1 = New OleDbDataAdapter(sqlString, OleDbConnection1)
    OleDbDataAdapter1.Fill(myDataSet, "Orders")

End Sub
```

With the data now in the dataset, we can set our report source and preview the report itself, by adding this code to the bottom of the `CrystalReportViewer1_Load` procedure:

```
    OleDbDataAdapter1.Fill(myDataSet, "Orders")

    Dim myReport = New adonet_sample()
    myReport.SetDataSource(myDataSet)
    CrystalReportViewer1.ReportSource = myReport

End Sub
```

When you run your application and view this form, your report will be filled with data from the ADO.NET dataset, and will be displayed within the viewer, as shown in the following screenshot:

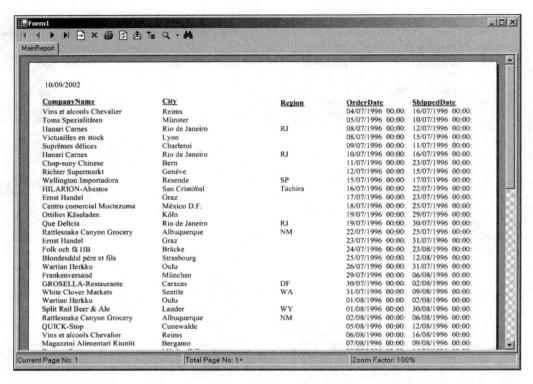

The only difference in integration between the Windows and the Web Crystal Report Viewer is that you will need to add the appropriate report viewer for the environment you are working with (discussed in Chapters 3 and 4). You can change the contents of the ADO.NET dataset numerous times within your application, and you can call the `DataSource` method at any time before previewing or refreshing your report.

Summary

In this chapter, we had a look at how Crystal Reports.NET accesses different data sources, as well as looking at some of the options for working with data within the Report Designer itself. We also had a brief look at creating ADO.NET datasets and walked through how to design and integrate reports using them.

With all of this behind us, it is time to look at one of the most time-consuming tasks when creating reports – integrating formulas and logic in our report, which is covered in Chapter 7.

Professional *Crystal Reports* for *Visual Studio .NET*

7

Formulas and Logic

In previous chapters, we've looked at creating and integrating reports, creating and consuming XML Report web services, and working with .NET data. In this chapter, we'll be narrowing our focus to look at where the majority of Crystal Reports development time is spent: writing formulas and logic. This will include:

- ❑ Deciding how to integrate logic into your report
- ❑ Working with the Formula Editor
- ❑ Creating formulas with Basic syntax
- ❑ Creating formulas with Crystal syntax
- ❑ Writing record selection formulas
- ❑ Using conditional formatting

At the end of this chapter, you will be able to identify the best way to add calculations and logic to your report, and understand enough syntax and code to handle most situations. You should also be able to differentiate between the two different 'flavors' of the Crystal Formula Language, and to write your own record selection and conditional formatting formulas.

Integrating Formulas and Logic into your Reports

Few reports are ever created just to list information on a page – most will include at least some basic calculations, summaries, and logic. You wouldn't want an invoice, for example, that didn't have a sales tax calculation and total at the bottom, or a sales summary without any totals. How this logic is incorporated into your report depends on the requirements set out by the eventual user. The following sections give an overview of the different ways that you can incorporate formulas and logic into your report.

The examples in this chapter deal specifically with creating and working with formulas. If you decide that you need to use a method other than writing formulas, turn back to Chapter 6 for examples of how to work with application data, SQL Commands, and SQL Expressions.

Database Structures

Since all reports are based on a data source, and the most common type of data source is a database, it follows that you might place the logic for your report in the database structures that you're using. In addition to creating reports from database tables, Crystal Reports.NET can also grab data from **views** and **stored procedures**. Using these devices, you can push most of the processing back to the database server. The advantage of doing this is that you can make further use of the investment you've made in your database server – all of that processing power will translate to reports that run faster and more efficiently (*if your server is any good!*).

In instances where you need to reuse logic and particular representations of the data between different reports, views, and stored procedures can provide a definite advantage over the raw data structures:

❑   Using a view, you can perform joins and consolidation at the level of the database, so that when you design your report, there are no messy joins to configure, and you don't have to figure out how the pieces fit back together. This is especially handy if you have a complex set of data structures, or if you foresee end users creating their own reports some day.

❑   If you have calculations or business logic that gets used repeatedly, a stored procedure can provide those calculations for a number of reports, without having to cut and paste Crystal formulas between the reports themselves. This is sometimes called **2½-tier logic**, rather than a true 3/n-tier situation, but the benefits are still tangible: the business logic can still be broken out and reused in other reports. You can also add parameters to your stored procedures, and Crystal Reports will accept input to these parameters as if they were a native Crystal Parameter field.

There will be times when you want a very specific report from multiple data sources, but find it difficult to select and display the data you need using Crystal Report's native features and formulas. For example, you may have data from three or four disparate order entry systems, and need to show information from all of them in one report. The data itself is stored in different formats and tables, with different primary keys and structure.

You could spend time creating Crystal Reports from these different data sources, and then attempt to use sub-reports to join the data together. This method would allow you to create composite keys, to pass variables back and forth between the different sub-reports, and to try to massage the information into the format you need. Alternatively, you could write a *stored procedure* to consolidate the data, and use that as the data source for your report.

For example, you could work with various Crystal features to create a report that would show data from the New York Stock Exchange alongside world economic indicators from the UN and your own company's sales – but what would happen if you wanted to add another data source or additional features to your report?

A key component of the report development lifecycle that we talked about in Chapter 2 was **technical review**. This is where you review the report's planned content, and determine the best way to deliver it. If the best method is to use a stored procedure or a view, don't be afraid to use the tools you have at hand. In an example with three data sources, it would probably make sense to consolidate all of these sources into one database, and then develop a view or a stored procedure to put them together in a format that could be used to create the required output.

Invariably, using stored procedures or views to return a result set will cause someone to ask, "If we're writing all these stored procedures, why do we need Crystal Reports at all?" We need Crystal Reports to do what it does best: creating information-rich, presentation-quality reports from the data provided. The better the dataset that we provide to Crystal Reports, the easier report development will be, and the more features we can incorporate into our report.

Application Data

Most applications today are developed on an underlying database or other data source, and Crystal Reports.NET can use this application data as the source for your reports, as we saw in the last chapter.

Probably the most compelling reason to use application data is that the logic from the application can be reused in your report. For example, if you have a data-bound grid that displays a number of orders together with calculated fields for order totals, sales tax, shipping, and so on, you could reuse this dataset as the source of your report.

If you didn't have access to this data, you would have to re-create the calculated fields using Crystal Reports formulas. When something changed in the application, it would also have to change in each report where it appeared. If you're developing an information-rich application, where the business logic is an integral part of creating that information, you may want to consider using the application data for the logic or calculations that appear in your report.

Crystal SQL Commands

As we saw in Chapter 6, something new to this version of Crystal Reports is the ability to use SQL commands as the basis of your report. In previous versions, all of the tables, joins, groups, fields, and so on that you selected for your report were translated into a SQL statement that was written by Crystal Reports itself. That request was submitted to the database, and the results returned to the report designer for formatting.

The problem was that while you could view the SQL statement generated within the Report Designer, you couldn't really change it, or use an existing statement in its place. Setting the SQL statement at run time provided one way of dealing with this limitation, but you still had to rely on Crystal Reports to create the initial SQL statement based on the tables, joins, and so on, that you selected in the report's design.

Clearly, there had to be a better way of doing things. With this release of Crystal Reports, you can now use SQL commands as the data source for your reports, (as opposed to tables, views, stored procedures, and so on).

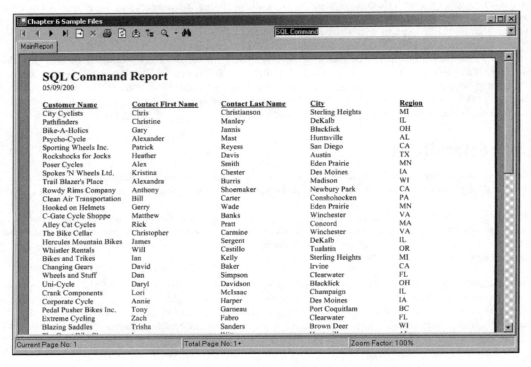

The report in the screenshot is from Chapter 6, and is based on a SQL Command.

The only drawback to creating a 'virtual table' with an SQL command is that when the database changes (when changing a field type, for example), you will need to go back to the report and change the SQL statement to reflect it.

Also, SQL commands cannot be shared between reports, so you could end up cutting and pasting the SQL statement between them. If you're considering implementing a report using a SQL command, you may want to consider creating a **database view** using that same SQL statement. In addition to being able to be used by multiple reports, a view is probably easier to maintain in the long run than individual SQL statements held within Crystal Reports.

Crystal SQL Expressions

Another key database feature of Crystal Reports is the ability to create SQL expressions using the purpose-built SQL Expression Editor, shown here:

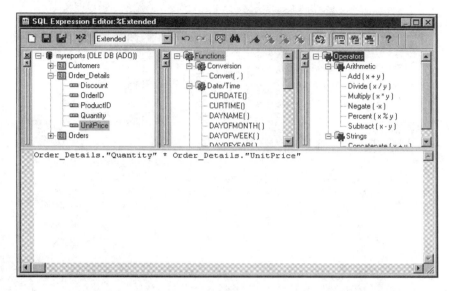

When creating a SQL expression field, you have access to all of the SQL functions and operators that are supported by your particular database server. These expressions are evaluated directly on the server, with their values returned to Crystal Reports. Be aware, though, that the same function or feature may not be available if you change the source of the report from one database platform to another.

If you're planning to use SQL expressions, you may want to turn back to Chapter 6 to review best practice for using this feature.

SQL expressions are a handy way to add discrete calculations to a report, but if you find yourself creating the same expressions for multiple reports, you may want to consider using a **stored procedure**, a **view**, or a **SQL command** to eliminate repetitive coding.

Formulas

Crystal Reports.NET has its own feature-rich formula language for adding calculations and logic to your report. Where the methods listed above can offer advantages in terms of sharing or reusing logic, or employing the power of a database server, Crystal's formula language has advantages of its own.

To start with, this language is fully integrated with all of the features in your report. We could use a field in a stored procedure to do a calculation such as computing Sales Tax, but it is with the Crystal Reports formula language that we can conditionally format that field, or print out text when the Sales Tax value is over $10,000, as shown overleaf:

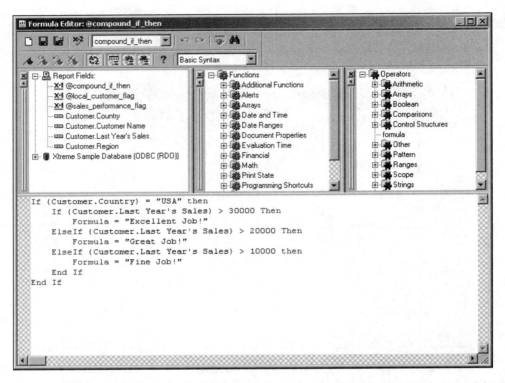

```
If {Customer.Country} = "USA" then
    If {Customer.Last Year's Sales} > 30000 Then
        Formula = "Excellent Job!"
    ElseIf {Customer.Last Year's Sales} > 20000 Then
        Formula = "Great Job!"
    ElseIf {Customer.Last Year's Sales} > 10000 then
        Formula = "Fine Job!"
    End If
End If
```

When working with a formula within Crystal Reports, you have access to the report's 'print state' and document properties, which include the page number, summary information, and so on. You could create a formula to print out a message on the last page of the report, showing the title, author, file name, path, and print date. This information is not available from any SQL data source – just the report itself.

Another example of where a formula is preferable to working with SQL is when you need to use some of the functions that are inherent to Crystal Reports.NET, like the ones for periods of time like MonthtoDate, YeartoDate, and so on, or financial ratios like current ratio, or A/R (Accounts Receivable) turnover, that would be difficult to create from scratch in SQL.

When choosing a method for integrating calculations or logic into your report, you're likely to use a combination of the methods listed above, based on their own merits. A good guideline to follow is that for complex calculations and data manipulation, you'll probably want to use your database server to its fullest capacity, and create summary tables, views and/or stored procedures to provide the information you need. If you're working with an information-rich application that already contains some logic, and performs calculations on a .NET dataset, you'll probably want to use the existing data in your application. But for calculations that can't be sourced from database structures or application data, or that are specific to Crystal Reports' features and functionality, the Crystal Reports formula language can surely hold its own.

Working with the Formula Editor

There are two basic types of formulas. First, there are **formula fields** that you can insert in your report (usually enclosed in braces and prefixed by the @ symbol, for example, {@SalesTax}). Second, there are formulas that appear "behind the scenes", like those for record selection or conditional formatting. From these two distinct types, you can create thousands of different formulas; but regardless of what you're working with, formulas are all created, debugged, and edited using the Crystal Reports formula editor.

Controlling the Editor's Appearance

The Crystal Reports formula editor has undergone a number of changes over the past few releases to move from a simple textbox to something that resembles a real code editor, including a customizable interface, color coding, and search and replace features.

To get things underway, the formula editor can be opened by either creating a new formula, or editing an existing formula. In this example, we're going to look at the formula editor by editing a formula that appears in a report (operators.rpt) that's included with the sample files for this chapter.

Open the report in the Report Designer and expand the **Formula Fields** section of the Field Explorer shown below.

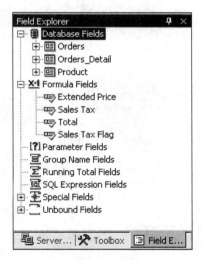

Locate the **Sales Tax** formula, right-click directly on it, and select **Edit**. This will open the Crystal Reports formula editor, the appearance of which is controlled by a set of default values.

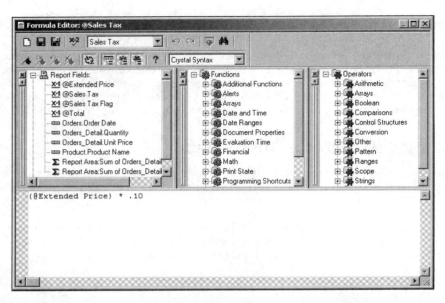

These values can be set in the Report Designer by right-clicking on the report and selecting **Designer |
Default Settings | Editors**. You can set the properties for comments, keywords, text, and selected text
using this dialog, including changes to the font size and color. Using these properties, the formula editor
can be modified to your preferences, for example, highlighting comments in a bright color, or keywords
in bold.

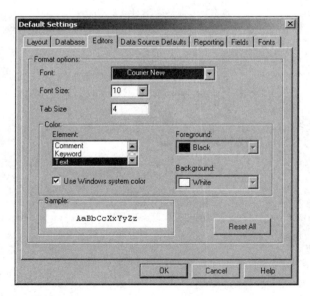

There's also a **Reset All** button that you can use if you'd like to reset the editor's settings to their
original defaults.

Controlling the Syntax Type

When working with the Crystal Reports formula language, there are two different types of syntax available to you: Basic syntax and Crystal syntax. We'll look at each of these in more detail later in the chapter.

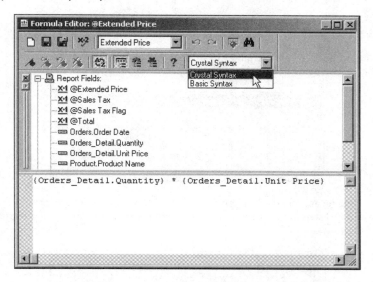

Which syntax you are working with is controlled by the drop-down list that appears in the upper right-hand corner, as shown in the previous screenshot. Each type of syntax has its own operators and functions that may (or may not!) overlap.

The code for the examples is in the Chapter07 folder:

- ❏ BasicSyntax_Basic – A viewing application that contains the reports discussed in this chapter that use Basic syntax.

- ❏ CrystalSyntax_Basic – An application that contains the reports discussed in this chapter that use Crystal syntax.

Checking for Syntax Errors

To check your formula for syntax errors, there is a Check icon (labeled X+2) that appears on the Formula Editor tool bar. This performs a syntax check on the formula in the window, but it doesn't guarantee that your formula will run, or produce the desired result. It just checks to make sure that you've spelled everything correctly, and that your code is well formed.

With the operators report open in the form designer, right-click on the Total formula under Formula Fields in the Field Explorer, to open the Formula Editor. Click on the Check icon and you will receive the following message:

Click on OK, and go back to the Formula Editor. Enter some random characters after the formula, and click on the Check icon again. This time an error dialog is displayed:

In this case, the checker has correctly identified an error where some characters have been inserted at the end of a formula. If you do not correct this error, you will receive another warning when you attempt to save the formula:

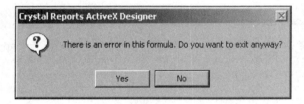

You can select Yes to leave the formula without correcting the error, but doing so may cause further errors when your report is run.

Creating Formulas with Basic Syntax

As mentioned above, Crystal Reports has two different types of formula syntax available for use. **Crystal syntax** was originally the only syntax available for use in formulas, but Visual Basic developers complained bitterly about having to learn yet another language – particularly one that seemed to be part Pascal and part Basic.

What is Basic Syntax?

With the introduction of Crystal Reports 7.0 came **Basic syntax**. This closely resembled Visual Basic code, using similar functions and operators, but with the ability to access all of the Crystal-specific functions and features. Over time, the two syntaxes have grown closer together, with the Crystal version having gone farther to reach its Basic cousin.

Which syntax you choose depends upon your background and experience. If you're a dyed-in-the-wool Crystal Reports developer, the chances are that you'll be more familiar with Crystal syntax. If you're a Visual Basic developer who has been pushed into report development as well, you'll be more comfortable using Basic syntax.

Since the two versions of syntax have grown closer together, we're going to concentrate our discussion here around the Basic version. A little later in the chapter, we'll look at the differences between the two, which should allow you to use the syntax of your choice.

Basic Syntax Coding Conventions

The structure used by Basic syntax in Crystal Reports closely resembles the structure used in Visual Basic, but there are a few slight differences. Open `operators.rpt` from the sample code, right-click on **Formula Fields** in the Field Explorer, and select **New**. Enter **LearnSyntax** in the dialog as the name of the formula:

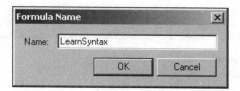

To start with, field names are enclosed in braces, and use the naming convention of `{tablename.fieldname}`, so enter the following formula that would calculate extended price in `operators.rpt`:

```
{Orders_Detail.Quantity} * {Orders_Detail.Unit Price}
```

Make sure that the crystal syntax is selected, and not basic syntax, and click on the check icon. The formula should be fine.

Other fields use a prefix to indicate the type of field you're working with. Parameter fields, for example, are prefixed by a question mark, and formula fields are prefixed with the @ character. Change your formula to calculate the sales tax using the extended price from this report by entering the following:

```
{@Extended Price} * .10
```

Click on the check icon again, to confirm that the formula is correct, as we were writing this formula in Crystal syntax. Now you can drag and drop the formula field onto the **Details** section of a report, it would be evaluated once for each record, and the value would be displayed.

Basic syntax, however, is slightly different. For each formula you write in Basic syntax, you need to use a special `Formula` variable to tell Crystal Reports what to return. Using the same `LearnSyntax` example in the Formula Editor, change the syntax to Basic syntax using the drop-down menu, and click on the **Check** icon.

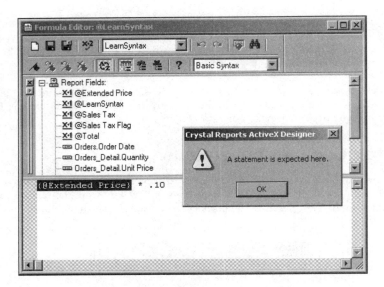

The correct code for our sales tax formula would be:

```
Formula = {Orders.OrderTotal} * {?SalesTax}
```

Enter this formula, and click on the Check icon to ensure this line of code is correct.

Even if you don't need to output a value, you still have to use the Formula variable and assign some value to it (even if you just make it up).

If, for example, we create a global variable and insert a calculation to add up the number of orders as we go down the page, but we don't actually want to print anything out until the end, we still have to set the Formula variable, to avoid getting a syntax error. Try the checker on the following code with and without the line that says Formula = 999.

```
Global TotalOrders as Number
TotalOrders = TotalOrders + {Orders_Detail.Quantity}
Formula = 999
```

As you've probably noticed, assignments are made using the equal operator. Just like other versions of the Basic language, you can add comments to your formulas with either the single quote, or the REM statement:

```
' This formula calculates the Total Sales
Global TotalOrders as Number
TotalOrders = TotalOrders + {Orders_Detail.Quantity}
Formula = 999
REM The formula variable is required
```

If you want to use REM on the same line as some formula text, you need to add a colon before you begin your REM statement, as shown below:

```
Formula = 999 : REM The formula variable is required
```

If you're using the apostrophe, you can just append it to the end of the line:

```
Formula = 999 ' The formula variable is required
```

Simple Operators

Now we need to look at a few of the simple operators that are available for use. Some of these are used in the sample reports that are included with the download files for this chapter. Many are self explanatory, and don't need much guidance for use, so we won't describe how to use every one. The easiest way to become familiar with the large number of operators is to actually use them, or play about with them in the Formula Editor, using the Check button to your ensure your syntax is correct.

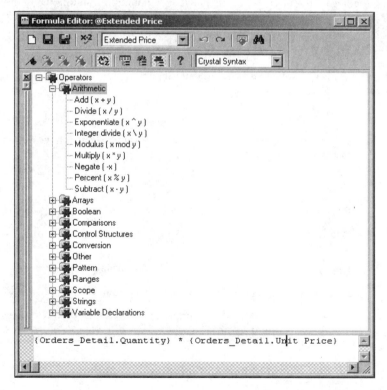

Although the majority are the same, Basic syntax and Crystal syntax occasionally utilize different operators. These differences are explained in Appendix C, *Crystal vs. Basic Syntax.*

Arithmetic

Crystal Reports .NET supports all of the basic arithmetic operators (including addition, subtraction, multiplication, and division), but also has support for a number of others, as discussed in the table below:

Operator	Symbol	Description
Integer Divide	\	Division where only the integer is returned (for example, 9\2 would return a result of 4)
Modulus	Mod	For dividing two numbers and returning the remainder
Negate	-( )	To negate or change the sign of a number
Exponentiate	^	For exponents, used for calculating squares, for example, 3^2 would return 9

Open operators.rpt in the report designer, and create a new formula by right-clicking on Formula Fields. By using the negate operator, we could calculate a value representing the number of items returned to the company from an order:

```
-({Orders_Detail.Quantity})
```

The negate function is also useful when working with financial information, where a negative amount may indicate a credit.

Boolean

For formulas and logic that need to return a True or False value, we also have a number of Boolean operators available within Basic syntax.

Operator	Description
Not	Reverses the value – for instance, Not(True) is False.
And	Where all conditions are True, returns True. Where one condition does not meet the criteria, returns False.
Or	Returns True if one or the other condition is met, or both.
Xor	Returns True if one and not the other condition is met.
Eqv	Returns True if both values compared are True, or if both values compared are False. If the two values compared are different, it returns False.

Comparison

For comparing two values, Basic syntax supports the usual comparison operators, including:

Operator	Symbol
Equal to	=
Not equal	<>
Less than	<
Greater than	>
Less or equal	<=
Greater or equal	>=

Type Conversion

Within Crystal Reports, there are eight different data types available for use:

- ❑ Boolean
- ❑ Number
- ❑ Currency
- ❑ Date
- ❑ Date-time
- ❑ Time
- ❑ String
- ❑ BLOB (Binary Large Object)

BLOB fields can be inserted into a report, but they cannot be converted to any other field type. They are handy when you need to insert non-traditional records into your report. (The sample database, for example, has a graphic file inserted into the Employee *table that, when placed on your report, will display the employee's photo. This can be seen in the* Employee_Listing.rpt *report that's included with the chapter's sample files.)*

When working with all of these different types of fields, we sometimes need to perform a conversion before we can use them in our formulas (for example, where a numeric value is stored as a string in the database). To convert field types, we have the following conversion functions:

Function	Use
CBool()	Returns True if the argument is positive or negative but not zero, and returns False if the argument is zero
CCur()	Converts Number, Currency, or String types to Currency

Table continued on following page

Function	Use
CDbl()	Converts Number, Currency, or String types to Number
CStr()	Converts Number, Currency, or Date types to String
CDate()	For converting to a true Date field
CTime()	For converting to a Time field
CDateTime()	For converting to a DateTime field
ToNumber()	For converting String and Boolean types to Number
ToText()	For converting Number, Currency, Date, Time, or Boolean to text
ToWords()	For spelling out numbers or currency values (for example, 101 is "One hundred and one")

> *In addition to these, there are also functions for converting* DateTime *strings – you'll find them in the Formula Editor, under the heading* **Additional Functions**. *These functions will accept a* DateTime *string and return a* Date *field, a* Time *field, or a number of seconds.*

So, to convert a number to a currency-format field, the formula would look something like this:

```
Formula = CCur({Orders.OrderAmount})
```

or, to use the ToWords() function to spell out the same currency amount:

```
Formula = ToWords(CCur({Orders.OrderAmount}))
```

which, for a value of 1001.50, would return the string One thousand and one and 50/100.

For date functions, you can pass the date in any number of formats, including the full date, days elapsed since 01/01/1900, date literals, and date components:

```
CDate("Sep. 05, 2002")
```

which returns a date value for September 5th, 2002,

```
CDate(#Jan. 01, 2005 12:02pm#)
```

which returns a date value for January 1st, 2005,

```
CDate(1960, 10, 10)
```

which returns a date value for October 10, 1960.

Summary Functions

When you insert a summary into your report, a corresponding summary function is used to create a specialized summary field. These summary fields can be used within your formulas just like any other field, and include sums, averages, and counts.

Summary fields are generally shown in one of two different ways. The first of these, where the summary function and a single field are shown, represents a grand total that may appear on your report (usually in the report footer). An example of this type would be:

```
Sum({Customer.Sales})
```

In addition to grand totals, summary fields can also be used at the group level. So in the same report that shows the summary above, you could also have a summary field that appears in the group header or footer. For example, if the group field were {Customer.Country}, the summary field would look like this:

```
Sum({Customer.Sales}, {Customer.Country})
```

For more information on inserting summary fields into your report, turn back to Chapter 2.

String Functions

The string functions within Crystal Reports are used to manipulate database and other fields that contain text. When working with strings, we can concatenate two strings together using either the plus operator (+), or the ampersand (&).

When working with two strings, we could use the plus operator, as shown:

```
Formula = "This is the Customer Name " + {Customer.Name}
```

To concatenate a string and another type of field with the plus operator, we would first have to do a type conversion to ensure that both of these fields were strings. Using the ampersand operator, you can concatenate strings with any other type of field, without performing a type conversion first:

```
Formula = "This is the Sales Amount " & {Customer.SalesTotal}
```

Although this method is easier, you may still need to perform a type conversion in order to have more control over how the field is converted (such as setting the number of decimal places when moving from a number to string).

In addition to concatenating strings, you can reference individual characters or sets of characters using the subscript operator, noted by square brackets ({fieldname}[n], where n is a position within the string).

To return the first letter of a customer's first name, the formula would look like this:

```
Formula = {Customer.FirstName}[1]
```

You'll notice here that Crystal treats strings as 1-based arrays (instead of 0-based). It also provides the ability to return a range of characters from the array – in this case, the first three letters:

```
Formula = {Customer.FirstName}[1 to 3]
```

In addition to concatenating and pulling strings apart using simple operators, we have a number of functions that can be used with string-type fields, including:

Function	Description
Len(*string*)	Finds the length of a string
Trim(*string*)	Trims extra spaces from either side of a string
LTrim(*string*)	Trims extra spaces from the left side of a string
RTrim(*string*)	Trims extra spaces from the right side of a string
UCase(*string*)	Converts a string to all uppercase letters
LCase(*string*)	Converts a string to all lowercase letters
StrReverse(string)	Reverses the order of a string
IsNumeric(*string*)	Tests to see if a field is numeric
InStr(*string1, string2*)	Searches for the position of *string2* inside *string1*
InStr(*start, string1, string2*)	Searches for the position of *string2* inside of *string1* using a numeric starting point

For example, to find the length of a string, you'd use the Len function:

```
Formula = Len({Customer.Country})
```

In the sample report shown below (employee_listing.rpt), some of these functions have been used to create an e-mail address to be displayed on a report that follows the naming convention of "first initial, last name", combined with the domain name:

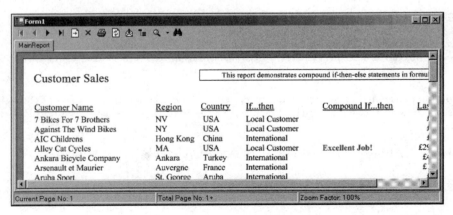

Date and Period Functions

Since most reports will involve date and time information in one form or another, Crystal Reports includes a number of predefined periods to help make life a little easier. You can think of the periods as pre-built arrays of dates, based on the current date. For example, you could use the period LastFullWeek in a comparison, and the range of date values from the Sunday to Saturday of the previous week would be included.

A complete list of these period functions appears below:

- ❏ WeekToDateFromSun
- ❏ MonthToDate
- ❏ YearToDate
- ❏ Last7Days
- ❏ Last4WeeksToSun
- ❏ LastFullWeek
- ❏ LastFullMonth
- ❏ AllDatesToToday
- ❏ AllDatesToYesterday
- ❏ AlDatesFromToday
- ❏ AllDatesFromTomorrow
- ❏ Aged0To30Days, Aged31To60Days, Aged61To90Days
- ❏ Over90Days
- ❏ Next30Days, Next31To60Days, Next61To90Days, Next91To365Days
- ❏ Calendar1stQtr, Calendar2ndQtr, Calendar3rdQtr, Calendar4thQtr
- ❏ Calendar1stHalf, Calendar2ndHalf
- ❏ LastYearMTD
- ❏ LastYearYTD

Just to drive the point home, all of the above functions act like arrays of dates. In the function AllDatesFromTomorrow, an array is created behind the scenes that includes all dates from tomorrow onwards. Likewise, when you access the function Aged0To30Days, an array is built of all dates that are 0 to 30 days behind the date you are comparing with. This is especially handy when working with financial reports, where you need to show aging of debts, invoices, and other time-sensitive documents.

We use these functions by comparing date-type fields against them, to determine whether those dates fall within the represented period. For example:

```
If {Orders.OrderDate} In Over90Days Then Formula = "Overdue"
```

This also can be used to create complex 'month-to-date' and 'year-to-date' reports, by displaying the data that falls in these periods in two separate columns.

In this chapter we will look at an example of a report has been created from the Customer and Orders tables within the Xtreme sample database (customer_orders.rpt, included with the code download). Some basic fields have been displayed on the report (like Customer Name, Order Date, and Order Amount), with a grouping inserted on Customer Name.

So, open the sample application, BasicSyntax_basic. You may prefer to build this example from scratch by creating your own project and viewer – it makes no difference to the finished result, as we will be working more or less exclusively in the Report Designer.

To display the two columns we need to create two separate formulas, which are then summarized, and the details of the report hidden. For the 'month-to-date' column, locate the Formula Field section of the Field Explorer, right-click and select New, and enter a name of MTD. The formula text looks something like this:

```
If {Orders.Order Date} In MonthToDate Then Formula = {Orders.OrderAmount}
```

For the year-to-date column, repeat the same process, but name the formula YTD, and enter the formula text shown here:

```
If {Orders.OrderDate} in YeartoDate Then Formula = {Orders.OrderAmount}
```

Having defined your two formula fields, you can drag and drop them onto your report in the 'details' section.

The next step in creating our summary report is to right-click directly on the MTD field and select Insert Subtotal from the context menu. Then repeat that for the YTD field

To finish off, right-click on the Details section in the Report Designer, select Hide Section, and then do the same for the Group Header #1 on Customer Name.

Your report should now show the two columns for month-to-date and year-to-date values; to get the customer name to appear as well, drag the Group #1 Name field out of the header into your Group Footer, and your report should appear as below.

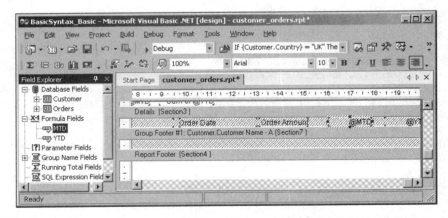

If you'd like to have a closer look, the complete report is available in the download file for this chapter.

Compile and run the report – but don't be alarmed if you get a nasty surprise!

Does your report look similar to the download? Probably not – there's one little trick that we forgot. Since the periods we used in this report are built from the current date and evaluated against the sample data (which is at least a couple of years old), the chances are that your MTD and YTD columns will be empty. Happily, you can set the system date in Crystal Reports by right-clicking on the report, selecting Report | Set Print Date, and entering a new date and time, as shown below.

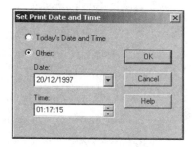

This allows you to change the internal date and time used by Crystal Reports to build the time periods, and some other date- and time-driven functionality. After setting the date, Crystal Reports will think that it's actually processing the report on that date, and behave accordingly. (This is especially handy if you need to do 'point in time' reports.)

In our case, if you set this date to 07/01/2001 or 20/12/1997 (either of these dates should be compatible with the sample data), your report should show both the MTD and YTD columns, with the totals for each customer.

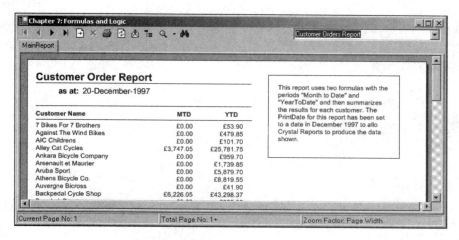

Print State and Document Properties

Crystal Reports has a number of special fields and properties that are generated by the system when a report is run. You will have already encountered some of these fields when adding page numbers, or summary information such as the report's title, author, etc.

Here is a list of these types of functions:

Function	Description
PreviousValue(*fieldname*)	The value of the previous field to appear
NextValue(*fieldname*)	The value of the next field to appear
IsNull(*fieldname*)	Tests whether a field is null
PreviousIsNull(*fieldname*)	Tests whether the previous field value is null
NextIsNull(*fieldname*)	Tests whether the next field value is null
PageNumber	Returns the current page number
TotalPageCount	Returns the total page count
PageNofM	Returns the current page number of the total page count
RecordNumber	Returns Crystal Reports internal reference of record number
GroupNumber	Returns Crystal Reports internal reference of group number
RecordSelection	Returns the current record selection formula for the report
GroupSelection	Returns the current group selection formula for the report
OnFirstRecord	Returns a True value when the first record is displayed
OnLastRecord	Returns a True value when the last record is displayed

Using these functions, you can quickly create formulas that can mark new records in a sorted list:

```
If Previous({Customer.CustomerName}) <> {Customer.CustomerName} Then _
    Formula = "New Customer Starts Here"
```

or you could print a text message at the end of your report:

```
If OnLastRecord = True Then _
    Formula = " ***** END OF REPORT ***** "
```

Control Structures

Crystal Reports supports a number of control structures that can control branching within a formula.

If...Then Statements

If...Then statements provide an easy method for controlling branching within your formula text. If...Then statements can work on the basis of a single condition, for instance:

```
If {Customer.Country} = "USA" Then Formula = "Local Customer"
```

In the customer sales report example that's included with this chapter (`customer_sales.rpt`), we can create a Formula Field that will assess if the value in the `Country` field is the USA. If it is, a message will be printed showing the customer as a "Local Customer". To do this, you merely open the Field Explorer, right-click on **Formula Fields | New**, and after giving the field a name (`local_customer_flag`), enter your formula into the editor.

You can also use an `Else` clause for when the condition is not met, for example:

```
If {Customer.Country} = "USA" Then Formula = "Local Customer" _
    Else "International"
```

Multi-line `If...Then...Else` statements can also be used, but keep in mind that once a condition is met, Crystal Reports will not process the rest of the formula text. For example, let's look at this early version of the formula field `sales_performance_flag` in `customer_sales.rpt`:

```
If {Customer.Last Year's Sales} > 30000 Then Formula = "Excellent job!" _
    Else If {Customer.Last Year's Sales} > 10000 Then Formula = "Fine job!" _
    Else If {Customer.Last Year's Sales} > 20000 Then Formula = "Great job!"
```

In this formula, if the value passed was 25,000, the formula would immediately stop on the second line (because the condition has been met), giving an incorrect result. In order to have a multi-line `If...Then...Else` formula work correctly, you need to put the conditions in the correct order, like so:

```
If {Customer.Last Year's Sales} > 30000 Then Formula = "Excellent job!" _
    Else If {Customer.Last Year's Sales} > 20000 Then Formula = "Great job!" _
    Else If {Customer.Last Year's Sales} > 10000 then Formula = "Fine job!"
```

In addition to multi-line use, you can also use compound `If...Then...Else` statements, nesting two or more statements in one formula, as shown below in the **compound_if_then** formula field from this report:

```
If {Customer.Country} = "USA" Then _
    If {Customer.Sales} > 30000 Then Formula = "Excellent job!" _
        Else If {Customer.Sales} > 20000 Then Formula = "Great job!" _
        Else If {Customer.Sales} > 10000 Then Formula = "Fine job!"
```

This would result in your report looking something like this:

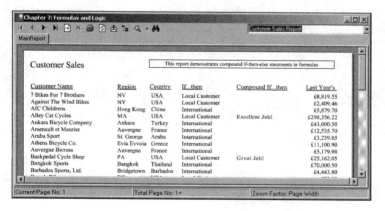

Select Statements

Another popular control structure is the `Select` statement, which can be used with `Case` to evaluate a particular condition. If that condition is `True`, control of the formula will go to the formula text for the met condition, as shown below:

```
Select Case {Customer.PriorityNumber}
  Case 1, 2, 3
    Formula = "high priority"
  Case 4
    Formula = "medium priority"
  Case Else
    Formula = "low priority"
```

Creating Formulas with Crystal Syntax

Over the past few releases, Crystal syntax and Basic syntax have moved closer together, through the development of similar functions and operators. In the next section, we'll have a look at some of the remaining differences.

We'll be using a project called `CrystalSyntax_basic` to look at this syntax. This project is available in the download code from **www.wrox.com**, or you could build it from scratch by following the instructions. If you decide to build it yourself, create a Windows Application now and call it `CrystalSyntax_basic`. Add the customer sales report (which should be in the download sample under the path `CrystalReports\Chapter07\customer_sales.rpt`) into the project by right-clicking on the project name in Visual Studio .NET and selecting **Add | Add Existing Item…** and then browsing to the report.

We're now in a position to drag and drop a **CrystalReportViewer** onto the Form, and also a **ReportDocument** component. When the dialog box opens to request which type of **ReportDocument** component you need, select **CrystalSyntax_basic.customer_sales**.

Insert the following code into the `Form_Load` event:

```
Private Sub Form1_Load(ByVal sender As System.Object, ByVal e As
    System.EventArgs) Handles MyBase.Load
  Dim myReport As New customer_sales()
  CrystalReportViewer1.ReportSource = myReport
  myReport.Load()
End Sub
```

Now compile and run it, to make sure all is well. It should look like this (we have set the **DisplayGroupTree** property in the **CrystalReportViewer** properties to `False` here, in the interests of visual clarity):

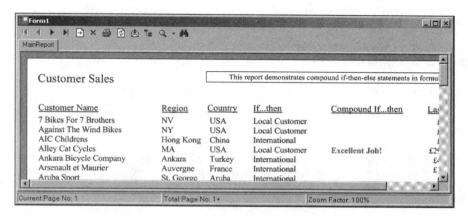

We are now ready to go and look at the syntax behind this report.

Differences from Basic Syntax

To start with, a Crystal syntax formula does not require the `Formula =` tag at the end to output the formula results. This is the statement from the Local_Customer_Flag formula field in the customer sales report. You can access this field by opening the report in Visual Studio .NET, selecting View | Other Windows | Document Outline from the main toolbar, and in the tree that appears selecting Formula Fields and right-clicking on Local_Customer_Flag, and then selecting Edit.

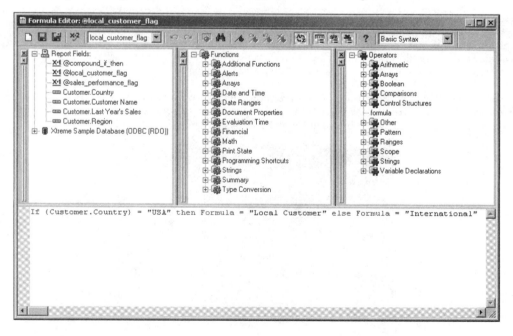

A Basic syntax statement is shown below:

```
If {Customer.Country} = "USA" Then Formula = "Local Customer" else Formula =
"International"
```

By default, a Crystal syntax formula will display the last value that is calculated within the formula, as shown below:

```
If {Customer.Country} = "USA" Then "Local Customer" else "International"
```

Also, since Crystal syntax was created before Basic syntax, there were a number of Crystal Reports functions that were actually reserved words within Visual Basic. These functions have been given alternative names, which means that a function in Crystal syntax and one in Basic syntax can now be named differently from each other.

A list of common functions that are different between the two syntaxes is available in Appendix C.

Creating Record Selection Formulas

Record selection is a key component of most reports, for it is here that the results are filtered to show only the information required. In Chapter 2, we had a first look at simple record selection, and at some of the operators that can be used to filter your report. Now that we're working with Crystal syntax, we can look at writing these formulas ourselves.

First, all record selection formulas *have* to be written in Crystal syntax – there is no option to use Basic syntax. This stems from the fact that Crystal Reports will take the record selection formula you create and write a SQL statement to retrieve the report results. Historically, Crystal syntax was the first type of syntax available, and most work has been done translating it to SQL. You may see Basic syntax supported in future releases, but that's up to Crystal Decisions!

To access or create record selection formulas, right-click on your report and select Report I Edit Selection Formula I Records. This should open up the following dialog box. Note that the drop-down box that enables you to switch between Crystal and Basic syntax is grayed out this time.

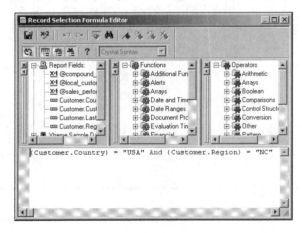

When working with record selection formulas, we use the same formula editor that you'd use to edit formulas that appear on your report, with one difference: a record selection formula will *never* have any type of output. The sole function of the record selection formula is to apply some condition against fields that appear in your report (where the condition is `True`, the record is returned), as shown in the examples below:

```
{Customer.Country} = "USA" And {Customer.Region} = "NC"
```

If you enter the above formula into the dialog box shown above (running a syntax check first of all by clicking on the X+2 icon), and then save and run the application, you should see the following output:

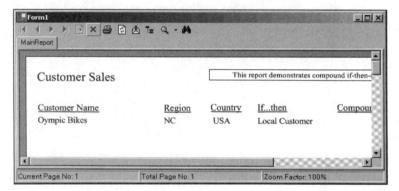

When working with a record selection formula, you have access to all of the fields, functions, and operators that are available within the formula language itself, including time periods, for instance:

```
{Orders.OrderDate} In MonthToDate
```

Best practice for record selection suggests that you only perform it on fields originating from your database. For example, imagine you have a formula in your report that translates the state or region names within the database to their 'long names' (so "CA" is shown as "California"). If you were going to create a record selection formula that used the state, you would definitely *not* want to use the 'long name' formula – if you did, the generated SQL statement would pull back every single record, evaluate the formula, and then use Crystal Reports' own inherent selection routines to filter the data.

On the other hand, if you were to create the record selection formula directly from the database fields, this in turn would be written to the SQL statement, and your report will run much more quickly.

Working with Conditional Formatting

Conditional formatting with Crystal Reports provides an effective method for highlighting data within the report. As you moved through the Report Designer, you may have noticed that a number of formatting options had the X+2 icon shown beside them. You can see one in the following dialog box, which is accessible by right-clicking on a textbox in the report, and selecting **Format**:

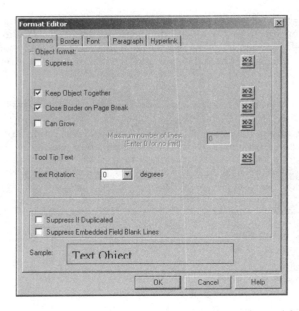

This indicates that these formatting properties can be used with conditional formatting: when some condition is True, the formatting property will be applied.

Understanding Conditional Formatting

There are two different kinds of conditional formatting available within Crystal Reports, based on the two different kinds of properties available for Crystal Reports elements. The first deals with Boolean properties, which include things like Suppress and Can Grow, and have an "on/off" state. The second deals with properties that can have multiple outcomes, like font or section colors. While the concepts behind using these two different types of properties are similar, the formulas behind them are different.

Conditional Formatting for Boolean Properties

With these properties, there is either a True or False status – if a field has the Suppress property checked, the property is True, and it will be suppressed. If not, the property is False, and the field is shown. When working with conditional formatting on these types of properties, all we need to do is specify a condition. If that condition is True, then the property will be set to True.

For the following walkthrough of conditional formatting, open the Customer Sales report (customer_sales.rpt) that's included with the sample files for this chapter.

In the case of Suppress, you can right-click on a field (in this case, the Last Year's Sales field (not the field in the report header, but the one in the report proper!), and select Format. On the Common property page, you will see the Suppress property checkbox. To start with, *don't* check the box – that would turn suppression on for every value. Instead, click the X+2 box that appears to the right of the property (shown opposite) to open the formula editor, and enter a conditional formatting formula.

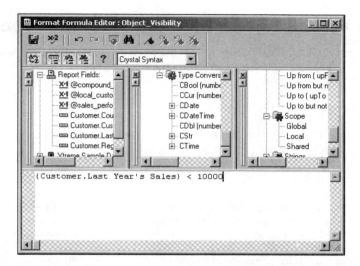

Since this is a Boolean-type property, all we need to do is enter a condition. When the condition is True, the formatting option will occur (in this case, the field will be suppressed). The formula would look like this:

```
{Customer.Last Year's Sales} < 10000
```

This would cause our report to show only the values that were greater than 10,000.

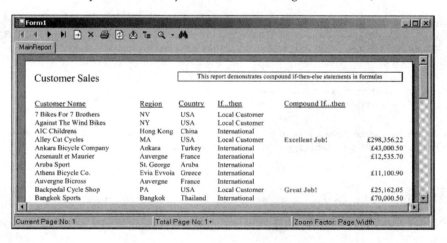

This conditional formatting formula was applied to an individual field, so only the field is suppressed – but you could apply it to an entire section. Be warned, though, that when you suppress a field or a section, it only suppresses the display of the field. It will still be included in any totals or formulas.

Conditional Formatting for Multiple-Outcome Properties

With properties that can have a multiple outcome, the conditional formatting formula needs to be a bit different. In our Boolean example above, only two things could happen: either the field was suppressed, or it wasn't. With multiple-outcome formulas dependent on the setting of a property, any number of things could happen. Using the same condition as above, if our value was over 10,000, we could have changed the field change color – but to which color?

When working with multiple-outcome properties, we have to use an If...Then statement to specify what will happen when the condition is True. For example:

```
If {Customer.Last Year's Sales} > 20000 Then Red
```

To apply this conditional formatting, right-click again on the **Last Year's Sales** field again, select **Format**, and then switch to the property tab for **Font** and click the **X+2** icon beside the font color. This will open the Formula Editor and allow you to enter your conditional formatting formula.

In the Formula Editor, all of the available values or constants for a particular property will appear in the functions list.

In addition to the constants (with a specific set for each attribute), you can also set the property to its CurrentFieldValue, or to its DefaultAttribute. For example, if you had a field in which the color property had already been set to **Green**, you could use this default in your formula:

```
If {Customer.Last Year's Sales} > 10000 Then Purple Else DefaultAttribute
```

With conditional formatting on multiple-outcome properties, you are not confined to a single If...Then statement. You can also used a compound If...Then, or an If...Then...Else statement, as shown below:

```
If {Customer.Last Year's Sales} > 100000 Then Blue _
  Else If {Customer.Last Year's Sales} > 50000 Then Orange _
  Else If {Customer.Last Year's Sales} > 20000 Then Red
```

Remember that the same rules apply to these formulas as to the formulas you create to display on your report. Once the condition has been met, Crystal Reports will stop evaluating the rest of the formula.

Summary

In this chapter, we've had a look at integrating formulas and logic into your report, and explored the topic of creating formulas to appear on your report, set record selection, and control conditional formatting. In the next chapter, we'll be looking at the Crystal Reports Engine, which is a selection of classes that can help give us much more power and control over our reports and their presentation.

Professional *Crystal Reports*
for *Visual Studio .NET*

Working with the Crystal Reports Engine

Earlier in the book, in the chapters about integrating reports for Windows and Web-based applications (Chapters 3 and 4), we looked at the different object models that were available and in turn, covered both of the object models for working with Windows and Web-based applications.

You may remember that there is actually a third object model that can be used, providing almost full control over the report itself and its contents. This object model, contained within the `CrystalDecisions.CrystalReports.Engine` namespace, is used in conjunction with the viewer object models and provides a powerful method to customize your report at run time.

In this chapter, we will be looking at the Crystal Reports engine, the functionality it provides, and some of the advanced integration techniques that you can use in your own application.

These will include:

- ❑ Crystal Reports Engine overview
- ❑ Printing and exporting
- ❑ Working with databases
- ❑ Formatting areas, sections, and fields
- ❑ Working with parameter fields
- ❑ Customizing formulas
- ❑ Working with other report components

At the end of this chapter, you will be able to identify when to use the Crystal Reports Engine namespace, know how to integrate it into your application, and understand how the features contained within can be used to customize reports within your application, using the properties, methods, and events associated with the engine.

Obtaining the Sample Files

All the example reports and code used in this chapter are available for download. The download file can be obtained from http://www.wrox.com.

You can use this solution to walk through the code examples in this chapter, or you can create your own solution by opening Visual Studio.NET and selecting File | New | Blank Solution. You can then use this solution to follow along with the instructions.

Understanding the CrystalDecisions.CrystalReports.Engine Namespace

If you have worked with Visual Basic and Crystal Reports before, you are probably familiar with the functionality within the Crystal Reports Engine. The Crystal Reports Engine provides a low-level interface into the report itself, and allows developers to control most aspects of the report programmatically.

Within Visual Studio .NET, the `CrystalDecisions.CrystalReports.Engine` namespace is used to expose this functionality. If you are integrating your reports in a simple view-only application, you may never need to delve into the Crystal Reports Engine, but for more complex integration and applications, you will find you'll need to use it almost every time.

Remember our earlier discussion in Chapters 3 and 4 about which namespace you should use for what function? One of the key points of that discussion was that you shouldn't mix the object models in your code. For example, if you do choose to use the `CrystalDecisions.CrystalReports.Engine` namespace, set all of your properties, methods, and events relating to the report using this namespace and use the `CrystalDecisions.Windows.Forms` namespace only for setting your report source, viewing the report and modifying viewer properties (such as toolbars and icons). Never the twain shall meet!

Customizing Reports Using the Report Engine

To get started, we will need to create a new project within our solution. To create a new project, select File | New | Project and in this instance, create a Windows Application and call the project `engine_basic` because, in the following sections, we are going to be looking at some basic Report Engine functionality.

We need a report object to work with. To add the sample reports to your project, select Project | Add Existing Item and select the folder where you unzipped the sample project. You will also need to change the file extension from VB Code Files to All files to see the report files we will be using in this chapter, including the first report, `CrystalReports\Chapter08\employee_listing.rpt`.

With a report to work with, we now need to reference the Report Engine so we can use it in our application. This reference may well add itself when you add the report to the project, but if not, or you are working with one of your custom reports, this will have to be added in Visual Studio .NET. To add a reference, select Project | Add Reference to open the dialog shown below:

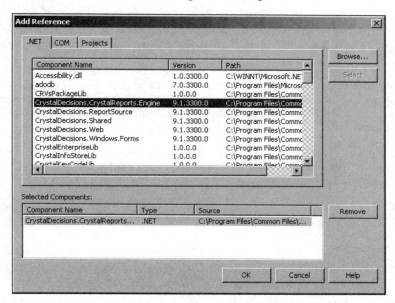

Highlight the CrystalDecisions.CrystalReports.Engine namespace and click the Select button and then the OK button to add the reference. The reference to the Crystal Report Engine should now appear in your project in the Solutions Explorer, under the References folder – we are now ready to go.

Getting Started

When working with the Crystal Reports Engine namespace, there is one class you will use most. The ReportDocument class is used to represent the report itself and contains all of the properties, methods, and events that allow you to define, load, export, and print your report.

So before we go any further, we need to start building our sample application form and then use the ReportDocument class to load a report to use during the course of our discussion about the Crystal Report Engine.

Building the Sample Application Form

We need to draw the Crystal Report Viewer on the bottom of our form – as we work through the different ways to use the Report Engine, we'll use the viewer on the form to view the resulting report.

We've also disabled the DisplayGroupTree property in the Properties window for now, to streamline presentation of the methods being used in this chapter. You can leave this enabled or disabled, as you like.

Loading a Report

Before we load the report, we need to have a report added it to our solution, which you did earlier when you added the employee_listing.rpt file.

To add the report to your form, switch to the **Design** view of the default form that was created with your project (Form1). In the toolbox on the left-hand side of the form designer, there is a tab marked **Components** and within that tab there should be a **ReportDocument** component that you can drag onto your form.

When you drag the **ReportDocument** component onto your form, it should open a second dialog and allow you to select a report document from a drop-down list – the employee listing report should appear here. Once you have selected a report, another section will appear underneath your form, showing the components you are using, and ReportDocument1 should be here.

With that out of the way, we are ready to declare and load our report for use with the Report Engine. Double-click your form to show the code view and locate the code for the Form_Load event – it is here that we are going to declare our report:

```
Private Sub Form1_Load(ByVal sender As System.Object, ByVal e As
    System.EventArgs) Handles MyBase.Load
  Dim myReport As New employee_listing()
  CrystalReportViewer1.ReportSource = myReport
  myReport.Load()
End Sub
```

That is all there is to it – once you have loaded a report, you have access to all of the properties, methods, and events associated with the ReportDocument object model. For example, if you wanted to extract the title of your report from the SummaryInfo (in the Report Designer, right-click and select **Report | Summary** Info to set this information) you could simply peek into the ReportDocument object model to grab the SummaryInfo collection (of which the ReportTitle is a member) by inserting this line of code at the end of the Form_Load event above:

```
MsgBox(myReport.SummaryInfo.ReportTitle.ToString())
```

There are actually five members of the SummaryInfo class:

Property	Description
KeywordsInReport	For returning or setting keywords
ReportAuthor	For returning or setting the report author
ReportComments	For returning or setting the report comments
ReportSubject	For returning or setting the report subject
ReportTitle	For returning or setting the report title

> Note: All of these properties can be viewed or set at run time, but remember, to actually write to the report file with these settings in place, you would need to use the **SaveAs** method, discussed a little later in this chapter.

Using the Initialization Event

Now in our example above, when we loaded the report, we had no way of knowing whether or not the report had been loaded. Luckily for us, there is an initialization event that is fired whenever a report is loaded.

We can use this initialization event to actually tell us when the report was loaded:

```
Private Sub report_InitReport(ByVal sender As Object, ByVal myEvent As
    System.EventArgs) Handles employee_listing1.InitReport
  MsgBox("Report loaded fine")
End Sub
```

This will save us time later when we try to troubleshoot our applications – if we know the report has been loaded safely, that is one less thing to check when problems occur.

Printing and Exporting

Within the Crystal Reports Engine, there are a number of different ways you can produce report output, even without the Crystal Report Viewer. This functionality provides an easy way for you to print directly from your application or print batches of reports without any user intervention.

We are going to start looking at this type of functionality with a simple print application, building on the sample application we are working with.

Printing Your Report

To print your report from your application, the `ReportDocument` class provides a simple `PrintToPrinter` method that can be used to print the report to the default printer. This method requires four parameters:

- ❑   Number of copies
- ❑   Collation flag (Boolean)
- ❑   Start Page
- ❑   End Page

So, adding to the form we were working with earlier, we could create a command button that would print your report to your default printer, as shown overleaf:

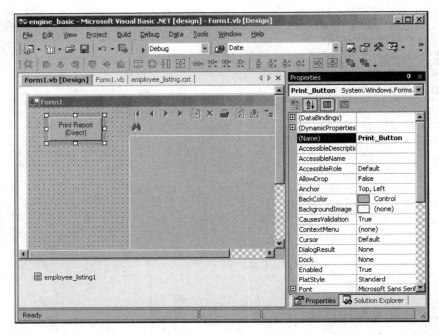

Call the button `Print_Button` and set the text as **Print Report (Direct)**. Now, double-click on the button to open the code behind it.

In this case, we are going to print one copy of pages 1 to 999 from our report to your default printer – if you double-click the command button you have added to the form, you can add the method call to the code view, and it would look like this:

```
Private Sub Print_Button_Click(ByVal sender As System.Object, ByVal e As
    System.EventArgs) Handles Print_Button.Click
    Dim myReport As New employee_listing()
    myReport.PrintToPrinter(1, True, 1, 999)
End Sub
```

Note: In this case, we used 999, assuming that that would be a good upper limit for the number of pages in your report.

If you need a little more control over the print process, there is also a `PrintOptions` class that comes in handy, allowing you to set the printer name to another printer (besides the default) and the number of copies, among other things. This class includes the following properties:

Property	Description
PageContentHeight	Returns the height of the pages content in twips.
PageContentWidth	Returns the width of the pages content in twips.

Property	Description
PageMargins	Returns or sets the page margins collection (including topMargin, bottomMargin, leftMargin, rightMargin).
PaperOrientation	Returns or sets the current printer paper orientation. Options are DefaultPaperOrientation (from the printer), Landscape, and Portrait.
PaperSize	Returns or sets the current paper size. Supports 42 different sizes, including PaperA4, PaperLegal, PaperLetter, etc.
PaperSource	Returns or sets the current paper source. Supports 13 different paper trays, including Auto (for the printer's automatic selection), Manual, Lower, Middle, Upper, etc.
PrinterDuplex	Returns or sets the current printer duplex option. Supports options for Default, Horizontal, Simplex, Vertical.
PrinterName	Returns or sets the printer name used by the report.

For a complete list of members in the PaperSize class, you can search the Visual Studio.NET Combined Help File for "PaperSize Enumeration" – for PaperSource, search for "PaperSource Enumeration".

> *Note: A lot of the printer-specific features (PaperSource, PrinterDuplex) will depend on your printer's capabilities and you may spend some time trying to figure out which members correspond with the different features on your printer. Usually, a printer will include a technical specification that will include this information but if you can't find it (or work it out) check the manufacturer's web site.*

So to put some of the options of the PrintOptions class together, and print a report duplex to a specific printer on A4 paper with a new set of margins, the code behind our command button would look something like this:

```
myReport.PrintOptions.PrinterName = ""
myReport.PrintOptions.PaperSize =
    CrystalDecisions.[Shared].PaperSize.PaperA4
myReport.PrintOptions.PrinterDuplex =
    CrystalDecisions.[Shared].PrinterDuplex.Default

Dim myMargins = myReport.PrintOptions.PageMargins
myMargins.topMargin = 10
myMargins.bottomMargin = 10
myMargins.leftMargin = 10
myMargins.rightMargin = 10

myReport.PrintOptions.ApplyPageMargins(myMargins)
myReport.PrintToPrinter(1, True, 1, 999)
```

If the PrinterName string is empty, the default printer is selected.

> Note: If you do change the page·margins, you will need to use the `PrintOptions`
> class's `ApplyPageMargins` method to apply your changes.

If you are migrating your code from Visual Basic 6.0, keep in mind that the Crystal Report Engine in Visual Studio .NET no longer supports the `SelectPrinter` method that was so handy in previous versions (it would pop up the standard **Select Printer** dialog for you). To use this functionality within Crystal Reports.NET, you will need to open the **Select Printer** dialog yourself and get the name of the printer and then set the `PrinterName` property of the `PrintOptions` class.

Exporting Your Report

In addition to printing your report without the viewer, you can also export your report without having to use the export button available on the Crystal Report viewer.

Within the `ReportDocument` methods, there is a method called `Export`, which can be used to export directly from your application. Unlike the `PrintReport` method, which would just print the report to the default printer, there are a number of properties that need to be set before you can actually call the `Export` method.

Here is a rundown of all of the properties and objects that are related to the `ExportOption` class:

Property	Description
DestinationOptions	Returns or sets the `DestinationOptions` object, including `DiskFileDestinationOptions`, `ExchangeFolderDestinationOptions`, and `MicrosoftMailDestinationOptions`
ExportDestinationType	Returns or sets the export destination type
ExportFormatType	Returns or sets the export format type
FormatOptions	Returns or sets the `FormatOptions` object, including `ExcelFormatOptions`, `HTMLFormatOptions`, and `PdfRtfWordFormatOptions`

So in another example, we could add another button to our form to export the report, as shown:

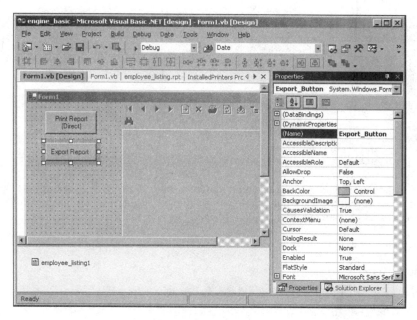

Name the button `Export_Button` and change the **Text** property to **Export Report**.

The code behind the button sets all of the properties and collections of information required. It then uses the `ExportReport` method to export our report. The first thing we need to do in our code is actually set up some variables to hold the different property collections that we will be setting, including properties for the `ExportOptions`, `DiskFileDestinationOptions`, and `FormatTypeOptions`.

```
Private Sub Export_Button_Click(ByVal sender As System.Object, ByVal e As
    System.EventArgs) Handles Export_Button.Click
    Dim myReport As New employee_listing()
    myReport.Load()

    Dim myExportOptions As New CrystalDecisions.Shared.ExportOptions()
    Dim myDiskFileDestinationOptions As New
        CrystalDecisions.Shared.DiskFileDestinationOptions()
    Dim myFormatTypeOptions As New
        CrystalDecisions.Shared.PdfRtfWordFormatOptions()
```

With some variables created, we now need to select where our exported file is going to be saved and what format it is going to be available in:

```
    myDiskFileDestinationOptions.DiskFileName =
        "C:\CrystalReports\Chapter08\test.pdf"
    myExportOptions = myReport.ExportOptions

    With myExportOptions
      .ExportDestinationType =
          CrystalDecisions.Shared.ExportDestinationType.DiskFile
```

```
    .ExportFormatType =
        CrystalDecisions.Shared.ExportFormatType.PortableDocFormat
    .DestinationOptions = myDiskFileDestinationOptions
    .FormatOptions = myFormatTypeOptions
End With
```

Finally, we call the `Export` method to actually export our report:

```
myReport.Export()
MsgBox("Your report has been exported in PDF format and saved to
    C:\CrystalReports\Chapter08\test.pdf")
```

When faced with a number of different property collection for destinations, format types and such, it can get a bit messy trying to figure out which combination of properties you need (for example, to export a report to an Exchange folder, in RTF format, but only the first two pages).

There are actually six export formats available for Crystal Reports.NET:

- ❏ Adobe Acrobat (`.pdf`)
- ❏ Crystal Reports within Visual Studio .NET, Crystal Reports 9.0 (`.rpt`)
- ❏ HTML 3.2 and 4.0 (`.html`)
- ❏ Microsoft Excel (`.xls`)
- ❏ Microsoft Rich Text (`.rtf`)
- ❏ Microsoft Word (`.doc`)

and two destinations for the exported report:

- ❏ Disk file
- ❏ Microsoft Exchange public folders

> For more information on the relationship between the objects involved in exporting, as well as the classes and members associated with each of the export formats and destinations, search the Visual Studio.NET Combined Help Collection using the keywords **CRYSTAL REPORT EXPORT**.

Some of the classes and members that are used with the Crystal Reports Engine are actually part of a `CrystalDecisions.Shared` namespace, which is shared between the Windows Forms Viewer, Web Forms Viewer, and the Crystal Reports Engine to reduce duplication in these namespaces.

Working with Databases

The strength of Crystal Reports.NET is its ability to extract information from a database (or other data source) and present the information in a report that users can view or print, so it stands to reason that most of your reports will be based on some database or data source within your application.

The Crystal Reports Engine provides a set of tools for working with databases, giving us the flexibility to change the database login information, location, and other features at run time, through the properties and methods associated with the Database object.

There are two classes associated with Database. They are Tables and Links. The Tables class contains all of the tables that are used in your report and the Links class contains all of the links between these tables as created within the report. Using these two classes, you can set the login information for your database, retrieve or change the location of tables, or change the table linking, among other functions.

We will start looking at these classes with one of the most common developer tasks – specifying the database connection information for your report. If you have established database security, you will want to pass the appropriate user name and password for the user who is viewing the report, and the following section will guide you through how this is done.

Logging on to a Database

When creating a report using Crystal Reports.NET, you can include data from multiple data sources in your report. While this feature makes for information-rich reports and can eliminate the need for multiple reports, it does pose a problem when customizing the report at run time.

It would be impossible to set one set of database credentials for all of the data sources in a report, so the Report Engine object model caters for these multiple data sources by allowing you to set the connection information for individual tables that appear in your report through the Tables class. This class has the following members:

Property	Description
Count	Returns the number of Table objects in the collection
Item	Returns the Table object at the specified index or with the specified name

Each Table object in the Tables collection has the following properties:

Property	Description
Fields	Returns the DatabaseFieldDefinitions collection (which we'll look at a little later in this chapter)
Location	Returns or sets the location of the database table
LogOnInfo	Returns the TableLogOnInfo object
Name	Returns the alias name for the database table used in the report

Now, at this point, you are probably wondering how the TableLogOnInfo actually gets set – there is a method associated with this class, ApplyLogOnInfo, that is used to apply any changes to the database login information for a table.

For collecting and setting the properties relating to TableLogonInfo and connection information, the CrystalDecisions.Shared namespace has a ConnectionInfo class that has the following properties:

Property	Description
DatabaseName	Returns or sets the name of the database
Password	Returns or sets the password for logging on to the data source
ServerName	Returns or sets the name of the server or ODBC data source where the database is located
UserID	Returns or sets a user name for logging on to the data source

We looked briefly at these properties and methods in Chapter 3, but we didn't tackle looping through the database. We'll look at that now.

Drag another button onto your Form, and call it Database_Button. Change the Text property to Northwind Report. We'll create a new Form with this button, so right-click on the project name, select Add | Add New Item.... and then out of the dialog box that pops up, select Windows Form. The default name will be Form2.vb, which is as good as any.

Double-click on our new button, and insert the following code:

```
Private Sub Database_Button_Click(ByVal sender As System.Object, ByVal e As
    System.EventArgs) Handles Database_Button.Click
  Dim Form2 As New Form2()
  Form2.Show()
End Sub
```

Now, drag a CrystalReportViewer onto Form2 in the Design mode, and right-click on the project to Add | Add Existing Item..., Browse to C:\CrystalReports\Chapter08\worldsales_northwind.rpt (this location will vary depending on where you have downloaded the sample code to) and add this report to the project.

Next, drag a ReportDocument component onto the Form and when the dialog box opens, select engine_basic.worldsales_northwind.

The next step is to add some additional code to set our ConnectionInfo class.

```
Private Sub Form1_Load(ByVal sender As System.Object, ByVal e As
    System.EventArgs) Handles MyBase.Load
  Dim myReport As New worldsales_northwind()
  CrystalReportViewer1.ReportSource = myReport
  myReport.Load()
  Dim myDBConnectionInfo As New CrystalDecisions.Shared.ConnectionInfo()

  With myDBConnectionInfo
    .ServerName = "localhost"
    .DatabaseName = "Northwind"
    .UserID = "sa"
    .Password = ""
  End With
```

Note: If you are using a secured Microsoft Access, Paradox, or other PC-type database, the same method can be used, except the `.ServerName` *and* `.DatabaseName` *are left blank.*

Then we can apply this `ConnectionInfo` by looping through all of the tables that appear in our report:

```
Dim myTableLogOnInfo As New CrystalDecisions.Shared.TableLogOnInfo()

Dim myDatabase = myReport.Database
Dim myTables = myDatabase.Tables
Dim myTable As CrystalDecisions.CrystalReports.Engine.Table

For Each myTable In myTables
  myTableLogOnInfo = myTable.LogOnInfo
  myTableLogOnInfo.ConnectionInfo = myDBConnectionInfo
  myTable.ApplyLogOnInfo(myTableLogOnInfo)
Next
End Sub
```

In this instance, we are looping through the tables using the table object – you can also loop through the tables through the item and the table name or index.

For instance:

```
myReport.Database.Tables.Item(i).ApplyLogOnInfo())
```

But it's up to you.

Setting a Table Location

Another handy trick that the Report Engine provides is the ability to set the location for tables that appear in our report. (This is the equivalent of going into the Report Designer, right-clicking, and selecting **Database I Set Location**.)

This can be useful for occasions when you have to put historical data into another table or want to separate out data in different tables for different business units, but the structure of the "source" and "target" table have to be the same, or you will get errors when the report is run.

When working with the location of a table, the `Location` property will both return and set where the table resides.

The example below demonstrates how the location of a table in a report could be changed to point to a "current" employee table.

We will build this example now. In your project, right-click on the project name and select **Add I Add New Item...** and choose **Windows Form**. The default name should be **Form3.vb**. Click OK. Drag a button onto the Design view of `Form1.vb` and call the button `Location_Button` and change the **Text** property to **Set Database Location**. Double-click on this button and insert the following code:

```
Private Sub Location_Button_Click(ByVal sender As System.Object, ByVal e As
    System.EventArgs) Handles Location_Button.Click
  Dim Form3 As New Form3()
  Form3.Show()
End Sub
```

We shall use `employee_listing.rpt` to demonstrate the point. This report is already attached to the project, so we do not need to add it. However, what we do need to do is to go into our Xtreme database and create a copy of the `Employee` table in Access. This copy should be named `Employee_Current`. Add a few more employee rows onto the end of the table, just so that the information is slightly different, and save it.

> There are several versions of Xtreme supplied from various sources, including the ones included with both Crystal Enterprise and Microsoft Visual Studio .NET. Make sure that the version you alter and the data source the report is referencing are the same!

The next thing to do is prepare `Form3.vb`. In the Design view of this Form, drag on a **CrystalReportViewer** and a **ReportDocument** component. When the dialog box for the `ReportDocument` comes up, select `engine_basic.employee_listing`.

All that remains is to insert the following code:

```
Private Sub Form3_Load(ByVal sender As System.Object, ByVal e As
    System.EventArgs) Handles MyBase.Load
  MsgBox("Note: To make this sample work, open the Xtreme sample database in
    Access and copy the Employee table to Employee_Current and change some
    values. You should see these changes when you view the report,
    indicating the set location worked correctly")

  Dim myReport As New employee_listing()
  CrystalReportViewer1.ReportSource = myReport
  myReport.Load()

  Dim myDatabase = myReport.Database

  Dim myConnectionInfo As New CrystalDecisions.Shared.ConnectionInfo()
  Dim myTableLogonInfo As New CrystalDecisions.Shared.TableLogOnInfo()

  Dim myTables = myDatabase.Tables
  Dim myTable As CrystalDecisions.CrystalReports.Engine.Table

  For Each myTable In myTables

    MsgBox("Before: " & myTable.Location.ToString())

    If myTable.Location.ToString() = "Employee" Then
      myTable.Location = "Employee_Current"
    End If
```

```
    myTable.ApplyLogOnInfo(myTableLogonInfo)

    MsgBox("After: " & myTable.Location.ToString())

  Next

  CrystalReportViewer1.ReportSource = myReport
  CrystalReportViewer1.Refresh()
End Sub
```

We're good to go. Run the application and click on the **Set Database Location** button. Various message boxes should appear, advising you on the changes in the location, as the tables cycle through the `For...` loop. Eventually the report will load, showing the changes you have made:

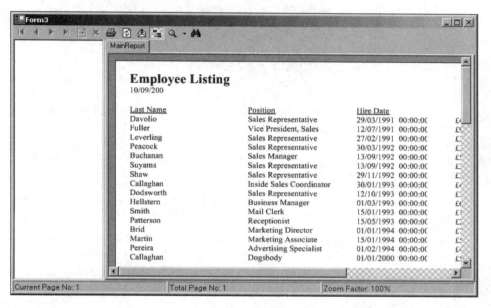

You could also use this feature to point to a table that resides on a completely different database platform (from SQL Server to Oracle for example), as long as the table definitions are compatible.

> *Note:If you want to ensure that your report has the most recent instance of the data you are reporting from, prior to your export you can use the* `Refresh` *method to refresh your report against the database.*

Setting the Join Type

For reports that are based on more than one table, Crystal Reports.NET has a visual linking tool that allows you to specify the links or joins between these tables:

247

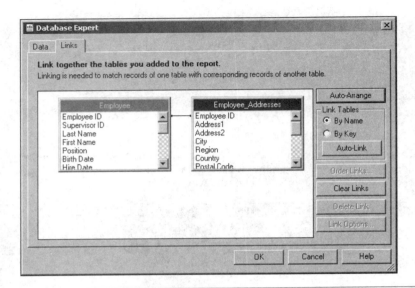

> Note: To see this dialog, open the Report Designer, right-click on your report and select **Database | Visual Linking Expert....**

When working with these tables and links at run time, it can be confusing when working with all of the different elements involved, so we'll break it down.

Similarly with `Tables`, there is a `TableLink` object that is contained in a `TableLinks` collection, which has one `TableLink` object for every link that appears in your report.

Keep in mind that tables can have multiple links between them – for example, you may have only two tables, but there may be three key fields that are linked together between those two tables.

A `TableLink` has the following properties:

Property	Description
DestinationFields	Returns a reference to table link destination `DatabaseFieldDefinitions` collection
DestinationTable	Returns a reference to the table link destination `Table` object
JoinType	Returns a summary of the linking used by the table
SourceFields	Returns a reference to table link source
SourceTable *Table*	Returns a reference to the table link source `Table` object

So to determine the tables and database fields used in linking our tables together, we can loop through all of the links used in our report. We'll look at how we do this now.

Drag another button onto Form1 in the Design view, and name it Links_Button. Change the Text property to Show Links. Double-click on the button and add the following code:

```
Private Sub Links_Button_Click(ByVal sender As System.Object, ByVal e As
    System.EventArgs) Handles Links_Button.Click
  Dim myReport As New employee_listing()
  myReport.Load()

  Dim myDatabase = myReport.Database
  Dim myTables = myDatabase.Tables
  Dim myTable As CrystalDecisions.CrystalReports.Engine.Table

  Dim myLinks = myDatabase.Links
  Dim myLink As CrystalDecisions.CrystalReports.Engine.TableLink

  For Each myLink In myLinks

    MsgBox("Destination Table: " & myLink.DestinationTable.Name.ToString &
        "." & myLink.DestinationFields.Item(1).Name.ToString())
    MsgBox("Source Table: " & myLink.SourceTable.Name.ToString & "." &
        myLink.SourceFields.Item(1).Name.ToString)
    MsgBox("Join Type: " & myLink.JoinType.ToString)

  Next
```

Compile and run. The message boxes should now appear, one after the other, bearing the name of the source and target links and also the join type.

Keep in mind that these properties are read-only – you will not be able to set the table linking using these properties. If you do want to change the database linking that is used, you may want to consider pushing the data into the report using a dataset.

Pushing Data into a Report

Earlier in our discussion of the different ways you could deploy a report in Chapter 1, we looked at "Push" and "Pull" type reports. Up until this point, we have been working exclusively with "Pull" reports, where we pull the information from the database and display it in our report.

For "Push" reports, you actually create the report the same way, except that when the report is run, you can "Push" a dataset to the report, as we did in Chapter 6. This works in a similar manner to actually setting the data source for an individual table, but instead of setting the property equal to another table, we are going to set it equal to another data source – in the example below, we are using our sample report that we have been working with, but instead of data from the Xtreme sample database, we are actually connecting to the Northwind database on SQL Server to get the data we need.

```
Dim query = "select * from Customer"

Dim MyOleConn As New System.Data.OleDb.OleDbConnection(conn)
Dim MyOleAdapter As New System.Data.OleDb.OleDbDataAdapter()
Dim MyDataSet As Data.DataSet

MyOleAdapter.SelectCommand = New System.Data.OleDb.OleDbCommand(query, MyOleConn)
MyOleAdapter.Fill(MyDataSet, "Customer")

myReport.Database.Tables.Item("Customer").SetDataSource(MyDataSet)
```

So instead of actually changing the links and tables that are used within the report, we are actually just pushing another set of data into those structures. As you work with this feature, you are going to pick up some tricks along the way and one of the most handy tricks is to use a SQL command as the basis of your report – this makes pushing data into the report easier, as a report based on SQL command treats the resulting data as if it were one big table.

From your application, you can then get a dataset that matches the fields in your SQL command and then push the data into that one table (instead of having to loop through multiple tables).

Working with Report Options

Another basic task when working with data sources and Crystal Reports is the setting of some generic database options for your report, which are set using the ReportOptions class that relates to the report you are working with – some of these options correspond to the options available in the report designer when you select Designer | Default Settings, but a few (like EnableSaveDataWithReport) are not available in the Report Designer, only through the object model.

Property	Description
EnableSaveDataWithReport	Returns or sets the Boolean option to automatically save database data with a report
EnableSavePreviewPicture	Returns or sets the Boolean option to save a thumbnail picture of a report
EnableSaveSummariesWithReport	Returns or sets the Boolean option to save the data summaries you create with the report
EnableUseDummyData	Returns or sets the Boolean option to use dummy data when viewing the report at design time. Dummy data is used when there is no data saved with the report.

A common use of these types of properties is for saving a report with data to send to other users. These properties can be used in conjunction with the Refresh and SaveAs methods to save a report with data that can be distributed to other users.

To test this, just alter the code in Print_Button code in Form1 as follows:

```
End With
myReport.Export()
```

```
myReport.ReportOptions.EnableSaveDataWithReport = True
myReport.Refresh()
myReport.SaveAs("c:\CrystalReports\Chapter08\saved.rpt",
    CrystalDecisions.[Shared].ReportFileFormat.VSNetFileFormat)

MsgBox("Your report has been exported in PDF format and saved to
    C:\CrystalReports\Chapter08\test.pdf and your original report has been
    saved to C:\CrystalReports\Chapter08\saved.rpt")
```

End Sub

Even if the user doesn't have Crystal Reports or Crystal Reports.NET, a simple viewer application created with Visual Studio.NET is all you need to view the report in its native format (or if you export to PDF, the Acrobat viewer) – the code for a sample viewer is included in the code samples for this chapter.

Setting Report Record Selection

When working with Crystal Reports, you will probably want to use record selection to filter the records that are returned. This record selection formula translates to the WHERE clause in the SQL statement that is generated by Crystal Reports.

You can see the record selection formula for a report by right-clicking on your report and selecting **Report | Edit Selection Formula | Records**. This will open the formula editor and allow you to edit your record selection formula.

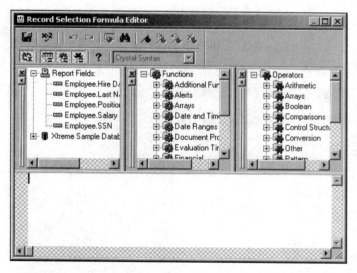

Note: The record selection formula within Crystal Reports is written using Crystal Syntax, so you may want to review the section on Crystal Syntax in the previous chapter.

You can retrieve the report's record selection and set it using the same property, as we saw in the examples in Chapter 3:

```
myReport.RecordSelectionFormula = "{Employee_Addresses.Country} = 'USA'"
```

Whenever the report is run, this record selection formula will be applied and the report filtered using the formula specified.

> *Note: You may look through the object model trying to find where to set the SQL statement that Crystal generates. At this point, your only two options for working with the SQL are to set the record selection (using the method just discussed) which will set the WHERE clause, or creating your own dataset using your own SQL statement and then "pushing" the data into the report.*

Working with Areas and Sections

Another often-used class is the ReportDefinition class, which is used to retrieve all of the areas, sections, and report objects shown in your report. An **Area** within the context of a Crystal Report corresponds to the types of sections we talked about earlier in the book in Chapter 2. There seven different types of areas, including:

- ❑ Detail
- ❑ GroupFooter
- ❑ GroupHeader
- ❑ PageFooter
- ❑ PageHeader
- ❑ ReportFooter
- ❑ ReportHeader

You may remember from Chapter 2 that all of these different types of areas can also have multiple sections within them (Details A, Details B, etc.), as shown below:

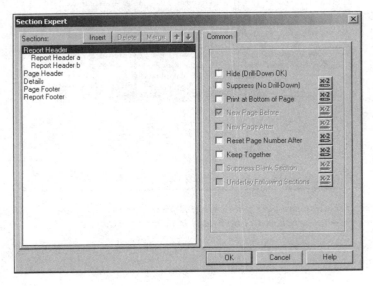

All of the areas within your report are held within the `Areas` collection of the `ReportDefinition`, which can be accessed through the name of the area or by the number. For example, if you wanted to work with the report header area, you could access it using:

```
myReport.ReportDefinition.Areas("ReportHeader")
```

likewise, you could access it using its item number as well:

```
myReport.ReportDefinition.Areas(1)
```

So, to start looking at how we can control these areas and sections at run time, we will take a look at areas first.

Formatting Areas

To get a feel for some of the formatting options that are available for sections, open the `employee_listing` report in the Report Designer, right-click on a section heading and select **Format Section...**:

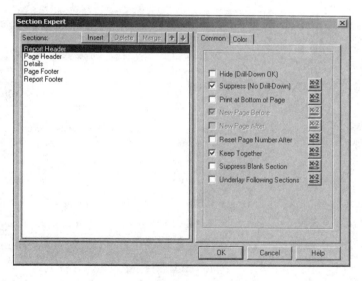

Most of the formatting options shown in this dialog can be directly read or set using the properties associated with the `AreaFormat` class, including:

Property	Description
EnableHideForDrillDown	Returns or sets hide for drill down option
EnableKeepTogether	Returns or sets the keep area together option
EnableNewPageAfter	Returns or sets the new page after option

Table continued on following page

Property	Description
EnableNewPageBefore	Returns or sets the new page before option
EnablePrintAtBottomOfPage	Returns or sets the print at bottom of page option
EnableResetPageNumberAfter	Returns or sets the reset page number after option
EnableSuppress	Returns or sets the area visibility

So to format our report so that we are suppressing the page header, the code would look something like this:

```
myReport.ReportDefinition.Areas.Item(1).AreaFormat.EnableSuppress = True
```

Keep in mind that any properties we set for an area also apply for all of the sections within that area (for example, any formatting applied to the "Report Header" would also apply to "Report Header A", "Report Header B", etc.)

Formatting Sections

For sections within an area, we also have a number of properties within a SectionFormat class that can control an individual section's appearance, including:

Property	Description
BackGroundColor	Returns or sets the background color of the object using System.Drawing.Color
EnableKeepTogether	Returns or sets the option that indicates whether to keep the entire section on the same page if it is split into two pages
EnableNewPageAfter	Returns or sets the new page after options
EnableNewPageBefore	Returns or sets the new page before option
EnablePrintAtBottomOfPage	Returns or sets the print at bottom of page option
EnableResetPageNumberAfter	Returns or sets the reset page number after option
EnableSuppress	Returns or sets the area visibility
EnableSuppressIfBlank	Returns or sets the option that indicates whether to suppress the current section if it is blank
EnableUnderlaySection	Returns or sets the underlay following section option

All of these properties work just like their counterparts within the Area class. The only one that is not Boolean is the BackGroundColor property, which is set using the System.Drawing.Color palette. If you haven't used this palette before, you may want to review the constants for the different colors available by searching the combined help on "System.Drawing.Color" and looking through its members.

So to illustrate the use of these properties, we could change the color of our page header and also suppress the page footer for our report. To accomplish this, pull another button onto your form (the final one!) and name it Format_Button. Change the Text property to Format Header Color. In the code behind this button, insert the following:

```
Private Sub Format_Button_Click(ByVal sender As System.Object, ByVal e As
    System.EventArgs) Handles Format_Button.Click
  Dim myReport As New worldsales_northwind()
  myReport.Load()

  myReport.ReportDefinition.Sections.Item(1).SectionFormat.BackgroundColor =
      System.Drawing.Color.AliceBlue
  CrystalReportViewer1.ReportSource = myReport

End Sub
```

Compile and run, and the result should resemble the screenshot below:

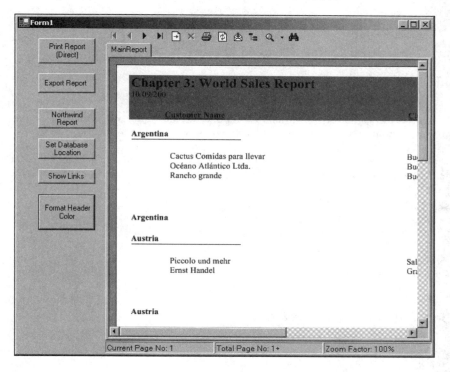

Note: If you are unsure of what number a particular section is, open the Report Designer and the section numbers will appear on the horizontal divider that marks the top of the section.

Working with Report Objects

Within the sections of your report, there are a number of report objects – you are probably already familiar with these objects, as they are the fields, graphs, and cross-tab objects, (among others) that appear on your report.

These are:

- ❑ BlobFieldObject
- ❑ BoxObject
- ❑ ChartObject
- ❑ CrossTabObject
- ❑ FieldObject
- ❑ LineObject
- ❑ MapObject
- ❑ OlapGridObject
- ❑ PictureObject
- ❑ SubreportObject
- ❑ TextObject

Each of the particular object types within your report has its own unique formatting properties, and may also share common formatting options with other types of objects as well.

To determine what type of object you are working with (and subsequently understand what options are available for each type), you can use the Kind property of the ReportObject to determine the ObjectType:

```
If section.ReportObjects(1).Kind = ReportObjectKind.FieldObject Then
        MsgBox("The first object is a Field Object")
    End If
```

To get started with looking at ReportObjects, we are going to look at the most common type, FieldObjects.

Formatting Common Field Objects

The main content on a Crystal Report is usually a number of fields that have been inserted and shown on your report. These could be database fields, formula fields, or parameter fields and are used to display the data returned by the report.

When working with these fields at run time, there are two different areas in which we can control the field – the content of the field and the format of the field. As most fields share some of the same formatting options, we will look at the formatting first and then break down by field type to see how we can change the content of these fields.

To start with, fields are contained within the `ReportDefinition` object and can be referenced by either the field name or by an item number:

```
myReport.ReportDefinition.ReportObjects.Item("Field1")
```

or:

```
myReport.ReportDefinition.ReportObjects.Item(1)
```

You may be tempted to refer to these fields by their name within Crystal Reports (`ReportTitle`) but keep in mind that you can add a field to your report multiple times, so in Crystal Reports.NET whenever you add a field to your report, a unique number and name are assigned to that field.

You can see the name of the field by looking at its properties within the Crystal Report Designer, as shown below:

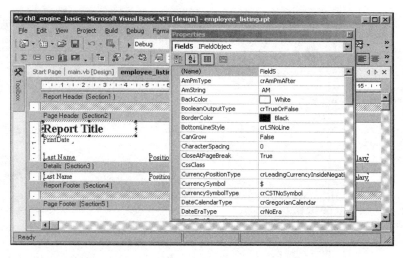

If your development follows a set naming convention, you also can change the name of the field to something other than the default Field1, Field2, etc. Keep in mind that there is no way to change the default naming convention, so you may find changing all of the names to be a bit tedious.

To reference the formatting options for a `FieldObject`, we need to access common field properties by referencing the `FieldObject` class, which has the following basic members:

Property	Description
Border	Returns the `Border` object
Color	Returns or sets the color of the object
DataSource	Returns the `FieldDefinition` object, which can be used to return and set format information specific to the kind of field

Table continued on following page

Property	Description
FieldFormat	Returns the `FieldFormat` object, which can be used to get and set format information specific to the type of field
Font	Returns the `Font` object (Note: Use the `ApplyFont` method to apply the changes)
Height	Returns or sets the object height
Left	Returns or sets the object upper left position
Name (inherited from ReportObject)	Returns the object name
ObjectFormat	Returns the `ObjectFormat` object that contains all of the formatting attributes of the object
Top	Returns or sets the object upper top position
Width	Returns or sets the object width

So we can set some of the common formatting properties (such as font and color) directly, as shown in the code example here (it's not included in the sample application, but you should play around with these properties to see what they can do):

```
If section.ReportObjects("field1").Kind = ReportObjectKind.FieldObject Then
    fieldObject = section.ReportObjects("field1")
    fieldObject.Color = Color.Blue
End If
```

There are specific properties that apply to the `FieldFormat` depending on what type of field you are working with. When you retrieve the `FieldFormat`, you will be able to set options that are specific to that field – there are five format types (in addition to a "common" type):

Property	Description
BooleanFormat *BooleanFieldFormat*	Gets the `BooleanFieldFormat` object
DateFormat *DateFieldFormat*	Gets the `DateFieldFormat` object
DateTimeFormat *DateTimeFieldFormat*	Gets the `DateTimeFieldFormat` object
NumericFormat *NumericFieldFormat*	Gets the `NumericFieldFormat` object
TimeFormat *TimeFieldFormat*	Gets the `TimeFieldFormat` object

In the following sections we are going to look at how to format the different types of fields using their `FieldFormat`.

Formatting Boolean Fields

With Boolean fields, and the `BooleanFieldFormat` formatting class, there is only one property, `OutputType`, which can be set to the following values:

Value	Description
OneOrZero	Boolean value to be displayed as a 1 or 0; 1 = True, 0 = False
TOrF	Boolean value to be displayed as a T or F; T = True, F = False
TrueOrFalse	Boolean value to be displayed as True or False
YesOrNo	Boolean value to be displayed as Yes or No
YOrN	Boolean value to be displayed as a Y or N; Y = True, N = False

So to change a Boolean field that appears on your report from displaying a binary representation to the text `True/False`, we could set this property to:

```
fieldObject.FieldFormat.BooleanFormat.OutputType = BooleanOutputType.TrueOrFalse
```

If you do need to see other values (such as **On** or **Off**, or **Active** or **Inactive**) you will probably want to create a formula in your report that translates these values for you:

```
If {Customer.Active} = True then "Active" else "Inactive")
```

Formatting Date Fields

Date fields within Crystal Reports have their own unique set of formatting properties that can be viewed in the Report Designer by right-clicking a date field and selecting **Format**. You can format date fields by example (picking a date format that looks similar to what you want) or you can customize most aspects of the date field using the dialog shown here:

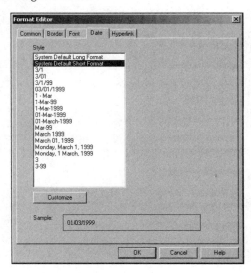

To bring this some of the same functionality at run time, the formatting of a date field has been broken up into multiple classes, all members of the `DateFieldFormat` class:

Property	Description
DayFormat	Returns or sets the day format
MonthFormat	Returns or sets the month format
YearFormat	Returns or sets the year format

All of the properties in these classes can be set separately, so you don't need to set the month format, for example, if you only want to change how the years are displayed. To start building up a format for a date field within our report, we are going look at the day format first. For the `DayFormat` property, we have three options:

- `LeadingZeroNumericDay` – A single digit day will be printed with a leading zero (for example, 07)
- `NoDay` – A day is not printed
- `NumericDay` – A day is printed in numeric format with no leading zero

For the `MonthFormat`, we have five options:

- `LeadingZeroNumericMonth` – The month is printed as a number with a leading 0, for single digit months
- `LongMonth` – The month is printed as text
- `NoMonth` – The month is not printed
- `NumericMonth` – The month is printed as a number with no leading 0
- `ShortMonth` – The month is printed as text in abbreviated format

For the `YearFormat`, another three:

- `LongYear` – The year is printed in long format with four digits
- `NoYear` – The year is not displayed
- `ShortYear` – The year is printed in short format with two digits

So, to put it all together, here are some examples of how these can produce some commonly requested date formats. To display the date with the days and months with a leading zero, and the full 4-digit year, the code would look like this (again, the next two code snippets are for example only and not included in a sample application of their own, but it is recommended that you experiment with these properties):

```
With fieldObject.FieldFormat.DateFormat

    .DayFormat = DayFormat.LeadingZeroNumericDay
    .MonthFormat = MonthFormat.LeadingZeroNumericMonth
    .YearFormat = YearFormat.LongYear

End With
```

The resulting date field would be displayed as "01/01/2003". For displaying only the month and year, we could change the code to read:

```
With fieldObject.FieldFormat.DateFormat

    .DayFormat = DayFormat.NoDay
    .MonthFormat = MonthFormat.LeadingZeroNumericMonth
    .YearFormat = YearFormat.LongYear

End With
```

This in turn would display the date as "01/2003". At this point, you have got to be asking yourself – how do I change the separator character? Or, if you have looked at the formatting properties associated with the field in the Report Designer, you might be wondering how you would set some of the other formatting features.

Unfortunately, the object model does not extend to cover all of the formatting features available for every type of field. If you want to change the format of a particular field and don't see the property listed, you can always create a formula based on the formula field to do the formatting work for you instead.

Formatting Time Fields

For formatting the time fields, the same concept applies, except there is only one class, TimeFieldFormat, which has the following properties:

Property	Description
AMPMFormat	Returns or sets the AM/PM type (either AMPMAfter or AMPMBefore) for 12:00am or am12:00
AMString	Returns or sets the AM string
HourFormat	Returns or sets the hour type (NoHour, NumericHour, NumericHourNoLeadingZero)
HourMinuteSeparator	Returns or sets the hour-minute separator
MinuteFormat	Returns or sets the minute type (NoMinute, NumericMinute, NumericMinuteNoLeadingZero)
MinuteSecondSeparator	Returns or sets minute-second separator
PMString	Returns or sets the PM string
SecondFormat	Returns or sets the seconds type (NumericNoSecond, NumericSecond, NumericSecondNoLeadingZero)
TimeBase	Returns or sets the time base (On12Hour, On24Hour)

So again, by combining all of these formatting properties, you can set the appearance for any time fields that appear in your report. For example, if you wanted to display the time in 24-hour notation, you could simply set the TimeBase property, as shown here:

```
fieldObject.FieldFormat.TimeFormat.TimeBase = TimeBase.On24Hour
```

Or to display any times that would normally be shown as "PM" as "-Evening", you could set the `PMstring` as shown:

```
fieldObject.FieldFormat.TimeFormat.PMString = "-Evening"
```

Which would cause the time field to read "07:13:42-Evening".

Formatting Date-Time Fields

And finally, for date-time fields, all of the classes available for both date and time fields are consolidated under the `DateTimeFieldFormat` class. The only addition to this class that we haven't looked at yet is the separator character that will appear between the date and time, which can be set using the `DateTimeSeparator` property, as shown here:

```
fieldObject.FieldFormat.DateTimeFormat.DateTimeSeparator = "="
```

If your report uses date-time fields and you would prefer not to see the date or time component, there is a setting available within the report designer to handle the way date-time fields are processed. Within the Report Designer, right-click on the report and select Report | Report Options to open the dialog shown below:

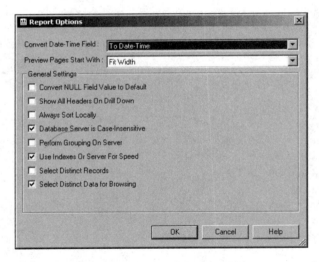

Use the first drop-down list to select how date-time fields should be interpreted in your report. You can also set this option globally by right-clicking on the report in the Report Designer and selecting Designer | Default Settings. Within the Reporting tab, there is an option for converting date-time fields.

Formatting Currency Fields

Currency fields within Crystal Reports have a number of formatting properties that can be set to create financial reports, statements, and other fiscal information and display the data in the correct format for the type of report that is being created.

You can format a number or currency field in your report by right-clicking on the field in the Report Designer and selecting Format, which will open a dialog that will allow you to format the field, and show a sample of the field in whichever format is chosen from the list. Or you can click the Customize button to control the granular properties associated with formatting.

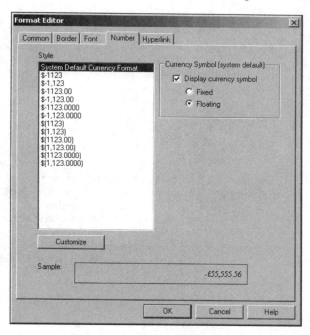

Unfortunately, not all of these properties can be changed programmatically, but the following properties of the NumericFieldFormat class are supported:

Property	Description
CurrencySymbolFormat	Returns or sets the currency symbol type (FixedSymbol, FloatingSymbol, or NoSymbol).
DecimalPlaces	Returns or sets the number of decimal places.
EnableUseLeadingZero	Returns or sets the option to use a leading zero for decimal values.
NegativeFormat	Returns or sets the negative format type (Bracketed, LeadingMinus, NotNegative, TrailingMinus).
RoundingFormat	Returns or sets the rounding format type. *Note: to see all of the different types available, search the Visual Studio Combined Help for "RoundingFormat Enumeration".*

So to change the format of a numeric field, showing a fixed currency symbol with two decimal places and rounding to the second decimal place (tenth), the code would look like this (again, for illustration only and not included in the sample application):

```
With fieldObject.FieldFormat.NumericFormat
   .CurrencySymbolFormat = CurrencySymbolFormat.FixedSymbol
   .DecimalPlaces = 2
   .RoundingFormat = RoundingFormat.RoundToTenth

End With
```

Keep in mind that we don't have the ability to actually change the currency symbol itself through the object model – you will need to set this in the report design itself or use a formula (for instance, `If {Customer.Country}` = "USA" then "US$" else "UKP") and position the formula immediately before the numeric field (or use yet another formula to concatenate the currency symbol formula and the field itself together.)

Summary

The Crystal Report Engine encompasses a lot of the functionality you will need when it comes time to integrate reporting into your application. Throughout the chapter, we have looked at some of the most common uses of the Report Engine, and hopefully have built a foundation where you should be able to feel comfortable applying the same concepts to other areas of the Report Engine's functionality.

In our next chapter, we will be looking at how to manage the distribution of applications that use Crystal Reports, and examining some of the issues that may arise out of such a distribution.

Professional *Crystal Reports*
for *Visual Studio .NET*

Distributing Your Application

Finally, with your development and testing finished, one of the last steps in the software development lifecycle is the actual deployment of your application to the end users.

In this chapter, we will look at the tools Visual Studio .NET provides to help distribute applications, and how these tools can be used to distribute applications that integrate Crystal Reports. This will include:

❑   Distribution Overview

❑   Deploying Windows Applications

❑   Deploying Web Applications

This chapter has been designed so that if you are interested in deploying Windows Applications, you can turn immediately to that section and get started. Likewise, if you are developing Web Applications, there is a separate section for web deployment – although this section is not comprehensive, to avoid repeating details which can be found in the section covering Windows Applications.

By the end of this chapter, you will be able to identify the setup and distribution tools within Visual Studio and understand how they can be used to package and distribute your application. You should also be able to create a setup program from an application that integrates Crystal Reports and successfully install the same application on a target machine.

Distribution Overview

If you come from a background where you have developed Visual Basic 6.0 applications, you will be familiar with the Packaging and Deployment Wizard that was available with the Enterprise editions of the product, and may even have used these tools to create script-based setups for your own applications.

It probably only took one or two attempts at distributing reporting applications with the Packaging and Deployment Wizard, to tell that there had to be a better way of doing things. To start with, it was difficult to determine which run-time files needed to be included with your report, and then once those same files were identified, you had to ensure that the files didn't conflict with or overwrite any other files on the target system.

Developers often added every Crystal-related file they could find to the setup (just to be on the safe side) but the size of the setup program and distributable files would blow out of proportion to the functionality Crystal Reports provided. Clearly, there had to be a better way of distributing reporting applications.

One of the design goals of Visual Studio .NET was to introduce a new set of powerful, integrated tools for developers that provided the majority of the functionality required to create and distribute applications. With that in mind, Visual Studio .NET enhances the ability to create deployment projects using Windows Installer technology that can generate an `.msi` file for your application, providing a manageable framework for distributing your application.

> *For more information on Windows Installer, check out the MSDN library and search under .NET Framework Deployment or Windows Installer.*

To get us started, we are going to take a look at some of the deployment tools within Visual Studio .NET and then later in the chapter, see how they can be used to deploy our own applications.

Getting Started

To start, the tools available for creating setup program and for deployment are now integrated within the Visual Studio IDE. You may have noticed that within Visual Studio .NET, there are some new project types. If you select File | New | Project and choose the folder for Setup and Deployment Projects, you can see that we have a number of different templates available for use when creating setup projects.

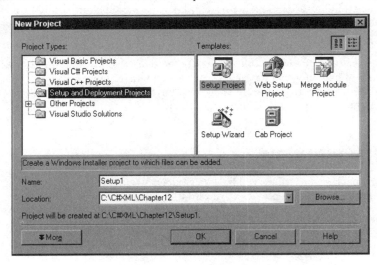

Setup Projects

If you are developing Windows-based applications, you could use a **Setup Project** to create a Windows Installer file for your application. Using this, you could deploy your application to a number of different Windows platforms and allow users to install all of the files required by your application on their local machine.

Web Setup Projects

For web-based applications, there is also a **Web Setup Project** that can also be used to create a Windows Installer file, but with a different target. For Windows applications, the associated files are usually installed on the local machine; for web-based applications, the required files will be installed in a virtual directory on (or accessible by) your web server.

Merge Module Project

Merge modules provide a container for application components and make it easy to distribute a number of files at once. An example of where a merge file could be used is with report distribution – you could create a merge file with all of your reports and simply add the merge file to our setup program (instead of adding them as individual reports).

Merge modules have a number of inherent benefits, including version control and portability between projects – when you are ready to update your application with a new version of all of the reports, you could simply create another merge module and include that in your setup program, making a neat transition between different versions of files.

Crystal Reports.NET includes a number of merge modules for its own framework and runtime files that we will be using a little later with our own setup projects.

> *The creation and distribution of Merge modules and CAB files is outside of the scope of this book, but you can find more information in the Visual Studio .NET Environment documentation within the combined help collection.*

Setup Wizard

To make things a bit easier, there is a **Setup Wizard** that can guide you through creating a setup project for your application. The Setup Wizard can be selected through the **File | New | Project** menu, and then choosing the **Setup and Deployment Projects** folder, which we saw in the previous screen shot.

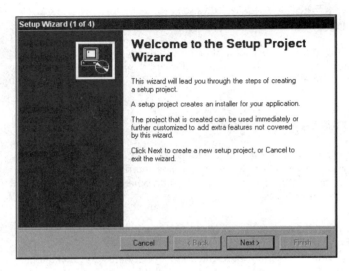

The **Setup Wizard** will guide you through the creation of your project, selecting a project type, and the files that are to be distributed. When you have finished, you will have a new setup project that you can customize as required.

Before we get into actually working with these different types of projects and the walk-throughs for this chapter, we are going to look at some of the basic deployment requirements.

Basic Deployment Requirements

To start, applications created in Visual Studio .NET require that the .NET Framework is installed prior to the application installation. The installer we are going to create actually needs the .NET Framework itself.

Microsoft provides a re-distributable file (`Dotnetfx.exe`) that will need to be installed before you install your setup and which includes its own merge module. This module is not used for distributing the framework, just for checking that it is has been installed.

> The .NET Framework contains all of the underlying system files that make it possible for .NET applications to run on your computer. For operating systems released after Visual Studio .NET, the .NET Framework will already be installed.

A launch condition (which we will look at later) called `MsiNetAssemblySupport` automatically gets added to any setup project you may create – its sole purpose is to check for the .NET Framework. If it doesn't exist, it halts the installation – you must have the framework installed from the redistribute file for your application to work.

The most common scenario for installing this re-distributable file is either using a batch file or a splash page (through a web page or other method) for your application, giving a link to both the re-distributable and your own setup program with instructions on how to install the framework and subsequently your own application.

Operating System

Windows applications created with Visual Studio .NET and the .NET Framework can be deployed on most Windows operating systems, with the exception of Windows 95 or earlier.

If you plan to deploy Web applications, Windows 2000 Server or Advanced Server is recommended (and of course, IIS!).

Hardware

The minimum hardware requirements for the .NET Framework and your application depend a lot on the type of application you have created and the response time you expect (you wouldn't want a form that pulled back 10,000 rows of data to be on a client machine with 64Mb of RAM).

For the minimum requirements for the .NET Framework, you can consult the Visual Studio .NET Framework Developers Guide online, but the following details the recommended requirements, based on experience deploying Windows applications that integrate reporting:

❑ Processor: Pentium 100MHz or above

❑ Memory: 128Mb or above

❑ Hard Disk: 80Mb available, plus report file size

For web-based applications, you would probably want to size the server based on the number of concurrent users. For a small workgroup application, the system requirements above may be adequate. For organization-wide applications, you will probably want to make a significant investment in both the processor and memory.

> *For large applications that need to scale beyond a single server, you may want to consider moving your application to Crystal Enterprise.*

With a quick look at the types of setup projects we can create, and the basic requirements for our target client and server machines out of the way, we can jump in to actually creating our first set up.

Deploying Windows Applications

This section details how to create an installer to distribute a simple reporting application.

To get started, we need a simple reporting application to play around with. For our walk-through, we are going to use the sample Windows project that can be found within the downloadable files for this chapter. In the download files, there is a single solution file for this chapter (Chapter10.sln) and within the solution file, there is a project called ch10_app, which contains a sample application that we will be using to demonstrate distributing a Windows application.

The application consists of a single form that hosts the Windows Crystal Report Viewer and when run will display a preview of an Employee Listing Report, as shown below:

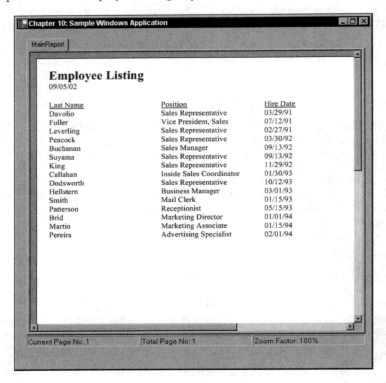

Creating a New Setup Project

As we stated earlier, to create a new Setup Project for an application, select File | Add Project | New Project and open the Setup and Deployment Projects folder and select Setup Project from the available templates. To keep things simple, we have already created the one for our application, and have called the setup project ch10_Setup.

This will open the design environment and the File System Explorer, shown in the following screenshot, which we will come back to:

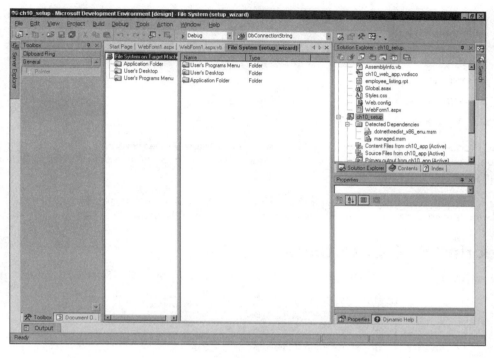

For now, we will see how to set some basic properties for our setup project – select View | **Properties Window** and then in the Solution Explorer, click on the name of your setup project, which will open the property page shown below:

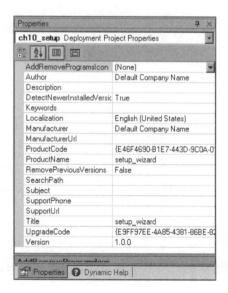

As you can see there are a number of properties available. We won't change any of them here, but the most commonly used ones are:

- ❑ Author
- ❑ Manufacturer
- ❑ Product Name
- ❑ Version

The **Product Name** property controls how your application will be advertised on the **Add/Remove Programs** menu in Control Panel, and other properties are also used for registry entries, and other application properties.

Anywhere you see a property in square brackets (for instance, [Manufacturer]), it means that this property is being treated as a variable and its value will be inserted when the application setup is created.

Selecting Project Outputs

When you first create the setup project, the IDE is opened to show the File System Explorer:

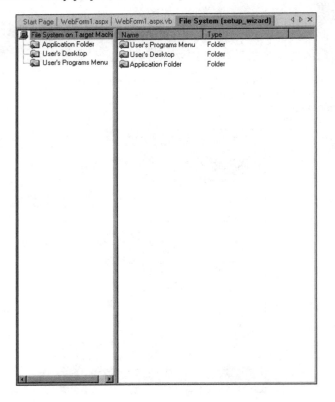

The **File System Explorer** is used to add the various types of files (.exe, .dll, .rpt) to your setup project, and when your setup program is run, the files will be copied to the location you specify.

In the File System Explorer, the majority of files from your project will be targeted at the Application Folder. By default, any items added to this folder will be copied to drive:\[ProgramFilesFolder]\[Manufacturer]\[ProductName], but you can change this default, if you like, by editing the respective properties in the Properties dialog.

To add files to the Application Folder, you would click on it and select Action | Add | Project Output – again this has already been done for this example. This will open the dialog shown below and allow you to add a Project Output Group.

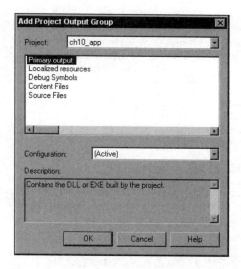

If you select Primary output, this will add the primary EXE and DLL files from your application. You would need to repeat the process and select Content Files to actually pick up the report files within your application.

Determining Runtime File Requirements

With the main components of your application added to the setup project and all of the report files as well, you would now need to determine what runtime files are required to make those same reports work on the target machine.

When looking at the runtime file requirements for Crystal Reports, there are a number of considerations, including the data source for your report (and any drivers in use), and export formats you wish to support, among other things.

There are three different types of merge files that can be used to help you determine these requirements:

❑   `Managed.msm` – The managed component MSM handles the distribution of all the managed components, which include the Windows Form Viewer, Web Forms Viewer, and all of the Crystal Decisions namespaces.

❑   `Database_Access_enu.msm` – The database access MSM handles the distribution of all of the other files that are needed to get the reports to run. This includes the database, export, and charting drivers.

❑   `Regwiz.msm` – Handles the installation of the Crystal Decisions keycode, so that your users are not asked to register their versions of Crystal Reports when viewing reports.

> In the documentation for Crystal Reports.NET, the `regwiz.msm` module is referred to as `keycode.msm` and it also mentions there are 19 different merge modules available for Crystal Reports.NET – all of these modules are iterations of the same merge modules to support additional (human) languages.

These merge files will do most of the work for you when deciding what files should be included in your setup program, but you should always double-check the files that the merge module has specified, just to make sure they have them all.

Adding Merge Modules

If you look in the Solutions Explorer under your setup project, these modules will appear in one of two places. If your setup project has detected a dependency that has already been detected (from the files you added earlier), the corresponding merge module can be found in the Detected Dependencies folder, as shown below:

If the merge module you require hasn't been automatically detected, you can add a merge module to your setup project by selecting Project I Add I Merge Module and browsing for the merge module you want using the dialog shown here:

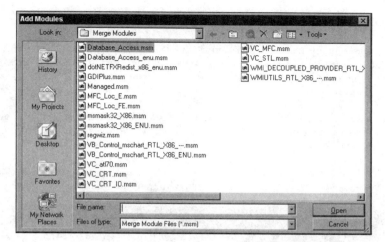

Select the merge module you want to add and click Open to add the module to the list.

If you would like to see what files are included with a module, view the Properties and check out the Files property, shown here:

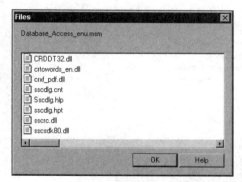

You can also see any dependencies that a module has by viewing the ModuleDependencies property, which will give the dialog below:

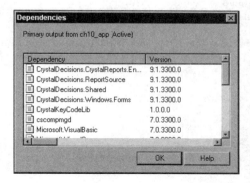

Working with Licensing

One of the requirements for using Crystal Reports.NET and distributing the free runtime and reports with your application is that you register the software and your personal details with Crystal Decisions. What better way to enforce registration than with a nag screen that appears whenever you open the report designer (charming, I know!).

In order to successfully distribute your application and get rid of the nag screen, you are going to need to register with Crystal Decisions and obtain a registration number. When you first started the Crystal Reports designer, chances are you were prompted to register at that point.

If you just clicked Cancel (like most people) you can still register by opening the Report Designer, and selecting Register from the right-click menu, which will open the dialog shown below:

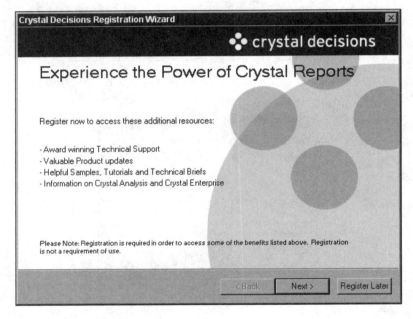

If you have registered, we need to take the registration number you were given and enter it into the `Regwiz.msn` merge module.

To copy your registration number (or to find out if you are registered), select Help | About Microsoft Development Environment to display a list of all of the Visual Studio .NET products you have installed.

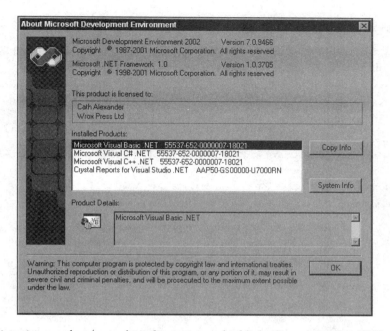

Note the registration number (or to do it the easy way, highlight Crystal Reports.NET and click on the Copy Info button). From that point, click OK to return to your project and locate the License Key property under Regwiz.msm merge module. You will need to enter or paste this license key before you build your setup project.

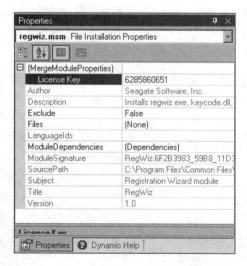

This is one of the most common errors when deploying applications that use Crystal Reports, so don't forget to do it every time you create a setup project.

Building your Setup Project

The last step of creating our setup project is to actually build the setup project. To build your setup, select Build | Build ch10_Setup and keep an eye on the Output window.

> The default Project Configuration is **Debug** and **Projectname** is the name of the deployment project – in our instance, if you had unzipped the sample files for this chapter into a `CrystalReports` directory on your machine, the setup directory would be found at
> `C:\CrystalReports\Chapter10\code\setup_wizard\Debug`.

Along with the MSI file that has been generated, there are also some additional files that should be in the same directory:

- ❏ `setup.exe` – serves as a wrapper for the .MSI file that has been created and for a utility that verifies the correct Windows Installer version and installs the correct version

- ❏ `setup.ini` – an `.ini` file containing the location of the Windows Installer files

- ❏ `Instmsia.exe` – the Windows Installer files for Windows 95, 98, and ME

- ❏ `Instmsiw.exe` – the Windows Installer files for Windows NT

If the setup finds that Windows Installer is not present or the correct version, it will launch the correct executable (`Instmsia.exe` or `instmsiw.exe`) to install or update the Windows Installer service before installing your own application.

Testing and Deploying your Setup Project

To test your generated deployment package, copy the entire directory to another computer or CD and run the `setup.exe` file, as shown here:

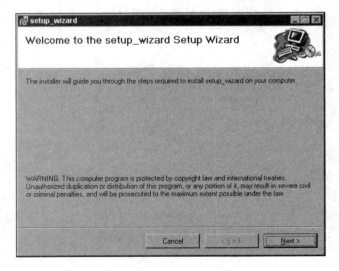

To test your application set up, you should be able to see where your files were installed and verify that they are present. Also, the application should appear under the **Add/Remove Programs** option in the Windows Control Panel.

In addition, if you have added a shortcut to your application, you should be able to select the shortcut you have created and it should launch the application. Make sure that you test the reports themselves, viewing a number of different reports and trying out the features such as drill-down and exporting.

Once you are satisfied that the application is installed and that it and the reports run correctly, you can distribute the setup files within the subdirectory to users as required.

Deploying Web Applications

This section details how to create an installer to distribute a simple reporting application. We won't cover the steps in much detail here, as most of the information is the same as for Windows applications; so if you have jumped straight to this part of the chapter, then please refer to *Deploying Windows Applications* above to fill in the details.

Preparing Your Web Server

Before you can install a new web application, the web server you are installing to needs to have the .NET Framework installed first. Just as with Windows applications, there is no automated way to install this from your setup project, so you will probably have to create a batch file or install it manually.

In addition to the .NET Framework, if your web application accesses data from a database or other data source, you will need to install MDAC 2.6 or greater in order for your application to work.

> **You can download the latest MDAC components from the Microsoft web site at http://www.microsoft.com/data/.**

Finally, when exporting directly from Crystal Reports and the Web Forms Viewer, you may need to configure some additional MIME types on your web server to associate a file extension (such as a PDF file) with its "helper" application (in this case, `Acrobat32.exe`).

> **Note: For more information on configuring MIME types for your version of IIS, visit the MSDN library at http://msdn.microsoft.com and search for "MIME".**

Creating the Setup Project

❑ Firstly, just as in the section on Windows deployment, we need a simple web reporting application to deploy and one has been included for you in the downloadable files for this chapter, in a project named `ch10_web_app`. This application consists of a single Web Form that has the web version of the Crystal Report Viewer embedded and allows you to preview the same Employee Listing report that we looked at when working with the sample Windows application earlier.

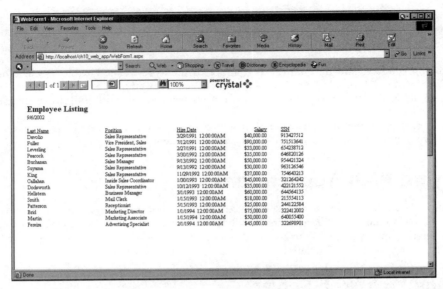

❑　Again we need a Setup Project for this web application – as before, we have already added this to our sample project – called ch10_web_setup.

❑　If you need to set some basic properties for your setup project – click on the name of your setup project, and select View | Properties Window, which will open the property pages.

There are a number of properties available; the most commonly used ones are the same as for Windows applications, except for Restart WWW Service that controls whether or not the WWW Service for IIS will be restarted when you install your web application. Whether this option is required or not is up to you and the requirements of the components you are installing on the web server itself.

❑　After this, you will need to consider selecting the Project Outputs, determining Runtime File Requirements, and adding Merge Modules, following the instructions in the *Deploying Windows Applications* section. While these have already been done for this example, you should know about them for your future projects.

❑　Next we will consider licensing. In order to successfully distribute your applications, you are going to need to first register with Crystal Decisions and obtain a registration number, as we covered in the section on Windows Applications.

Again, just like when deploying Windows Applications, this is one of the most common errors when deploying applications that use Crystal Reports, so don't forget to do it every time!

Building your Setup Project

❑　To build your setup, select Build | Build ch10_web_setup.

The default Project Configuration is Debug and Projectname is the name of the deployment project – in our instance, the directory would be ch10_web_setup\Debug\ch10_web_setup.msi.

As we saw when we built our Windows application setup, there are also some additional files that have been generated along with the `.msi` file, which will be in the same directory. For more details about these files see *Deploying Windows Applications.*

Testing and Deploying your Setup

❏   To test your generated deployment package, copy the entire directory to another computer or CD and run the `Setup.Exe` file.

You must have install permissions on the web server you are using in order to run the installer, and in addition, you must also have the correct IIS permissions to create a virtual directory and install this application.

❏   To test your web application setup, you should be able to see where your files were installed on the web server and verify that they are present. Also, the application should appear under the Add/Remove Programs option in the Windows Control Panel.

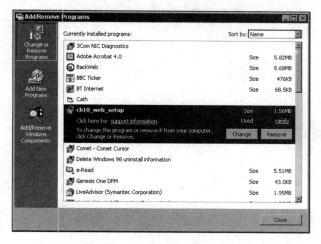

❏   To test the application itself, open Internet Explorer and type the URL http://ComputerName/ch10_web_app. Make sure that you test the reports themselves, viewing a number of different reports and trying out the features like drill-down, exporting, and so on.

❏   Once you are satisfied that the application is installed and that it and the reports run correctly, you can distribute the setup files within the subdirectory to users as required.

Summary

In this chapter, we had a look at deploying both Windows and Web applications using the tools available within Visual Studio .NET (and with a little help from Crystal Reports). Throughout the chapter, we looked at some of the tools that are available to make creating setup programs easier and walked through examples of creating setups for both Windows and Web-based applications, including how to build, test and deploy these setup files. With the skills gained from this chapter, you should be able to successfully deploy and configure reporting applications for one user or for one hundred.

Professional *Crystal Reports*
for *Visual Studio .NET*

Troubleshooting

When working with any development environment or tool, you are going to spend a fair amount of time troubleshooting to diagnose problems, resolve conflicts, and so on. Crystal Reports.NET is no different. This appendix lists some of the resources available to help you troubleshoot your reporting application, as well as some common problems you may experience.

Troubleshooting Resources

There are a number of resources available to help you work out any issues or problems you may encounter, and a good place to start is with the resources provided by Crystal Decisions.

Crystal Decisions Knowledge Base

http://support.crystaldecisions.com/kbase/

The Crystal Decisions Knowledge Base provides a comprehensive selection of articles across the range of Crystal Decisions products, and is updated twice a week with over 100 documents relating to Crystal Reports.NET. To search for articles related to Crystal Reports.NET, search on the keywords dotnet or .NET or VB.NET or CSHARP.

Crystal Decisions Library

http://support.crystaldecisions.com/docs/

For the Crystal product range, this provides a library of technical briefs, release notes, FAQs, how-tos, and so on. To search for articles on Crystal Reports.NET, use the drop-down menus provided or search for a document name like CRNET*. This will provide a list of available documents, most of which are in Adobe Acrobat (.pdf) format. It is here you will also find summary lists of items such as articles, or sample applications, that relate to Crystal Reports.NET.

Crystal Decisions Downloads

http://support.crystaldecisions.com/updates/

Includes a number of downloads of drivers, utilities, and sample applications available for use with Crystal Reports.NET. There are sample applications available that use both Visual Basic .NET and C# code, as well as any software updates and hot fixes that are available.

Crystal Decisions Technical Support

http://community.crystaldecisions.com/support/answers.asp

As a registered user of Crystal Reports.NET, you are entitled to use Answers By Email, Crystal Decisions' interactive online support service.

Microsoft Newsgroups

Microsoft.public.vb.crystal
Microsoft.public.dotnet.general

Microsoft provides a public newsgroup for using Crystal Reports with VB. You will find a number of postings that relate to older version of Crystal Reports, but there is still some good information contained within the group.

MSDN

http://msdn.microsoft.com/library/en-us/crystlmn/html/crconcrystalreports.asp

MSDN provides a duplication of the documentation found with Crystal Reports.NET and is available in the online MSDN library. You can also find links on MSDN to other resources, including articles from MSDN magazine, other web sites and dot net resources like www.gotdotnet.com.

Google Groups

public.seagate.crystal-reports.general
public.seagate.crystal-reports.programming

These are two groups that were migrated from Deja-News to Google Groups, providing helpful hints and postings from other Crystal Reports.NET users. Again, like the Microsoft newsgroups, there is a lot to wade through but occasionally you will find the gem of information that makes it all worthwhile.

Sources of Errors

Existing Reports

If you have existing Crystal Reports you have created using a previous version of Crystal Reports (8.5 or below) you can use these reports with Crystal Reports.NET by importing them into your project or leave them as external and reference them within your application. Below are some of the most common errors that occur with reports and Crystal Reports.NET:

Error	Interpretation
Opening a .NET report in a previous version (8.5 or below) causes a fault	Once you have saved a report in Crystal Reports.NET, the report cannot be opened in previous versions of Crystal Reports. You should keep a copy of the report if you wish to open it in a previous version.
	You cannot open Crystal Reports.NET reports in Crystal Reports 8.5 or below because the file format for a .NET report is different from that for previous versions.
	The Crystal Knowledge Base recommends two different strategies for using reports you also need to edit outside of Crystal Reports.NET:
	If you add the report as an Existing item and don't change the report's structures, you should be able to edit the report with the previous version designer (8.5 or below) as the report file remains in its original report format.
	If you know you need to edit the report outside of Crystal Reports.NET, the best method is to leave the report file alone and reference the file at run time. Rather than importing or creating a new report, you can load the previous version report file into the application at run time and view the reports. If you were to set the report source property with the path and name of the report, the report could then be viewed within your .NET application, but still be edited externally with the previous version's Report Designer.
Crystal Dictionary is not supported in this version	Crystal Reports.NET does not support Crystal Dictionaries (or Seagate Info Views) as a data source for reports. If you attempt to import an existing report that uses either of these data sources, you will receive this error message. To utilize this report, you need to either set the location of the report to a valid data source, or you could re-create the report within the Crystal Reports.NET Report Designer.

Table continued on following page

Error	Interpretation
The formatting of graphs is lost in Crystal Reports.NET	When importing a report from a previous version of Crystal Reports that includes a graph, the graph formatting you have specified may not translate with the rest of the report. Crystal Reports.NET is missing the Chart Analyzer from the retail version of Crystal Reports, which allows you to use advanced formatting options on your graph. Crystal Reports.NET cannot understand this advanced formatting.
OLAP grids disappear from the report when it is imported into Crystal Reports.NET	When you attempt to import a report from a previous version of Crystal Reports (Crystal Reports 8.5 or below) that utilizes an OLAP grid, the grid will be dropped when you import your report into Crystal Reports.NET. This happens because Crystal Reports.NET does not support OLAP data at the time of going to press, and there is currently no workaround available.
Geographic maps disappear from the report when it is imported into Crystal Reports.NET	Like OLAP grids, Geographic mapping is not supported within Crystal Reports.NET. Any existing reports that have a map in them can be used, but the map area will appear blank if you import them into the Crystal Reports.NET designer.

Report Designer

Within the Report Designer itself, there are a number of areas that can be a problem, and sometimes make you think you have done something wrong (even when you haven't!). Like any product in its first release, there are still some issues to work out.

Error	Interpretation
The Field Explorer disappears	When working in the Crystal Report Designer, you can access the fields that are available for use with your report from the Field Explorer. If you accidentally close this window, you can get it back by selecting View	Other Windows	Document Outline or by pressing *Ctrl-Alt-T*.
Delete button does not function properly in the Field Explorer	Normally, when you highlight a formula or parameter field in the Field Explorer and click the *Delete* key, the field will be deleted. With Crystal Reports.NET, this behavior does not work. To delete the field, you will need to highlight it and press the *Delete* key twice. This behavior has been noted and should be fixed with future releases of the project.
Sort order of fields can not be set	When working with record-level sorting in your report, there is no way to set the sort order or precedence, other than removing and adding the fields again in order.

Error	Interpretation
The priority of the sort order in the Record Sort Order Control cannot be set directly	In Crystal Reports.NET, the Record Sort Order control offers no direct method to set the priority order of two or more fields in the Sort Fields list. For example, there are no up or down buttons that allow you to change the list order in the Sort Fields list. If you need to modify the priority in which fields are sorted, manually remove the fields from the Sort Fields list and add them again in the desired order.

Database and Data-related

Error	Interpretation
Problems with string lengths in XML DataSets	When using XML DataSets as the data source for your reports, Crystal Reports.NET will treat all of the fields as if they have the maximum length, and think they contain 65,000+ characters. If you need to use the length for any of these fields, make sure you use trim in the Crystal Reports formula language prior to applying the record.
Errors using Set Location functionality	When using the Set Location functionality within Crystal Reports.NET, you can set an existing table location to a new location, for example, pointing a report from a test database to a production database. After you have finished setting the location of your data, the user interface within Crystal Reports will not be updated with this information. This is a known error and should be fixed in future releases.

Subreports

Error	Interpretation
Locating your subreport in Crystal Reports.NET	When editing a subreport within Crystal Reports.NET (by right-clicking on the subreport and selecting Edit Subreport), a tab is added to the **bottom** of the page. Previous versions of Crystal Reports would open a tab at the **top** of the page. You can use these tabs to navigate between different subreports that exist within your main report.

Table continued on following page

Error	Interpretation
A report with a subreport runs slowly or indefinitely	With subreports, performance can be a problem if your subreport is processed multiple times. When you create a subreport and place it on a report, keep in mind that its position determines how many times that subreport will be run. For example, a subreport placed in the Report Header will only run once (as the Report Header itself only appears once).
	A subreport placed in the Details section, however, will run once for each detail record that is shown. In a large report, this can mean that a subeport runs hundreds of times over.
	If you are using subreports to display information in the Details section of your report, consider creating a SQL command, database view, or stored procedure to provide this information instead of using subreports to display the data.
	In addition, if you don't need to see the subreport immediately, then consider turning the report into an on-demand subreport, by right-clicking on the subreport, selecting Format I Subreport, and checking the appropriate option.

Exporting

Error	Interpretation
Formatting errors occur when exporting to Adobe Acrobat	When exporting to Adobe Acrobat (.pdf) format, you may encounter a number of formatting errors, including:
	❑ Boxes drawn on your report lose their formatting
	❑ Double-line borders appears as single-lines
	❑ Cross-tab header only appears on first page
	These are known errors with exporting to .pdf, and should be fixed in future versions of Crystal Reports.

Windows Forms Viewer

Error	Interpretation
Cancel button in the print dialog does not work	When you preview your report in the Windows Forms Viewer, there is a print button that will allow you to print your report to the printer of your choice. You can print from this dialog with no problems, but the cancel button does not cancel the dialog.

Web Forms Viewer

Error	Interpretation
Cannot drill down into the group tree after using the `ShowGroupTree` method	If you use the `ShowGroupTree` method, there is a bug in Crystal Reports.NET that will not allow you to drill down into the group tree. This issue has been tracked by Crystal Decisions and should be fixed in future releases of the product.
Improving the quality of images in the Web Forms Viewer	When working with reports that contain graphs and other pictures in the Web Form, the default resolution is 96dpi. This resolution was picked based on a number of factors, including file sizing, and download times, but will often turn graphs and other images a bit grainy.
	There is a setting in the registry that can be changed to alter the magnification ratio for images. For more information on the necessary registry changes, go to the Crystal Decisions Knowledge Base and search for document number c2010317 for complete instructions.

XML Report Web Services

Error	Interpretation
Web Service ignores the record selection formula	When working with a report that has been published as an XML Report Web Service, the report's record selection formula cannot start with a commented line, as the Web Service will ignore the rest of the record selection formula and return all available records.
	The example below shows an incorrect record selection formula:

```
' This sets the record selection formula
{Customer.Country} = "USA"
```

and the correct version:

```
{Customer.Country} = "USA"
' This sets the record selection formula
```

Comments can appear anywhere after the first line, but never on the first line.

Table continued on following page

Error	Interpretation
Access Denied Error Message	When working with Server File Reports (reports accessed through the generic report Web Service) you may encounter the error message: **Request Failed with HTTP Status 401: Access Denied.** To correct this error, you will need to ensure that the **CrystalReportWebFormViewer** directory is enabled for anonymous access in IIS. You will also need to restart the WWW Publishing Service before this change will take effect.

Professional *Crystal Reports* for *Visual Studio .NET*

Migrating Applications to Crystal Reports.NET

One of the most common situations that a developer will face, at least with regard to Visual Basic or Active Server Pages programming and the .NET Framework, is the conversion of Crystal Reports into the new Crystal Reports.NET format and design in Visual Studio .NET. While this is a fairly simple operation in general, there is a path to follow, and several pitfalls wait to ensnare the unwary. If you have looked at Appendix A then you will already be aware of most of these, but if not, don't worry, we'll cover all of this and the following in this short appendix:

❑   An example of using a Crystal 8.5 report in Visual Studio .NET

❑   Migrating a VB6 application with Crystal 8.5 to Visual Basic .NET using the Upgrade Wizard

This doesn't seem like much, but it covers the two most common conversion efforts for VB programmers. Most likely, we'll be engineering a new application using existing reports. This is fairly easy, because unless the report uses a feature not supported in Crystal Reports.NET, we only have the data pipeline to worry about.

The second case is more hairy, however, because VB code will have to change. We'll take a simple application and see what the Upgrade Wizard does to the code.

On a personal note, I began this appendix with the commonly held proposition that the problems would be in the areas of data access methods. After fighting the good fight over and over, I discovered that this is not the case – actually, as we'll see, the example converted with the minimum of changes to the report. In fact, only a change in attitude by the programmer is necessary. Visual Basic .NET is an object-oriented language, and now the report files are treated as objects. The data access methods, however, are pretty much the same, provided we don't let Visual Studio .NET change the report to a Crystal Reports.NET format.

Using Crystal Reports 8.5 in Visual Studio .NET

As stated above, the most likely scenario is using existing Crystal Reports in new Visual Studio .NET applications. The essential goal here is adding existing .RPT files to a new Visual Basic .NET project, and viewing them using the Crystal Reports Windows Forms Viewer. Initially, this is made complex by the basic constraint of the Crystal Report Viewer in Visual Studio .NET and its poor support of the ODBC and OLEDB methods of data access.

As part of this appendix, we'll add two existing Crystal 8.5 reports to a new Visual Basic .NET Windows Application, using the Crystal Reports Windows Forms Viewer. We'll start by looking at our sample reports, then build our viewer, including the reports, and change the data connection as needed. Finally, we'll consider some advanced topics.

> Keep in mind that the biggest change in the use of Crystal 8.5 reports in Visual Studio .NET is the new object model of the .NET Framework.

Our Sample Reports

The first report, Sample 8.5.rpt, is a simple report drawn from the Pubs database in a local SQL Server. The Pubs database is available from the Microsoft site, or you can download the SQL Script as part of the code samples in this appendix.

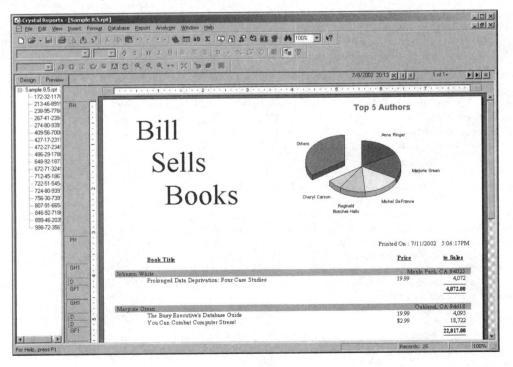

This report uses the three basic features of any report, grouped data, charts, and text. It is a collation of sales by author, including a pie chart of the Top 5 Authors by Volume. There are a few formulas – mostly text concatenations – included to prove that this functionality works in Visual Studio .NET. More complex algorithms would only confuse matters, as all formulas are executed in the same way.

A More Complex Example

To stir things up a little, we have added `Complex Sample 8.5.rpt`. This report uses some of the features not supported in Visual Studio .NET, just to see what happens to them. These features include:

- ❑ Office Connectivity
- ❑ OLAP
- ❑ Mapping
- ❑ Alerts
- ❑ XML

For this example, we'll include some mapping, offer some XML Export, and take a look at how Visual Studio .NET handles these changes. See the sample files for a copy of this report, which is essentially the same as `Sample 8.5.rpt`, with a map of sales rather than a chart.

A New Visual Basic .NET Report Viewer

First we need to build a very simple single-form Windows Application that will handle these two reports.

Create a new Visual Basic .NET Windows Application called `ReportViewer`. Next, add the two report files, `Sample 8.5.RPT` and `Complex Sample 8.5.RPT`, to the project. Enlarge the form, and add a **CrystalReportViewer**, a **ComboBox**, and a **Button** control as below. Set the **CrystalReportViewer** control's visibility to **False**.

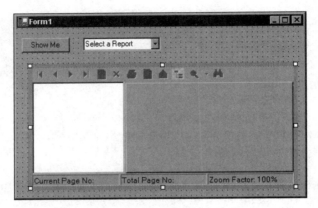

In the `Form1_Load` event handler, fill `ComboBox1` with our two report types:

```
Private Sub Form1_Load(ByVal sender As System.Object, & _
                    ByVal e As System.EventArgs) Handles MyBase.Load
    ComboBox1.Items.Add("Simple Report")
    ComboBox1.Items.Add("Complex Report")
End Sub
```

In the `Button1_Click` event handler, we'll check the value of `ComboBox1` and fire up the viewer:

```
Private Sub Button1_Click(ByVal sender As System.Object, & _
                    ByVal e As System.EventArgs) Handles Button1.Click
    Select Case ComboBox1.SelectedItem
        Case "Simple Report"
            CrystalReportViewer1.ReportSource = "Sample 8.5.rpt"
            CrystalReportViewer1.Visible = True
        Case "Complex Report"
            CrystalReportViewer1.ReportSource = "Complex Sample 8.5.rpt"
            CrystalReportViewer1.Visible = True
        Case Else
            MsgBox("Select a report")
    End Select
End Sub
```

Finally, run the report in debug mode by hitting *F5*.

Select a report from the drop-down list, and click on the **Show Me** button to open the selected report. The following dialog will appear:

So what happened here? The dialog doesn't give you much information – just typical of Crystal Reports, isn't it? Even in debug mode, you don't get any good information about what actually happened, so, if you are like me, you'll attempt to **Verify Database** by loading the report into Visual Studio .NET and right-clicking on the data connections.

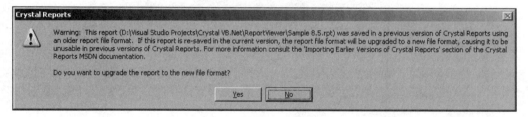

We find that Crystal Reports still provides us with a wonderful cryptic error message – Unable to Load Report. So what's up? As it turns out, the problem wasn't the data connection at all, and in fact the use of the data wizard isn't necessary.

What this comes down to is a difference between using a Crystal Reports 8.5 report in a .NET application, and using a Crystal Reports.NET report. Until we did the data fix-up, essentially we still had a Crystal Reports 8.5 report, residing in a .NET application.

> **Crystal 8.5 reports are still usable in .NET applications and have all of the same data features as if they were in VB6. Only reports changed to .NET format lose the ODBC functionality.**

The best lessons are lessons learned the hard way, but we get to re-download the report and try again. We need to begin again with a new report, with a new name, in order to change our attitude.

Changing our Visual Basic .NET Report Viewer

Visual Basic .NET is an object-oriented language, and we need to treat it as so when dealing with Crystal Reports. Let's try a few new steps that may help us with the new paradigm.

Begin by renaming the report files to `simple.rpt` and `complex.rpt`. The Visual Studio .NET designer will use the names of our files as report names. Remove the old reports from the designer by right-clicking on them and selecting **Remove From Project**, and then add the two new files. The Solution Explorer should look something like this:

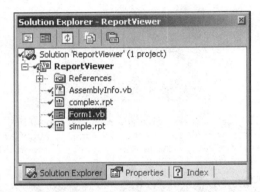

Build the solution (the shortcut keys are *Ctrl+Shift+B*). Now change the `Button1_Click` event handler to something more object oriented, so it looks like this:

```
Private Sub Button1_Click(ByVal sender As System.Object, & _
                          ByVal e As System.EventArgs) Handles Button1.Click
    Select Case ComboBox1.SelectedItem
        Case "Simple Report"
            Dim simpleReport As New simple()
            CrystalReportViewer1.ReportSource = simpleReport
            CrystalReportViewer1.Visible = True
        Case "Complex Report"
            Dim complexReport As New complex()
            CrystalReportViewer1.ReportSource = complexReport
            CrystalReportViewer1.Visible = True
        Case Else
            MsgBox("Select a report")
    End Select
End Sub
```

Next build and run the program. When the application has loaded, select the simple report, and the report loads in the viewer as it should.

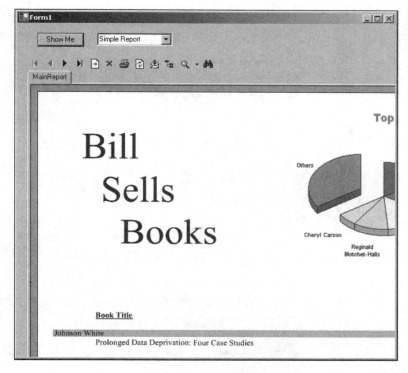

Admittedly, using some of the more esoteric data drivers like Btrieve, and perhaps some of the more out of date drivers, such as DB2 drivers, will cause problems. The good word from the nice people at Crystal Decisions is that if it doesn't simply work when this protocol is tried, it may be necessary to fix-up the report, delete the existing data bindings, and replace all of the fields in the reports. Upgrades can be like that – you can only go so far before you have to start over from scratch.

Invalid Features in the Complex Report

So now, we need to implement the same type of functionality in the complex sample. Largely, everything in the two reports is the same, with the exception of two new requirements – namely the map and the XML Export.

The Map Graphic

The map is a simple examination. If we open the `complex.rpt` file in Visual Studio .NET, we discover that the software simply doesn't recognize it.

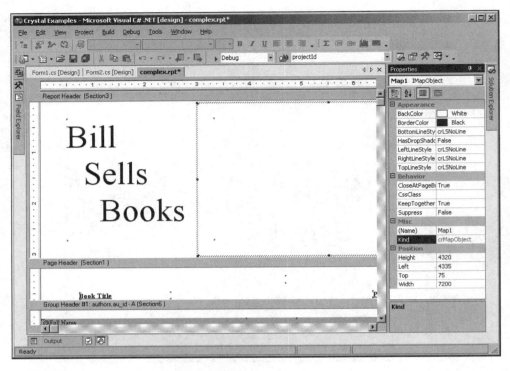

We can see that the object is referenced, but it is a kind of `crMapObject`, and none of the operational parameters that we see in Crystal Reports 8.5 are available. Also, the object isn't viewable in preview mode in the designer, although it will still run in a viewer – so long as we don't convert the report file from the previous file format to a .NET format, as we discussed above.

> You will also find that Crystal Dictionaries and Crystal Queries are not supported in .NET, and will not actually run. Reports using these technologies will probably need to be rewritten to use `DataSet`s, as described in Chapter 6 of the book.

The XML Export

The XML Export is constrained by the Property Explorer of the CrystalReportViewer object itself, in our Visual Basic .NET Windows Application – just as it is in VB6. Checking the Property Explorer, we discover that some features, including XML Export – simply aren't there, irrespective of the version of the report contained in the viewer.

The export to XML just isn't an option, and as described by Crystal Decisions, exports only work to:

❑ RTF

❑ DOC (Microsoft Word)

❑ PDF

❑ XLS

❏   RPT

❏   HTML

❏   DHTML

This is still an excellent selection of formats for most uses.

Migrating from VB6

The Upgrade Wizard is a tool provided by Microsoft as part of the Visual Studio .NET package, to assist us with migrating existing applications to the .NET Framework. It's not, as we will see, crammed full of functionality for Crystal Reports.

Our Sample Application

Let's go back to the original application we had open before. Go ahead and start up Visual Studio .NET, and select Open Project. Navigate to the folder with the original VB6 project, and open it. We are greeted with the Visual Basic Upgrade Wizard.

The Upgrade Wizard

Go through the steps, agreeing that you want to create an .EXE (only option) file, and selecting your destination folder. As you watch, keep in mind that all it is doing is rewriting what we just created in the section above. It takes a while doesn't it? I am on a really fast machine too, so I think I'll go and check my e-mail.

The New Code

OK, folks, we're back. Build the resulting solution. What? Errors?

❑ Crystal8.5Designer.vb(93): Type 'CrystalReport1' is not defined.

❑ ComplexCrystal8.5Designer.vb(93): Type 'CrystalReport2' is not defined.

We have a problem. The DSR files that we created with VB6 didn't convert into anything, and that needs to change.

The Problem with DSRs

A dig into the Knowledge Base for Crystal Reports.NET uncovered this interesting piece of information.

> **A DSR file (from the Report Designer Component) must be manually converted to a standard Crystal Report (RPT) file.**

To convert a DSR file to a RPT file:

❑ From the VB6 project, load the report by double-clicking the DSR file from the Project window.

❑ Right-click on the report, and from the pop-up menu, select Report | Save to Crystal Reports File.

A quick check finds that Knowledge Base is right. If we drop the DSR files from the project and insert our converted Crystal files, everything does work to some level of satisfaction. To get an eyeful, however, check out the source code from the Crystal8.5Designer.vb file, and all of the linked help files:

```
'UPGRADE_ISSUE: CrystalReport1 object was not upgraded. Click for more: 'ms-
help://MS.VSCC/commoner/redir/redirect.htm?keyword="vbup2068"'
Dim Report As New CrystalReport1

Private Sub Form2_Load(ByVal eventSender As System.Object,
                       ByVal eventArgs As System.EventArgs)
                       Handles MyBase.Load
    'UPGRADE_WARNING: Screen property Screen.MousePointer has a new behavior.
    'Click for more:
    'ms-help://MS.VSCC/commoner/redir/redirect.htm?keyword="vbup2065"'
```

```
     System.Windows.Forms.Cursor.Current=System.Windows.Forms.Cursors.WaitCursor
     'UPGRADE_WARNING: Couldn't resolve default property of object
     'CRViewer1.ReportSource.
     'Click for more:
     'ms-help://MS.VSCC/commoner/redir/redirect.htm?keyword="vbup1037"'

     'UPGRADE_WARNING: Couldn't resolve default property of object Report.
     'Click for more:
     'ms-help://MS.VSCC/commoner/redir/redirect.htm?keyword="vbup1037"'

     CRViewer1.ReportSource = Report
     CRViewer1.ViewReport()
     'UPGRADE_WARNING: Screen property Screen.MousePointer has a new behavior.
     'Click for more:
     'ms-help://MS.VSCC/commoner/redir/redirect.htm?keyword="vbup2065"'

     System.Windows.Forms.Cursor.Current = System.Windows.Forms.Cursors.Default
End Sub

'UPGRADE_WARNING: Event Form2.Resize may fire when form is intialized.
'Click for more:
'ms-help://MS.VSCC/commoner/redir/redirect.htm?keyword="vbup2075"'
Private Sub Form2_Resize(ByVal eventSender As System.Object,
                         ByVal eventArgs As System.EventArgs)
                         Handles MyBase.Resize
     CRViewer1.Top = 0
     CRViewer1.Left = 0
     CRViewer1.Height = ClientRectangle.Height
     CRViewer1.Width = ClientRectangle.Width
End Sub
```

Summary

This author tries to refrain from bold, sweeping statements about personal topics, but in this case, though, I'll make an exception. I don't know about you, but I sure did learn something:

❑   If the Crystal Reports 8.5 report you are working from is using up-to-date database access methods, there aren't really any problems with the connectivity – despite many rumors to the contrary.

❑   Once you save a Crystal Reports 8.5 report in Visual Basic .NET, you can no longer open it in Crystal 8.5.

❑   Think objects. Crystal files, like DataSets, become objects in the world of .NET. Understanding that conceptually will give a programmer a much greater understanding of how to manipulate third-party structures like Crystal Reports.

❑   The Upgrade Wizard, while a file tool, probably isn't worth the effort for programs using the Crystal Reports Designer. Export the reports, and recode the application by hand. It will turn out much cleaner, and simpler.

There are a number of articles recommended for further reading on this topic.

- ❑ .NET VB Migration tool does not convert DSR files to RPT files
  http://support.crystaldecisions.com/library/kbase/articles/c2010234.asp

- ❑ Saving an existing report causes the .NET Report Designer to close unexpectedly
  http://support.crystaldecisions.com/library/kbase/articles/c2010272.asp

- ❑ Changes to a Version 6 Report with saved data may not save correctly in VB .NET
  http://support.crystaldecisions.com/library/kbase/articles/c2010273.asp

- ❑ Err Msg: "Crystal Dictionary not supported in this version" in .NET Designer
  http://support.crystaldecisions.com/library/kbase/articles/c2010338.asp

- ❑ Err Msg: "Invalid report version" when opening a .NET report in CR 8.x
  http://support.crystaldecisions.com/library/kbase/articles/c2010775.asp

- ❑ Err Msg: "Query engine error" when connecting to AS400 via OLE DB in VS .NET
  http://support.crystaldecisions.com/library/kbase/articles/c2011092.asp

After spending a little more time with the product, you might note that accessing reports via ASP.NET rather that in a Windows Application causes a few more data problems than encountered in this appendix.

In working with clients on the issue of converting Crystal Reports 8.5 reports to a .NET environment, the general consensus is that conversion is good, but the creation of a reporting system with the .NET Framework, or use of Crystal Enterprise, is even better.

Professional *Crystal Reports* for *Visual Studio .NET*

Crystal vs. Basic Syntax

In Chapter 7, we had a look at creating formulas using both Basic Syntax and Crystal Syntax. This appendix has been put together as a handy reference for the differences between the two and provides listings of the functions and operators in each different syntax.

This list is by no means exhaustive, but hopes to provide you with some idea of the main and most-used syntax in cases where Basic and Crystal syntax differ.

> **Remember that you cannot combine both syntaxes in a single formula, and that it is only possible to use Crystal Syntax in a record selection formula.**

Functions

Crystal Reports includes a number of pre-built functions that are available for use within a formula. The majority of these functions are the same in both Basic and Crystal Syntax, with the exception of the functions below.

Note: Where there is more than one equivalent function, they are all listed.

Mathemetical

Basic	Crystal
Fix(n)	Truncate(n)
Fix(n, #places)	Truncate(n, #places)

Where *n* is a number-type field, both `Fix()` and `Truncate()` will truncate a number to a specified number of decimal places.

For example `Fix({field}, 2)` would trim the field to two decimal places.

String Functions

Basic	Crystal	Notes
Len(string)	Length(string)	Returns the length of a string
LTrim (string)	TrimLeft(string)	Trims all spaces from the left-hand side of a string
RTrim (string)	TrimRight(string)	Trims all spaces from the right-hand side of a string
UCase (string)	Uppercase (string)	Converts a string to all uppercase characters
LCase (string)	Lowercase(string)	Converts a string to all lowercase characters
IsNumeric (string)	n/a	Boolean – determines whether a string is numeric or not
CStr(field), ToText(field)	CStr(field), ToText(field)	Converts different types of fields to string

Date/Time Functions

Basic	Crystal	Notes
CDate, DataValue	CDate, DateValue	Date
CTime, TimeValue	Ctime, TimeValue, Time	Time
CDateTime, DateTimeValue	DateTime, CDateTime, DateTimeValue	Date-Time
WeekDay	DayofWeek	Returns the day of week

Arrays

Basic	Crystal	Notes
Array (x,...)	MakeArray (x,...)	For creating arrays of different types within your formula

Operators

In addition to different types of functions, Basic and Crystal occasionally utilize different operators:

Arithmetic

Basic	Crystal
n/a	x%y

This is the percent operator, and it calculates the percent that X is of Y.

Conversion

Basic	Crystal
n/a	ToCurrency

This operator is for converting a field to a currency format with two decimal places.

String

Basic	Crystal	Notes
&	&, +	Similar in function, the ampersand can also be used to concatenate different types of fields, while the plus operator only works with string fields
(x(y))	x[y]	For referencing the subscript of arrays and strings, Basic uses parenthesis, while Crystal syntax uses brackets (for example {stringfield}[3] would return the character in the third position of the string)

Variable Declarations

Before we can use a variable in a formula, it has to be declared. Basic and Crystal Syntax both have different ways of declaring variables, based on the type and scope of the variable. The most common variable declarations are included below:

Basic	Crystal
Dim x	n/a
Dim x ()	n/a
Dim x As Boolean	Local BooleanVar x
Dim x As Number	Local NumberVar x
Dim x As Currency	Local CurrencyVar x
Dim x As Date	Local DateVar x
Dim x As Time	Local TimeVar x

Table continued on following page

Basic	Crystal
Dim x As DateTime	Local DateTimeVar x
Dim x As String	Local StringVar x
Dim x As Number Range	Local NumberVar range x
Dim x As Currency Range	Local CurrencyVar range x
Dim x As Date Range	Local DateVar range x
Dim x As Time Range	Local TimeVar range x
Dim x As DateTime Range	Local DateTimeVar range x
Dim x As String Range	Local StringVar range x
Dim x () As Boolean	Local BooleanVar array x
Dim x () As Number	Local NumberVar array x
Dim x () As Currency	Local CurrencyVar array x
Dim x () As Date	Local DateVar array x
Dim x () As Time	Local TimeVar array x
Dim x () As DateTime	Local DateTimeVar array x
Dim x () As String	Local StringVar array x
Dim x () As Number Range	Local NumberVar range array x
Dim x () As Currency Range	Local CurrencyVar range array x
Dim x () As Date Range	Local DateVar range array x
Dim x () As Time Range	Local TimeVar range array x
Dim x () As DateTime Range	Local DateTimeVar range array x
Dim x () As String Range	Local StringVar range array x

To select a scope for variables created in Basic syntax, you can use the following scope attributes in place of the Dim statement:

❑   Local – The variable is specific and can only be used in the formula in which it is defined.

❑   Global – The variable is available to formulas throughout the entire current report.

❑   Shared – The variable can be shared with a subreport as well as the entire current report.

Note: Dim is equivalent to using "Local".

Professional *Crystal Reports*
for *Visual Studio .NET*

Index

Important entries have page numbers in **bold** type.

C

Notes

Notes

Notes

Notes

C# Today

The daily knowledge site for professional C# programmers

p2p.wrox.com

The programmer's resource centre

A unique free service from Wrox Press
With the aim of helping programmers to help each other

Wrox Press aims to provide timely and practical information to today's programmer. P2P is a list server offering a host of targeted mailing lists where you can share knowledge with four fellow programmers and find solutions to your problems. Whatever the level of your programming knowledge, and whatever technology you use P2P can provide you with the information you need.

ASP — Support for beginners and professionals, including a resource page with hundreds of links, and a popular ASP.NET mailing list.

DATABASES — For database programmers, offering support on SQL Server, mySQL, and Oracle.

MOBILE — Software development for the mobile market is growing rapidly. We provide lists for the several current standards, including WAP, Windows CE, and Symbian.

JAVA — A complete set of Java lists, covering beginners, professionals, and server-side programmers (including JSP, servlets and EJBs)

.NET — Microsoft's new OS platform, covering topics such as ASP.NET, C#, and general .NET discussion.

VISUAL BASIC — Covers all aspects of VB programming, from programming Office macros to creating components for the .NET platform.

WEB DESIGN — As web page requirements become more complex, programmer's are taking a more important role in creating web sites. For these programmers, we offer lists covering technologies such as Flash, Coldfusion, and JavaScript.

XML — Covering all aspects of XML, including XSLT and schemas.

OPEN SOURCE — Many Open Source topics covered including PHP, Apache, Perl, Linux, Python and more.

FOREIGN LANGUAGE — Several lists dedicated to Spanish and German speaking programmers, categories include. NET, Java, XML, PHP and XML

How to subscribe:
Simply visit the P2P site, at http://p2p.wrox.com/

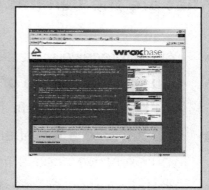

Programmer to Programmer™

Registration Code: 77446432IY262R02

Wrox writes books for you. Any suggestions, or ideas about how you want
information given in your ideal book will be studied by our team.
Your comments are always valued at Wrox.

Free phone in USA 800-USE-WROX
Fax (312) 893 8001

UK Tel.: (0121) 687 4100   Fax: (0121) 687 4101

Professional Crystal Reports for Visual Studio .NET – Registration Card

Name _____

Address _____

_____

_____

City _____ State/Region _____

Country _____ Postcode/Zip _____

E-Mail _____

Occupation _____

How did you hear about this book?

❏ Book review (name) _____

❏ Advertisement (name) _____

❏ Recommendation _____

❏ Catalog _____

❏ Other _____

Where did you buy this book?

❏ Bookstore (name) _____ City _____

❏ Computer store (name) _____

❏ Mail order _____

❏ Other _____

What influenced you in the purchase of this book?

❏ Cover Design   ❏ Contents   ❏ Other (please specify):

_____

How did you rate the overall content of this book?

❏ Excellent   ❏ Good   ❏ Average   ❏ Poor

What did you find most useful about this book? _____

_____

What did you find least useful about this book? _____

_____

Please add any additional comments. _____

_____

What other subjects will you buy a computer book on soon?

_____

What is the best computer book you have used this year?

_____

Note: This information will only be used to keep you updated
about new Wrox Press titles and will not be used for
any other purpose or passed to any other third party.

wrox

Programmer to Programmer™

Note: If you post the bounce back card below in the UK, please send it to:

Wrox Press Limited, Arden House, 1102 Warwick Road,
Acocks Green, Birmingham B27 6HB. UK.

Computer Book Publishers